PRESIDENTIAL SELECTION

PRESIDENTIAL SELECTION

Theory and Development

JAMES W. CEASER

PRINCETON
UNIVERSITY PRESS

The same ambition can destroy or save,
And makes a patriot as it makes a knave.

    —ALEXANDER POPE,
     An Essay on Man

TABLE OF CONTENTS

PREFACE

CONTEMPORARY scholarship on the presidential selection process has almost entirely ignored the thought of America's past statesmen and political theorists. The absence of what one might call a traditional approach to the study of presidential selection can be traced primarily to the extra-Constitutional status of most aspects of the current selection system. While the operations of the presidency and the Congress are still controlled in many crucial respects by the Constitution, the basic features of the selection process—including popular elections, parties, conventions, and campaigns—developed outside of, and largely in opposition to, the original Constitutional design. As a result, students of the selection process, unlike many of those studying our other institutions, have seen no need to consult the ideas of the Founders. Nor have they felt that any body of thought on the selection process since the Founding deserves serious consideration. In this they have followed the dominant view of party historians, who until very recently taught that the development of parties and the selection process was a product not of a conscious design of certain statesmen to fashion constitutional doctrine but rather of a search by pragmatic politicians for the most effective way to win power.

The study of the presidential selection system has thus been left to the domain of modern scholars without the assistance or constraint of any classical American conceptions of its purpose. This freedom from tradition has led to a kind of scholarly license, with nearly as many approaches to the topic as the number of scholars writing in the field. While some studies have produced valuable insights, it is apparent that the field lacks an approach that defines the basic elements of the selection process, indicates the relationship among them, and establishes criteria by which to judge proposals for change.

These deficiencies were apparent to anyone who compared the recent debates on the reform of the selection system with those on the scope of executive power. The contrast was striking: here were two areas of institutional analysis, both constitutional in the sense that they involved fundamental aspects of our political system, which were treated in entirely different ways. The debate on the presidency was informed by classical views of the nature of executive power and as it proceeded seemed to promote a deeper understanding of the issues. The debate on selection, on the other hand, developed without reference to past ideas and often degenerated into unreflective declamations in favor of or against direct democracy, as if this were the only value that merited consideration.

The dissatisfaction I felt with the quality of this debate and with some of the institutional changes that resulted from it led me to go back to the works of earlier American thinkers in search of a broader approach to the study of presidential selection. I was under no illusion that these sources could furnish immediate solutions to today's problems or even that they could offer the kind of direct guidance they sometimes provide in the case of questions relating to our other institutions. But I was hopeful, and soon became convinced, that traditional thought in this area could at least help to identify the range of issues necessary for any comprehensive treatment of the selection problem.

The goal, accordingly, that I have set for myself in this study is to integrate contemporary institutional analysis of the selection process with the relevant themes of American political thought. In attempting to combine what are now considered two distinct fields, I am aware that I will be addressing two different audiences. To those in the field of American political thought, this study offers a discussion of the ideas of four major thinkers on the question of presidential selection: the Founders, Thomas Jefferson, Martin Van Buren, and Woodrow Wilson. I intend to show not only that these thinkers gave the issue of selection a great deal of attention, but further that their ideas decisively shaped the development of the selection system. To those in the field of contemporary political parties and electoral politics, this study presents an account of the recent changes in the selection process and an analysis of their implications for the structure of political parties and for the nature of presidential leadership and executive power. It is my basic intention, however, not to address each of these audiences separately, but both together. The study of past political thought is designed to elucidate a perspective on the presidential selection process that can be used to analyze contemporary problems, while the discussion of contemporary problems serves to illustrate many of the difficulties that concerned past thinkers.

One final comment. This book concludes with a prescription for modern politics—a call for the reinstitution of strong electoral parties for the purposes of providing an informal check on the president and restraining the leadership appeals of presidential aspirants. This prescription represents what is admittedly a personal judgment about the most profound themes within the tradition of American political thought, and I have therefore tried to separate the analysis of past thinkers from the conclusions I ultimately draw. Some will certainly challenge these conclusions; my hope, however, is that they will not dismiss the sources from which they are taken, but will attempt to use these same sources to build a case for a different set of recommendations.

ACKNOWLEDGMENTS

THIS book grew out of my doctoral dissertation at Harvard University, and I would like to express my gratitude to my thesis advisors, James Q. Wilson and William Schneider, who gave so freely of their time, advice, and encouragement while I was writing and revising the manuscript. Arthur Maass read my original introduction and with his usual firmness and kindness helped me to rethink my basic objectives. My friend and former colleague at Kenyon College, Phil Marcus, read the manuscript in its entirety and made many suggestions which I incorporated into the book; his wife, Sally, handled the typing and to my great relief took the liberty of doing a substantial amount of editing. The book touches on a wide range of topics in American political thought and electoral behavior, and I could never have undertaken so extensive a project without the excellent background I received in these two areas from my teachers Robert Horwitz, Harry Clor, Harvey C. Mansfield, Jr., H. Douglas Price, and Walter Dean Burnham.

In revising the manuscript, I was fortunate to have the help of three excellent readers supplied by Princeton University Press: Hugh Heclo, Robert Nakamura, and the late Herbert Storing. Each offered valuable suggestions which I tried to take into account in my second writing. Just before his death, Professor Storing joined the faculty at the University of Virginia and in the very brief time that we were colleagues assisted me with many points in the early chapters. Two graduate students at Virginia, Jeffrey Mason and Stephanie Feazel, helped with proofreading and the preparation of an index. The Earhart Foundation and the University of Virginia kindly supplied me with financial assistance during the summers of 1976 and 1977.

Finally, I would like to thank my wife, Sue, who supported me financially and morally while I was writing the original draft and who endured with just the right degree of patience—but no more—the countless revisions of sentences and ideas.

JAMES W. CEASER
May 21, 1978 Charlottesville, Va.

PRESIDENTIAL SELECTION

INTRODUCTION

NEAR the end of the Constitutional Convention, when the delegates were still struggling over the provisions for choosing the president, James Wilson described the issue of presidential selection as "the most difficult of all on which we have had to decide . . . [one] that has greatly divided the House and will also divide the people out of doors."[1] Fortunately for the Founders Wilson's prediction of immediate controversy proved to be mistaken, and the selection system became one of the few features of the proposed Constitution to escape criticism. But Wilson's fears have certainly been borne out over the course of American history. If the selection system is defined to include both the nomination and final election stages, then it can probably be said that it has been the most unstable of all our major national institutions. The system has undergone at least four transformations since 1787, including one that has occurred over the past decade. For a people accustomed to relying on "prescription" to settle institutional crises, the current instability in the selection process poses an unusual challenge. Neither the institutions proposed in the Constitution nor the practices of the past generation offer a workable solution for the modern era. In order to provide guidance for those legislating on the process, the political scientist must undertake the unfamiliar task of the institutional theorist and inquire into the basic goals of the selection system.

The transformation currently taking place in the selection process began in the 1960s with the breakdown of the so-called "mixed" nominating system that had been in existence

---

[1] James Madison, *Notes of Debates in the Federal Convention of 1787*, ed. Adrienne Koch (New York: W. W. Norton, 1969), p. 578 (September 4).

since the second decade of this century.[2] The race for the Republican nomination in 1964 revealed a major new trend in the motivation of partisan participation. In many areas of the country dedicated "amateurs," distinguished by their commitment to attaining certain policy goals, replaced the traditional "professionals" or "regulars" who had been more concerned with organizational maintenance. The intervention of amateurs had occurred on several occasions in the past; yet because of the large increase in the number of educated, upper-middle class citizens and the decline in the amount of patronage available to the party organizations, there were strong grounds for concluding that a permanent shift to amateurism was about to take place.[3] This tendency was furthered in one respect but superceded in another by the emergence of the reform movement in the Democratic Party in 1968. Under the impetus of this movement, the national Democratic Party twice issued new guidelines governing the selection of delegates to the national convention. The reformers' two chief objectives were to diminish the power of the regulars and to enhance that of the amateurs. They succeeded in the former but largely failed in the latter. In response (or reaction) to the national party guidelines, a number of states changed their electoral laws on the selection of delegates. Between 1968 and 1976, fourteen states added primaries, bringing the total of delegates selected by primaries to over seventy percent in both parties, nearly double the

[2] The term "mixed system" is used by Nelson Polsby and Aaron Wildavsky to refer to the combined system of selecting delegates by primaries and by caucuses. See *Presidential Elections* (3rd ed., New York: Charles Scribner's Sons, 1971), p. 238. James Davis uses the synonymous terminology of a "hybrid system." See *Presidential Primaries* (New York: Thomas Y. Crowell, 1967), p. 269.

[3] The terms amateur and professional are taken from James Q. Wilson's, *The Amateur Democrat* (Chicago: University of Chicago Press, 1962). For an account of the rise of the amateur in American national parties, see Everett Ladd, Jr., *Transformations of the American Party System* (New York: W. W. Norton, 1975), pp. 304-31.

4

figure of 1968; and a number of states changed their existing primary laws to institute the novel principle of proportional representation and to strengthen the connection between the selection of the delegates and the voters' preference for a national candidate. The effect of these changes, to the surprise and dismay of many reformers, was to install "the people" as the sovereign force over the nomination, at the expense of the amateur no less than the professional.[4]

Over the past fifteen years the nominating process has thus been transformed from a mixed system, in which control over the nomination was shared by the people and the party organizations, to what can be termed a plebiscitary system in which the key actors are the people and the individual aspirants. Along with the emergence of this new institutional form has come a new method of generating support in presidential campaigns: "popular leadership," or the attempt by individual aspirants to carve out a personal mass constituency by their own programmatic and personality appeals and by the use of large personal campaign organizations of their own creation. At the nomination stage, this form of leadership takes place entirely without the filter of traditional partisan appeals, as the nomination race is in effect a national nonpartisan contest. But even at the final election stage, the personalistic aspects of the campaigns are becoming increasingly important relative to partisan appeals, a fact which follows in large measure from the way in which the candidates are now nominated.

It is still too soon, however, to claim that the new plebiscitary system has been firmly established. The new procedures have only recently been implemented, and there is as yet no firm consensus in their favor. A consensus on behalf of the selection system can be said to exist where the public and

---

[4] The disparity between the reformers' intentions and the results they helped to promote is discussed by Austin Ranney in "Changing the Rules of the Nominating Game" in James Barber, ed., *Choosing the President* (Englewood Cliffs, N.J.: Prentice Hall, 1974), pp. 73-74.

the candidates accept the existing rules as a matter of habit or where the public endorses—or at least does not reject—the principles that underlie the rules. Prior to 1964 the mixed system certainly enjoyed support on the first count and probably on the second as well. One prominent scholar writing in 1963 praised the system for its "tradition and legitimacy" and for the ease with which it allowed "both the electorate and the party politician [to] plan their actions in accord with accepted procedures"; and most students of the electoral process at the time argued that the system served the nation well, producing reasonably competent candidates and maintaining the strength and stability of the two-party system.[5] By contrast, recent nomination campaigns have been characterized by a good deal of uncertainty among the contestants about the basic strategy they should employ; and the public has registered some discontent, if public opinion polls on such questions can be regarded with any seriousness.[6] All this could be excused as a natural reaction to new rules and state laws if it were clear that there was agreement in the nation about what kind of selection process should finally emerge. But no such agreement exists. Some continue to press for further reforms in the name of more democracy, while others—among them a growing number of scholars and even some disillusioned reformers—have begun to question the wisdom of a fully "open," plebiscitary system.[7]

The election campaign of 1972, more than any other single event, caused scholars and political commentators to begin to question the wisdom of the new system. Critical attention

[5] Gerald Pomper, *Nominating the President* (New York: W. W. Norton, 1966), p. 215. For other favorable accounts see James Davis, *Presidential Primaries* (New York: Thomas Y. Crowell, 1967), pp. 269-71, and Nelson Polsby and Aaron Wildavsky, *op. cit.*

[6] See Austin Ranney, *Curing the Mischiefs of Faction* (Berkeley, University of California Press, 1975), p. 133.

[7] Ranney, "Changing the Rules," pp. 73-74, 77; Donald Matthews, "Presidential Nominations" in Barber, ed., *Choosing the President*, p. 34; and Denis Sullivan *et al., The Politics of Representation* (New York: St. Martin's Press, 1974), p. 114.

6

focused initially on two aspects of the campaign: the bitter intraparty split within the Democratic Party and the criminal acts committed by President Nixon's campaign organization. The difficulties experienced by the Democrats, many argued, were directly related to the inability of the new system to foster harmony among the factions of the party. The new system, it was said, encouraged and rewarded the more extreme appeals.[8] On the Republican side, the Watergate break-in and the other assortment of dirty tricks were also linked to certain features of the selection system. These acts were the work of a wholly personal organization dedicated to the election of a particular man. A party-run organization, it was often argued, would never have allowed itself to go to these extremes, as it would have been more independent of the candidate and less willing to sacrifice the long-term reputation of the party for the success of one individual. Although the large personal organization did not originate with the plebiscitary system, its use in the past occurred in just the kind of "outside" campaign that has now become the norm; and one finds today that these organizations are recognized as essential and fully legitimate elements in the selection process.[9] In addition to these two defects of the new system, some commentators posited a connection between the selection process and the rise of the "imperial" presidency. This connection was detected not simply in the particular instance of the Nixon Administration's shift of the plumbers unit from stopping leaks to springing them, but more fundamentally to the claims made by or on behalf of recent presidents to the possession of a personal electoral mandate; such claims, it was argued, were facilitated by the emphasis placed on the

[8] William R. Keech and Donald R. Matthews, *The Party's Choice* (Washington, D.C.: Brookings Institution, 1976), p. 156; Sullivan, *The Politics of Representation*, p. 114. As we shall see, however, the new institutional arrangements can also encourage, depending on the character of the times, a heavy reliance on "image-building."

[9] See Robert Agranoff's *The New Style in Election Campaigns* (Boston: Holbrook Press, 1976), pp. 3-49.

7

individual candidate under the current system.[10] Taken together, these problems of the 1972 campaign suggested a common underlying theme—the failure of the selection system to offer any restraint or provide a moderating influence on the pursuit and exercise of power.

The 1976 campaign was by almost any standard less disturbing than that of 1972, and for many it removed all doubts about the new system. The positive aspects of the nomination races were certainly evident: after initial tensions and divisions within both parties, the nominees held their respective party followings in the general election; and there were no obvious crises similar to 1972—no threats of walkouts, no protestations of illegitimate or unfair selection rules, and no criminal abuses. Yet there were still some troubling signs. The Democratic nominee once again won by running as an "outsider" against the party establishment. To some observers, and especially to the reformers who had intended to establish a system that emphasized substantive issues, there was the disconcerting fact that Jimmy Carter had gained his initial advantage by what was seen as an empty image appeal and by the mild exploitation of an anti-Washington "mood" that was irrelevant to the final election campaign and to the task of governing the nation.[11] If the 1972 campaign indicated that the new system was open to extreme issue appeals, the 1976 campaign suggested that, under different circumstances, it was susceptible to control by a soft, contentless style of politics. The reformers' "new politics" of issue appeals, if it existed in 1976, was to be found on the Republican side; but in this instance, too, the reformers might have professed disappointment that it did not concern the kind of positive moral questions they intended, but instead

[10] This is the implicit thesis in the Ripon Society's book on the 1972 election, *Jaws of Victory* (Boston: Little Brown, 1973).

[11] For a discussion of these charges, see Warren E. Miller and Teresa Levitin, *Leadership and Change* (Cambridge: Winthrop, 1976), pp. 199-203. See also the charges made against Carter by Rick Stearns in the *Wall Street Journal*, July 9, 1976.

an arousal of popular fears over giving up the Panama Canal. Finally, the length of the campaign left more than a few to wonder if the preoccupation with selecting a president had not intruded too much on the job of governing the nation.[12]

If there was perhaps too great a tendency after 1972 to attribute all of the failings of American politics to the influence of the selection system, there may now be, in light of the more favorable results of 1976, too strong an inclination to excuse the system of any faults whatsoever. The analytic mistake one must avoid is to draw general conclusions about the effects of the selection system from the results of a particular campaign. The outcome of any given race is determined not only by the prevailing selection system—understood as the laws, rules, and associated practices governing the process—but also by political factors, such as the mood of the electorate, the intensity of the issues, and the personalities of the candidates. These political factors are never constant. As they shift, they can obscure or accentuate certain institutional influences. The only way to determine the effects of the selection system would be to isolate its independent influence on the political system and on the character of the campaign, assuming a certain set of political variables. In practice, of course, this is impossible to do. But realizing the nature of the analytic problem is an important corrective to drawing hasty and erroneous conclusions. The campaigns of 1972 and 1976 should be analyzed with a view to attempting to discern the consequences of the selection system as such, with the best "test" of validity coming from the demonstration of a logical connection between institutional forms and posited effects.

The consequences of the new selection system thus remain to be determined. But the results of the campaigns conducted under it thus far justify James Barber's rather modest claim

---

[12] This thought, which was expressed frequently by certain columnists during the campaign, is treated in the scholarly literature by Richard Neustadt in the most recent edition of *Presidential Power* (New York: John Wiley's Sons, 1976), pp. 19-22.

9

that the "data emerging over the past few years make necessary a thorough examination of the way we choose our chief executive."[13] The starting point of such an inquiry must be with the simplest and most fundamental question: what is it that we want from our system of presidential selection? And if we are to avoid, at least initially, a mere restatement of the recent debate over reform, we must be willing to inquire not only into questions concerning the "inputs" into the system, i.e. matters of procedures, but into its "outputs" as well, i.e. the broader consequences of the selection process for the political system as a whole.[14] If this approach is adopted, most would probably agree on five general objectives for the selection system. It should: minimize the harmful effects of the pursuit of office by highly ambitious contenders; promote the proper kind of executive leadership and the proper nature of executive power; help secure an able president; ensure a legitimate accession; and provide for the proper amount of choice and change. These five goals are so integrally related to what are, or should be, the considerations that go into devising a selection system that they can properly be called its major "functions."

The first function, minimizing the harmful effects of the pursuit of power by highly ambitious contenders, is probably the most revealing about the selection problem as a whole. Almost every major politician will at one time or another fix attention on becoming president and adjust his behavior in a way that improves his chances of being considered. For those who enter the select circle of contenders, the tendency will be all the greater to adopt whichever strategies and tactics are legal and acceptable—and perhaps some that are not—if they appear to improve prospects of success. It is reasonable to assume, therefore, that the ambition of con-

[13] "Introduction" to Barber, ed., *Choosing the President*, p. 2.

[14] This terminology was used by Herbert J. Storing in testimony before the Subcommittee on the Constitution of the Senate Judiciary Committee, *The Electoral College and Direct Elections, Hearings* 95th Congress, 1st Session (1977), pp. 129-49.

tenders, if not properly guided, can lead to actions and political appeals that are destructive of one's party or of the general good. Such conduct, in fact, would seem to be the "natural" tendency of ambition, for the ambitious seek what in the first instance is advantageous for themselves. Realizing this general problem, legislators of political institutions have usually sought to discover some way to create a degree of harmony between behavior that satisfies personal ambition and behavior that promotes the public good. Every student of American politics is aware of this principle as it applies to the division of power among office holders, but it is surprising how many now ignore it or deny its applicability in the case of the process that governs office seekers.

The major problems posed by the ambition of presidential contenders can be classified under two broad headings. The first is the disruption of the proper functioning of a major institution that may result when office holders use their position to further their presidential aspirations. One striking instance of this problem was identified by James Sterling Young in his treatment of the caucus system of nomination in the early nineteenth century. Young shows how the caucus system led cabinet officers having presidential aspirations to court the members of Congress, with the consequence that the unity and independence of the executive branch were undermined. The failure of the selection system in this instance to structure presidential ambition in accord with the intended character of the Constitution very nearly led to a transformation of the entire political system.[15] A contemporary example of this general problem can perhaps be seen in the decline of the Senate as a serious deliberative body. In the view of a number of students of Congress, this transformation can be explained in large measure by the attempt of many senators to position themselves for a presidential candidacy by engaging in the kind of public "posturing" that the new selection system seems to require. More and more

[15] James Sterling Young, *The Washington Community* (New York: Harcourt, Brace, and World, 1966), pp. 245-49.

11

this has led senators, in the words of Norman Ornstein, to opt for "media coverage over legislative craftmanship."[16]

The second problem, by no means exclusive of the first, results when candidates attempt to build a popular following by the arts of popular leadership—by empty "image" appeals, by flattery, or by the exploitation of dangerous or ungovernable passions.[17] According to James Barber, one of the major problems of presidential politics today is the "kitsch and fakery" that so often characterize candidate appeals; and V. O. Key in his final book, *The Responsible Electorate*, warned of the need for vigilance against those "who have championed intolerance [and] stirred the passions and hatreds of people who have advocated causes known by decent men to be outrageous or dangerous in their long-range consequences."[18] The strongest term for such action is demagoguery, although the word is usually confined today to refer to harsh rhetoric that evokes anger and fear in connection with issues such as race prejudice or "law and order." It would be a mistake, however, to overlook the demagogic character of a mild flattery that tells the people they can do no wrong or of seductive appeals that hide behind a veil of liberality, making promises that can never be kept or raising hopes that can never be satisfied.

It is certainly not too much to ask of contenders that they

[16] Norman J. Ornstein, Robert Peabody, and David W. Rohde, "The Changing Senate: From the 1950s to the 1970s," in *Congress Reconsidered*, ed. Lawrence Dodd and Bruce Oppenheimer (New York: Praeger, 1977), p. 17. See also David Mayhew, *Congress and the Electoral Connection* (New Haven: Yale University Press, 1974); Nelson W. Polsby, *Congress and the Presidency*, 2nd ed. (Englewood Cliffs: Prentice Hall, 1971), pp. 67-69; and Senator Aiken's Senate retirement speech, *Congressional Record*, vol. 120, no. 172, 93rd Congress, 2nd Session, 1975.

[17] By popular leadership, we are referring to the effort to mobilize power or to govern by winning a mass constituency in support of one's programs or personality. The term will be elaborated below in chapters 1 and 4.

[18] Barber, "Introduction," p. 6. V. O. Key, *The Responsible Electorate* (New York: Random House, 1966), p. 2.

12

exercise self-restraint. No regime would want to relax the check imposed by a public standard that demands unselfish dedication of its politicians. But it takes no great deal of sophistication to realize the inadequacy of mere professions of high-mindedness for curbing excesses. Other means of restraint are therefore necessary. The approach relied on most today is to control candidate abuses by legal restrictions and penalties. This approach was used in the recent campaign finance legislation which was designed to protect the public interest from candidates' granting special privileges or favors to large contributors. Thus while one arm of the modern reform movement seeks to make the selection process more open, the other seeks to prevent abuses, often encouraged by that very openness, by means of new legal limitations and administrative agencies.[19] But whatever the merits of this legal approach for curbing certain abuses, it does not reach those which by their very nature cannot be classified as criminal or proscribed by legal statute. Into this category fall most of the excesses noted in the two problems discussed above.

If ambition in these instances cannot be checked by law, it might nevertheless be regulated by the general institutional structure of the selection system. Institutional regulation of behavior consists in establishing certain constraints and incentives—not criminal penalties—that promote desired habits and actions and discourage unwanted behavior. The selection system, conceived in this sense, is the "institution" that structures the behavior of presidential aspirants

[19] The extremely high costs of campaigns are attributable in large measure to the open nominating process, a fact cited by William J. Crotty in *Political Reform and the American Experiment* (New York: Thomas Y. Crowell, 1977), p. 106. More importantly, it has been frequently argued that the "dirty tricks" practiced by the Nixon campaign in 1972 were a natural if not inevitable outgrowth of the kind of personal campaign organizations that have now become standard under the open process. For this thesis, see especially The Ripon Society and Clifford W. Brown, Jr., *Jaws of Victory* (Boston: Little Brown, 1973), pp. 226-42.

13

and their supporters. It is likely to work most effectively where it can rely on the candidates' own strongest impulse: if matters can be arranged such that undesirable behavior will detract from the chances of success, candidates will turn "voluntarily" to other strategies. Properly channeled ambition can be used to curb its own natural excesses.

The second function, promoting the proper kind of executive leadership and power, can be discussed here only in a formal way without specifying the content of "proper." This function implies that, up to a certain point at least, the office should be thought of as the end and the selection process the means. Decisions about selection should be made with a view to how they affect the presidency. However alien this view may be to many modern theorists who hold citizen participation to be the highest goal of the selection process, it was often adopted as the central consideration in past debates about the selection problem.[20] Its perceived importance rested on the assumption that the way in which power is sought must have a profound influence on the way in which it is exercised.

One aspect of this function is the effect of the campaign on the behavior of incumbents and on the task of governing the nation. De Tocqueville, one of the first to discuss this question at any length, worried that campaigns drained constituted authority of its usual discretion. During the campaign everything hangs in a suspended state; or worse, the incumbent may become absorbed in the "task of defending himself [rather than] ruling in the interest of the state."[21] De Tocqueville's concern over the adverse influence of the campaign was so great that, in one of his few instances of disagreement with the Founders, he opposed reeligibility for an incumbent president. But one need not accept this pre-

[20] For a modern statement on behalf of the need for participation, see John S. Saloma III and Frederick H. Sontag, *Parties* (New York: Random House, 1973).

[21] Alexis de Tocqueville, *Democracy in America*, trans. by George Lawrence (Garden City: Doubleday, 1969), p. 135.

scription to apply the same reasoning to other aspects of the selection system. The length of time during which electoral considerations predominate will vary with the duration of the open canvass and the extent to which the nomination process is open or popular. These are factors that lie immediately within the control of the selection system narrowly conceived, and there is little question that the combined effect of the plebiscitary nominating system and the recent campaign finance legislation has extended the active and visible length of the campaign.[22]

The presidency is affected by the selection system in a number of other ways. The leadership appeals used to seek the office create habits and expectations that carry over into how both the public and the candidates understand the role of the presidency. Some of the most important debates on the place of political parties in our system have focused on how they influence the method of seeking the presidency and hence the presidency itself. George Washington and later John Quincy Adams opposed party competition on the grounds that partisan nominations and campaigns would force candidates to become identified with a part of the populace rather than the whole and would compel aspirants to make specific commitments. In their view this would undermine the independence of the presidency and curtail presidential discretion. Some Progressive thinkers objected to the way in which parties tied candidates to outmoded principles, thus preventing the possibility of change in response to new conditions. To "free" the candidates and thus the president from the constraints of parties, they proposed a national primary that would enable individual leaders to propose new programs and build new constituencies. Like

[22] Neustadt remarks that "Ford announced his candidacy and his campaign manager . . . in July 1975, thirteen months before his party's national convention, seven months before the first primary election, six months earlier than nonincumbent Kennedy had moved in 1960, with what was then regarded as unprecedented haste" (*Presidential Power*, p. 20).

15

Washington and Adams, the Progressives also sought to increase the discretion of the president, though this discretion now rested on the ability of individual leaders to win public support for their program during the campaign.

The selection system will also influence the kind of claim to authority a president can assert. The more popular the mode of selection, the more likely it becomes that a president will invoke the informal title of representative of the people's will along with—or perhaps in place of—the Constitutional powers of the office. If the claim to embody the popular will is made by the candidate on behalf of his own standing or program, rather than on behalf of a party, then the mandate asserted may be a personal one, as that claimed by some recent presidents. The attempt to influence the power of the presidency by changing the basis on which its authority is claimed is again a factor that has figured prominently in past revisions of the selection system. The rise of permanent party competition and direct popular selection of the electors were measures that in some cases were deliberately favored as a way of strengthening a candidate's claim to being the "people's president."[23] The Progressives sought to add even further to this claim by weakening traditional parties through direct democracy in the nomination process.

Finally, the method of selection affects the power of the president in a more immediate sense by determining the groups and constituencies to which the candidates, including an incumbent seeking reelection, must appeal. As the system changes, candidates incur different obligations and operate under different constraints. When nominations were dominated by party organization, a president was compelled to deal with specific power brokers within his party and to take account of the interests they represented. Traditional parties, whatever their faults, offered an informal check on

[23] From the title of Neil Pierce's book, which calls for abolition of the electoral college and a direct election of the president: *The People's President* (New York: Simon and Schuster, 1968).

16

the exercise of presidential power. At the same time they also provided the president with a valuable resource for gaining support with the public and with members of Congress.[24] Under the current plebiscitary system in which candidates campaign directly for the nomination and build their own personal mass constituencies and organizations, the check provided against the executive by the party has been weakened. This may give modern presidents greater discretion, although they may now be forced to deal directly with interest-group leaders without having the benefit of the "buffer" provided by the party power brokers. To the extent that they can avoid this constraint, it will be by their ability to appeal directly to the public through techniques of mass persuasion. Presidents are also likely to lose the support that the parties formerly provided, the consequence being that their effective power will in some ways be more limited than before. The means again by which they are most likely to attempt to overcome this weakness is through mass appeals and the assertion of a "special" relationship with the people. Modern presidents now stand directly before the bar of public opinion, and one should not be surprised if they become more assertive in their claim to authority and more "popular" or demagogic in their leadership appeals, if only to compensate for their loss of partisan support.[25]

The third function of the selection system, securing an able executive, refers to the personal qualities desired of a president. What transforms this function from a meaningless expression of a general concern to a legitimate institutional

[24] For a persuasive argument on this point, see Aaron Wildavsky, "The Past and Future President," *The Public Interest* 41 (Fall 1975): 56-76. For indirect support of this point, see Leo M. Snowiss, "Congressional Recruitment and Representation," *American Political Science Review* 60 (Fall 1966), pp. 627-39.

[25] This argument was made long before the current wave of reform by James Q. Wilson, *The Amateur Democrat*, pp. 344-47; and Edward Banfield, "In Defense of the American Party System" in Robert Goldwin, ed., *Political Parties, U.S.A.* (Chicago: Rand McNally, 1961), pp. 34-36.

consideration is the reasonable assumption, backed by comparative research into selection in various liberal democracies, that different systems influence the type of person who is apt to compete and succeed. An open nomination system, it has been argued, places a greater premium on those qualities that appeal to a mass audience, such as an appearance or aura of sanctimony; "closed" systems will value to a greater degree those qualities that are esteemed by the group empowered to select: for example, "keeping one's word" in the case of American politicians or trustworthiness in the case of British parliamentarians.[26]

Of course what constitutes a qualified person is, beyond a broad consensus on certain basic qualities such as honesty and intelligence, a matter of dispute. Different theorists have advocated very different character qualifications. After a long period of neglect, this issue has reemerged as a major concern of political scientists, especially since Watergate. The dominant contemporary school within political science classifies character according to different "personality types." These are defined not in terms of the attributes employed in ordinary political discourse, e.g. courage, decisiveness, or virtue, but rather by reference to categories that derive from modern psychological theory. Whatever this approach may have added to the field of biography, it has thus far been of no assistance in informing the debate on the institutions of the selection process. The only concrete institutional proposal to emerge from these studies—a board of "elite gatekeepers" to screen presidential aspirants—is so impractical and contrary to republican principles that the one scholar who made the suggestion did so, one suspects, only to indicate the limits of the approach.[27]

[26] Hugh Heclo, "Presidential and Prime Ministerial Selection" in Donald R. Matthews, ed., *Perspectives on Presidential Selection* (Washington, D.C.: Brookings Institution, 1973), p. 37.

[27] See Edwin C. Hargrove, "What Manner of Men" in Barker, ed., *Choosing the President*, pp. 30-33. Hargrove seems to be fully aware of the difficulties involved in the "personality approach" and

It is quite apparent, then, that in a popular regime no one "personality type" can be mandated by law or institutional arrangement. The selection system can only exert its influence by indirect means, through such general injunctions as the Constitution's age requirement, the determination of who has the power to nominate, and the establishment of certain norms of leadership style having some implications for character attributes. The indirect and general nature of such influences combined with the many and indeterminate factors that bear on the relationship between the people and their leaders make this function the least susceptible of institutional regulation. Character, to the extent it can be influenced by the selection system, can be affected only within a very broad range.

The fourth function of the selection process is to help ensure an accession of power that is unproblematic and widely regarded as legitimate. By unproblematic we refer to the "mechanical" aspects of the process, most notably to those relating to its capacity to produce a winner without confusion or delay. An example of an aspect of the process frequently charged as being defective is the method by which the president is chosen when the election goes to the House: because the choice is made from among the top three candidates and because a majority of states is required for election, there is no assurance of avoiding a stalemate, a possibility that worried both Madison and de Tocqueville.[28]

The larger issue, however, concerns the problem of legitimacy—whether the people consider the selection process to be basically fair and in accord with their understanding of republican principles. A system that is widely regarded as corrupt or undemocratic imposes a heavy burden on its

---

his own work has shown a great emphasis on the role of institutional restraints. See *The Power of the Modern Presidency* (New York: Alfred A. Knopf, 1974), pp. 295-98 and pp. 308-12.

[28] Madison, letter to George Hay, August 23, 1823: *Letters and Other Writings of James Madison*, 4 vols. (Worthington, 1884), 3:333; de Tocqueville, *Democracy in America*, p. 134.

choice, whether at the nomination stage, as Taft learned in 1912, or at the final election, as John Quincy Adams discovered after 1824. It is important, accordingly, that the selection system conform generally with the prevailing standard of republicanism. This, however, must be distinguished from attempts to change the system in response to ephemeral interpretations of republican principles that are fostered by candidates or factions seeking a short-term advantage and which may temporarily win public acceptance. The selection system, whatever its actual legal status, plays a crucial "constitutional" function in molding people's views about the nature of the republican principle, and quick changes in the system without due regard for their effect on people's understanding of democratic government pose a clear threat to the concept of constitutional government. This threat is obviously greatest at the nomination stage, which has escaped direct Constitutional regulation but which nonetheless influences public attitudes on this fundamental issue.

Disputes about the legitimacy of the selection process have taken place over both the methods of electing and of nominating. In respect to the final election process, supporters of the original parties attacked the discretion that electors were given under the Constitution and by 1800 succeeded in making them serve as agents of their electorate, whether the people or the state legislatures. The method of selecting electors by the state legislatures was then challenged and by 1828 the electors were being selected directly by the people in all but one of the states. The system of determining the winner by electoral votes rather than popular votes continues to be questioned by direct-election advocates who insist that a crisis of legitimacy would ensue if the Constitutionally designated winner ever failed to win a plurality of the popular vote.

At the nominating stage, the legitimacy of party nominations was widely contested through the election of 1836; and the specific nominating agency used by the Jeffersonian-Re-

20

publican Party after 1800, the caucus, was overthrown in 1824 after the public became convinced that it was an "oligarchic" institution. From 1840 until 1912 nominations made by conventions dominated by party politicians became an accepted part of the political system. But the Progressives overturned this consensus by arguing that nominations by party leaders were undemocratic. In 1912 they mounted an attack on this system and managed to weaken the party organizations by passing primary laws in some states. They were only partially successful, however, and in 1968 the nomination process was again denounced on the grounds that it was undemocratic and insufficiently open. These attacks created the original impetus for the recent reform movement which began by supporting the principle of direct democracy in the nomination process.

In addition to disputes about the meaning of republican government, there is another consideration that bears on the question of legitimacy. It is clear that the task of legitimation will be greatly facilitated if a candidate emerges with widespread support, assuring him of something approaching a majority, before the time that public law becomes involved in determining a winner. Wherever the government, by use of its own legally devised machinery, must act in a conspicuous way to "create" a majority where one does not appear to exist naturally, the likelihood increases that the legitimacy of the accession will be called into question. This problem was faced when the auxiliary system of selecting the president by the House was used in 1824. It is also at issue in the debate over the various proposals for direct election of the president. Either the direct election plan must allow for a candidate to win by a simple plurality, in which case the victor might be chosen, and quite visibly, with a percentage far less than a majority; or else there must be a provision made for a run-off, in which case there is an incentive for more parties to enter the initial election and a danger in the run-off of unseemly deals between the successful contenders and those defeated in the first round.[29] The function of legitimacy must accordingly be defined to include not only the formal problem of designing a system that conforms with the standards of republicanism but also what we may call the "informal problem" of obtaining support for the candidates prior to the direct involvement of the legal mechanisms of the state.

The final function, providing for the proper amount of choice and change, can again be introduced only in general terms, for the meaning of "proper" in this case has been the source of the greatest dispute about the nature and role of parties over the last quarter century. There have been two basic schools of thought on this question. The "consensual school," associated with the names of Pendleton Herring, V. O. Key, Edward Banfield, and James Q. Wilson, argues that parties, meaning the major parties, play their most constructive role when they avoid taking ideological stands and manage to incorporate the major groups of society into broad coalitions.[30] The "choice school," originally associated with the doctrine of party government and now with the more nebulous doctrine of reform, emphasizes the need for parties to take clear stands on principles and the issues of the day and to offer the electorate a significant or "meaning-

[29] The amendment that most direct election advocates now have agreed on is Senator Birch Bayh's plan, which calls for a run-off election between the top two vote getters in the event that no candidate receives over forty percent of the vote on the first ballot. The possibility of pushing the election into a run-off could constitute a major change in the "psychology" of the voter, since he could at least have some hope—as he does not under the current system—that his vote was not final but only the indication of a provisional first choice.

[30] Pendleton Herring, *The Politics of Democracy* (New York: W. W. Norton, 1965), pp. 100-16; V. O. Key, *Politics, Parties, and Pressure Groups*, 5th ed. (New York: Thomas Y. Crowell, 1964), pp. 199-227; Edward Banfield, "In Defense of the American Party System"; and James Q. Wilson, *The Amateur Democrat*, pp. 340-70.

ful" choice at each election.[31] For the consensual school, it is sufficient for democracy that there be a responsible "out" party that is able to replace the "in" party when the incumbent fails to win the public's support. For the choice school elections play a much grander role: parties must offer coherent programs so that the people, in making their selection for the president, actually chart the subsequent direction of public policy.

The terms of this debate as they were found in the 1950s and early 1960s have been altered but not entirely superceded by more recent scholarship on the theory of critical realignment.[32] Proponents of this theory have shown that "underneath" all questions relating to the institutional role of parties lies the dynamic movement of historical forces which, whatever the prescribed role of parties, may compel them at some periods to express fundamental choices and may make it unlikely that they will do so at other periods. Sometimes our parties behave as the consensual school would like and sometimes as the choice school would prefer. Certain advocates of this approach have even suggested that the entire debate about the institutional role of parties is irrelevant: the only true explanatory variable of the character of parties lies in the cleavages within society and how these develop over time.[33] This formulation, however, certainly goes too far. The "discovery" of the critical election

[31] See, James MacGregor Burns, *The Deadlock of Democracy* (Englewood Cliffs, N.J.: Prentice Hall, 1963); Stephen K. Bailey, "Our National Political Parties" in Goldwin, ed., *Political Parties U.S.A.*, Saloma and Sontag, *Parties.*

[32] Walter Dean Burnham, *Critical Elections and the Mainsprings of American Politics* (New York: W. W. Norton, 1970), James Sundquist, *Dynamics of the Party System* (Washington, D.C.: Brookings Institution, 1973), Harry Jaffa, "The Nature and Origin of the American Party System" in Goldwin, ed., *Political Parties U.S.A.*

[33] Sundquist offers the strongest statement of this position in his *Dynamics*, pp. 304-5.

23

theorists has quite properly placed the institutional debate into proper perspective by showing that the study of parties cannot be divorced from an analysis of historical forces influencing electoral politics. The character that parties will assume is constrained by the movement of history, and no institutional analysis can by itself explain all one wants to know about the question of electoral choice. The times may decisively dictate the degree of choice. On the other hand, however, the dynamic of historical movement cannot entirely account for the role of parties and the amount of choice they offer. At the very least, the original dispute between the two schools continues in respect to whether the institutional arrangements of the selection system should encourage the most rapid expressions of electoral changes or retard their course; and beyond this, it may be argued, and probably correctly, that the party system itself has an independent effect if not in creating, then at least in measurably stimulating or dampening, the cleavages within society. Neither an historical nor an institutional perspective on parties, then, is entirely adequate for comprehending the subject. Both forms of analysis are needed and must be combined into a more general theory that gives each its proper weight. Since, however, the movement of history lies outside the control of the institutional theorist, it is only natural that the debate on the selection system should focus on questions of institutional arrangements, for it is in this area that the legislator possesses a degree of choice.

The institutional dispute cannot be settled here, but some points of clarification can be offered. First, it is necessary to keep in mind just what role the selection of the president plays in initiating fundamental changes in the direction of public policy. The proponents of the choice school are correct in identifying presidential elections as one of the major sources of fundamental change or "renewal" in our system. One need only cite the elections of 1800 and 1860 as clear evidence of this fact. But it is incorrect to imply, as some of these same theorists have done, that national elections are the only source for such changes. Major changes in our system have been initiated from "above" the electoral process by the decisions of constituted authorities and from "below" the electoral process by temporary political movements that are not in any immediate way electoral agents. The initiation of the change to the welfare state and the modern civil rights revolution are better explained by one or both of these factors than by recourse to any decisions made in presidential elections. Presidential elections will usually play at least a secondary role in all such changes through a retrospective judgment of the initiatives taken by a president or even by the Court, but it inflates the importance of the selection process to claim that it is the only institution to consider when discussing the question of major change.

All further points of clarification require that one accept the distinction between normal and unusual times that lies at the heart of the theory of critical realignments. In normal times, the differences between the two schools of thought identified above are most clear-cut. Advocates of the consensual school worry about the threats to a democratic system that emanate from the "darker" side of democratic politics—from demagogues and from radical and intolerant movements. There is no justifiable reason, according to this school, to open the electoral process to these influences, which is exactly what would occur under any institutional arrangement that deliberately sought to magnify choice. Moreover, the magnification of choice, even when it manages to avoid extremism, actually conflicts with the goal of promoting a responsible electoral system. To foster responsibility, the electoral system must allow the citizens to express dissatisfaction with the incumbent by turning him out of office. If, however, the parties are ideological in character, voters may refrain from making the change they would like out of fear of the principles of the opposing party. Moderate differences between the positions of the parties provide the necessary flexibility that

25

allows citizens to punish one party without spiting themselves. The choice school responds to these arguments by declaring that it is precisely the failure to take on issues in normal times that leads to periodic crises and to a governing process characterized by "fits and starts."

Unusual times naturally confuse the debate between these two schools. By unusual times we are referring to those moments in which the division between elements of society and the nature of the issues are such that moderate choice is impossible. These major or critical elections constitute America's "mini-revolutions" and illustrate the central proposition of the critical-alignment theorists that all elections are not equal, even in a democracy. The existence of these elections has obviously created greater problems for the consensual school, and some of its proponents have justifiably been criticized for ignoring such elections altogether.[34] Yet certain spokesmen for this school, most notably V. O. Key and James Q. Wilson, have articulated a broader statement of the consensual position that encompasses such elections.[35] In their view there is no reason to structure the major parties in order to deliberately encourage change. Change will come—insofar as any institution can provide for it—when it is needed. Change derives from an open electoral system and not necessarily from intraparty democracy. For these theorists, the role of the third party is crucial in the dynamics of change. Change, in fact, comes from the least "institutionalized" aspects of the selection system, from third parties, movements that impinge on the major parties, and individual acts of leadership. The choice school, on the other hand, proceeds on the assumption that it is possible and desirable to institutionalize the function of change by the way in which the major parties are constituted, although members of this school are by no means

[34] See Jaffa, "The Nature and Origin," pp. 60-63.

[35] V. O. Key, Jr., "A Theory of Critical Elections," *Journal of Politics* 17 (February 1955), pp. 3-18; James Q. Wilson, *The Amateur Democrat*, see especially pp. 359-60.

in agreement about how this could be done. Because the major parties, if properly constituted, would provide for the proper amount of choice and change, one finds, curiously enough, that the role of third parties is usually less significant for the choice school theorists than for those of the consensual school. The choice school regards critical elections as in one sense representative of the kind of significant alternatives we always should have, although in another sense these elections go too far. The radical character of such elections, combined with the emergence of volatile movements and third parties, is a symptom of the failure of the two parties to regulate the proper degree of choice in normal times. A more rational arrangement would give us more serious elections but perhaps fewer critical ones.

The subject of this book is the development of the selection system from the founding of the republic to the present day. The developmental process is traced and explained by reference to the theories of the selection process of the Founders, Thomas Jefferson, Martin Van Buren and Woodrow Wilson. These statesmen were chosen either because they themselves were most influential in shaping the character of the selection process or because they best articulated the views of those who did play an active role. The Founders established the original system, and though they were less successful in this endeavor than in any other of their major initiatives, their structure still partly governs the process today and their ideas played a major role in the subsequent revisions of the selection system in the nineteenth century. Thomas Jefferson is less a theorist of the selection problem than the others included in this study. Yet as the principal leader of America's first political party, he had to justify certain changes from the original system that subsequently were developed by his follower, Martin Van Buren, into a more comprehensive doctrine. Martin Van Buren may justly be called the founder of the idea of permanent party

27

competition in America and of the consensual theory of the role of parties. His thought, which has only recently been "discovered" by historians, is crucial to understanding the workings of the selection process during the nineteenth century and indeed for most of this century as well. Woodrow Wilson offered the most coherent and certainly the most influential statement of the Progressive view of parties, selection, leadership, and change. In one form or another many of his ideas have filtered down and been accepted, often unknowingly, by modern advocates of reform.

In tracing the development of the selection system from the point of view of ideas, no claim is being made that this approach is comprehensive. The development of any institution, it hardly needs saying, is a product of much more than rational thought. Accident, circumstance, the striving of politicians for political advantage, and technological and sociological change have all played an important role in shaping the evolution of the selection system, as standard institutional histories of the process have amply documented.[36] In contrast to the view in these histories, however, it will be argued that the ideas of the statesmen considered in this study exercised an important and often a decisive influence in shaping the broad outlines of the development of the system. And whatever may be the limitations of this focus from the standpoint of the historian, it certainly offers the historical approach that is best suited for helping us deal with contemporary issues in the selection process. Theories about the selection process, much more than past events, can provide us with an understanding of the general problems of this institution and assist the legislator in making choices about its future character.

[36] See Eugene H. Roseboom, *A History of Presidential Elections* (New York: Macmillan, 1970), Paul David, Ralph Goldman and Richard Bain, *The Politics of National Party Conventions* (Washington, D.C.: Brookings Institution, 1960), chap. 2; and Roy F. Nichols, *The Invention of the American Political Parties* (New York: Free Press, 1967).

An outline of the historical development for each of the five functions identified earlier can briefly be described. In regard to structuring the ambitions of presidential aspirants, the Founders sought to devise a system that would prevent electoral contests that turned on the use of the "popular arts," meaning issue arousal and the emphasis on those aspects of character that played to popular passions for an attractive or interesting leader. Such contests, the Founders believed, would undermine the intended role for the president and introduce the danger of unnecessary electoral divisions. The direction of their solution was to base the choice of the president not on momentary campaign appeals, but on the candidates' reputation as determined largely by previous public service. Their electoral system was designed to divert the ambition of aspirants from making issue appeals and channel it in the direction of establishing a distinguished record.

Jefferson took a step toward admitting issue formation in the selection process. Popular leadership in this sense, he believed, was necessary in 1800 to counteract the oligarchic bias of the existing nonpartisan system and to rescue republican government from what he considered to be the seditious designs of the Federalists. But with the advent of the Missouri debates in 1819, Jefferson began to stress the dangers of unregulated popular leadership, fearing that unscrupulous leaders of the opposition party would seize on popular passions in an effort to raise themselves to the presidency. Jefferson's solution, to which he never consistently adhered, was to establish the dominance in the nomination process of two parties—the Republicans and the Federalists. This would force Federalist leaders to attach themselves openly to the principles of their party, which Jefferson thought were less dangerous, at least after 1816, than some of the temporary issues these leaders might exploit under nonpartisan competition.

Van Buren developed Jefferson's suggestion into a general solution to the problem of ambition in the pursuit of the presidency. The catalytic event for Van Buren was the election of 1824 in which the Republican Party ceased to nominate or function as a meaningful organization, and in which as a consequence the candidates found themselves "free" to solicit the presidency in the most expedient fashion. Van Buren shared Jefferson's views about the dangerous consequences of nonpartisan politics, which he felt would lead to campaigns based on demagoguery or "image" appeals, but he did not accept Jefferson's contention that the problem was restricted only to leaders of the opposition party. The issue as he saw it was a more general one of unregulated ambition in pursuit of the presidency. Following Jefferson's briefly held view, Van Buren proposed the establishment of permanent competition between two parties that were safe and moderate in their principles and that together would normally control the path of access to the presidency. Aspirants would then be forced to adopt the principles of one or another of these parties, thereby avoiding appeals to more dangerous currents of opinion. The selection of leaders could best be determined in the initial preselection phase by knowledgeable politicians, and it was to such persons that Van Buren assigned the task of nomination, at first (unsuccessfully) in the form of the Congressional caucus and later in the form of the national convention. The final test between the candidates would come at the final election stage, where the voters, shielded from the confusion likely to characterize a race among numerous candidate factions, could make their choice between two tested and well-known parties. The electorate, as envisioned by Van Buren, would consist mainly of partisans whose voting decision would be based as much on their attachment to their party as on an independent determination of each candidate's qualification and merit.

Wilson focused on the absence of strong leadership in the government, a fact which he attributed in part to the overbearing power of the party organizations in relationship to the individual aspirants. To provide for stronger leadership,

Wilson sought by means of the national primary to enhance the status of individual candidates during the electoral process, freeing them from the constraints of traditional parties and allowing them to create a popular constituency of their own making. The political party, understood in an entirely different way from the nineteenth century, would form around the successful candidate and his program. Wilson expressed concern over the dangers of excessive popular appeals and demagoguery, which his solution seemed to invite, but he abandoned any attempt to control them by institutional means, relying instead on the good sense of the people and the self-restraint of the leaders. The rejection of institutional controls on leadership appeals marked a decisive break with previous theories and laid the foundation for the modern view of "openness" in the selection process.

In regard to the effect of the selection system on presidential leadership and executive power, the Founders saw their system as consistent with maintaining the "independence" of the executive. Choice by electors avoided dependence on Congress (except in the event of recourse to the auxiliary plan); and election by reputation would foreclose the need to make specific commitments to voters. The Founders also understood that the executive would often have to withstand popular demands. For this, too, selection on the basis of reputation along with some degree of indirectness respecting the popular vote would provide the president with the necessary degree of insulation.

Jefferson's views on the connection between the selection system and the presidency were never fully developed, but certain implications can be drawn from his general position. Jefferson sought to move the president into closer contact with the immediate opinions of the people and saw that a national election could provide a direct test of the people's will. Victory in such a contest provided the president with the added weight of popular authority, although in his interpretation of the formal powers of the presidency Jefferson

favored a more limited role than that envisioned by his prede-
cessors. Jefferson also introduced the idea of selection according to party principle, with the leader being chosen
initially by fellow partisans and distinguished in large measure by his fidelity to partisan goals. Executive power, in this
view, would likewise be used to accomplish partisan ends.
Yet it is important to note that, except for a brief period,
Jefferson did not intend partisanship to be permanent. His
objective, at least up until 1819, was to end active opposition
by a second party and to establish the principles of his own
party as the consensual basis of a new nonpartisan order.
There was little difference, then, between Jefferson's initial
ideas on party competition and those of the Founders, though
his justifications for some of his short-term actions were not
without important long-term effects.

Van Buren was less concerned with the selection system's
effect on the presidency than with some of the other functions, but once again certain general ideas concerning presidential leadership follow from his other positions. In Van
Buren's view, the party leader would be a "politician" skilled
at holding together the conflicting interests of a diverse coalition. His concept of a partisan leader was thus much less
that of the principled spokesman of partisan ideals embodied
by Jefferson and more that of a pluralist broker. The president would have certain obligations for maintaining his
party's organization which included the distribution of patronage. The executive would also be limited by the principles
of his party, although these principles were of such a general
character that room would still exist for the exercise of considerable discretion. Van Buren also appreciated, though in
a limited way, that the strength of the party could be of some
assistance to the executive in carrying his view with Congress.

Woodrow Wilson reacted against the constraints on leadership that the nineteenth-century parties imposed and against
the limited role for the executive that had grown up over the
course of the century. Wilson sought to devise a selection
system that would give the executive a new basis of authority

which could expand both the president's power and discretion and thereby transform the presidency from the "errand boy" of Congress into the preeminent institution of the national government. The key to the president's new authority lay with his claim to being a public opinion leader embodying personally the will or mandate of the people. Under a national primary system, Wilson hoped to focus attention once again on the qualities of the individual leader rather than on the traditions or principles of the party. Unlike the Founders, however, Wilson stressed the importance of the leader's programs or general "vision" in soliciting popular support. Selection of the candidates would turn on how leaders "interpreted" the popular will, with interpretation understood as a function transcending established party lines and resting on direct communication between the individual leader and the public. This understanding of political leadership coincided perfectly with Wilson's concept of executive leadership: the foundation of presidential authority would exist not so much in the formal powers of the office as in the informal claim of popular leadership. The technique of winning office was much the same as the technique of governing.

Corresponding to these different conceptions of presidential leadership were different ideas about the character attributes expected of the candidates. These ideas were very general and were embedded in the conceptions of leadership, a fact that suggests that these statesmen recognized the impossibility of specifying a single character type for the presidency. The line of development on this function follows a movement from the Founders' conception of maturity and "virtue," to Van Buren's more democratic emphasis on the compatibility or likeness between the leader and the people, to Wilson's democratic but antipopulist ideal of excellence in the service of the popular will. Wilson's understanding of excellence was linked to the quality of inspirational leadership, meaning the ability to convey a moral sense or vision to the people. The Wilsonian ideal continues to dominate today, though it has been mixed with a more populist con-

33

ception of compatibility and has at times been replaced in practice by certain "image" characteristics. These are both results which Wilson would have deplored, but which his own open system seems to encourage.

On the function of ensuring legitimacy, we have already noted the increased emphasis on the principle of direct democracy down to the present-day insistence by some on a direct election of the president and a full-scale plebiscitary nominating system. The "informal" aspect of legitimacy, which refers to the problem of securing a candidate with sufficient popular support to avoid having the state create a majority, has been equally important in explaining the development of the selection system. The Founders made every effort to devise a system that would, if necessary, create a majority that would appear as natural as possible. The system of choice by electors, each having two votes, was central to their plan. Yet even this system could not guarantee a majority, and the Founders, over the objections of Madison and Hamilton, devised a cumbersome and undemocratic auxiliary plan of election by the House. The belief of many of the Founders was that the auxiliary plan would seldom need to be used because the nationalizing effect of the new Constitution would ensure, in James Wilson's words, that "continental characters will multiply . . . so as to enable the electors in every part of the union to know and judge them."[37] This assessment was probably too optimistic. In any event, the apparent failure of such characters to emerge automatically, together with certain institutional changes from the Founders' plan, made it appear after the election of 1824 that the choice of the president might usually be made by the House. To avoid this result, Martin Van Buren and his followers argued that parties were needed to narrow the field of contestants and provide national support for the candidates.

With the acceptance of parties, the problem of securing a nominee with sufficient backing to be a legitimate choice disappeared. It was replaced, however, with disputes over

[37] Madison, *Notes*, p. 578 (September 4).

34

the legitimacy of the nomination process and with a concern over the quality of the persons selected by parties that bordered on a concern for legitimacy. The Progressives decried the monopoly over nomination by bodies that subordinated considerations of leadership qualifications to the parochial and often corrupt interests of the party organizations. The nominees chosen by these bodies were said to be undistinguished and to lack, if not legitimacy for the office they sought, then at least the stature that could claim for the office its rightful place as the central institution in the American system. The return to a focus on individual leaders in the selection of the president would not, according to Wilson, pose any problems relating to the informal aspect of legitimacy. Parties would still be in existence at the final election stage to ensure a national following; and at the nominating stage one could now be confident that with the development at last of a truly national political community, individual leaders would emerge from a popular vote with broad national support.

On the final function, providing for choice and change, it has already been said that the Founders envisioned a nonpartisan selection process in which the outcome would turn less on issues than on a judgment of the qualifications of well-known statesmen. Yet the Founders did foresee an important role for a popular pronouncement on policy and hence to some extent on change in the case of elections in which an incumbent wished to be returned. In these elections, the Founders believed their system would allow for a retrospective judgment of the incumbent's performance and a change in leadership (and policy) if there was general dissatisfaction. The Founders never spoke, however, of the use of national elections for the purpose of making "critical" changes or implementing new principles emanating from a popular movement. Jefferson, of course, employed a national election for one such change in the "revolution of 1800," and his writings were filled with constant reminders of the need for periodic revisions of the laws and general policies. Yet for all this he never developed a doctrine of selection in which presidential elections were seen as the natural occasion for such changes. And in fact, as time went on, he increasingly emphasized the threat presidential elections posed for fomenting dangerous divisions.

Martin Van Buren purposely established parties to control or manage change. Parties would be moderating agencies that would place impediments in the way of new and upsetting electoral divisions. They would not, however, fully close the door to critical change, as a challenge by a third party was still a possibility. It would be more correct to say that the doctrine of party competition was designed by Van Buren to introduce a bias against change. Wilson sought to reverse this presumption and to open the electoral system to new initiatives on a regular basis. But unlike the modern party-government school—of which he was, ironically, the founder— Wilson saw the source of change as emanating in the first instance from individual leaders and not parties. With Wilson the selection process achieves a new importance, which it continues to hold today, as the "institution" in the regime that provides for dynamic transformations. For Wilson it might be said that the selection process becomes an institution of equal importance with the formal institutions, having a positive function to perform that no other institution can.

From this survey of the functions of the selection system it may be observed that the development of ideas about the presidential selection process strongly influenced, and in turn were strongly influenced by, ideas about the role of political parties. While there is a certain merit in treating the development of parties as an independent concern, as some well-known historians have done, it should be clear that many of the decisive changes in the "idea" of party in America were related to the effect of parties on presidential selection.[38] A complete understanding of the development of parties and

[38] The history of the development of the idea of party is best treated in Richard Hofstadter's *The Idea of a Party System* (Berkeley: University of California Press, 1969).

of the presidential selection system therefore requires that the two be treated together.

For the Founders, parties and popular leadership were viewed largely as distinct problems with each being considered a political evil for independent reasons. The two problems intersected, however, at the point of presidential selection, where the Founders held that popular leadership in the pursuit of office would cause or facilitate the formation of national parties. Candidates making use of the popular arts would raise national issue constituencies, which, in light of the excesses brought on by the open bidding for popular approval, might ultimately lead to parties in the most dreaded sense of seditious alternatives to the existing regime. To Jefferson in his later years and to Van Buren, party became the beneficial instrument for controlling popular leadership during selection. Two dominant parties, each with relatively safe principles, would absorb the nation's partisan energies and force leadership to occupy predetermined grounds. This solution required a change both in the kind of parties that existed and in the attitude toward parties on the part of active partisans. Parties could no longer do battle over first principles but had to conform to the basic principles of the regime; and partisans could no longer concern themselves simply with the fate of their own party, but also had to consider the well-being of the party system as a whole.

The objective shared by the Founders and Van Buren on the crucial point of using the selection process to control personal factions and demagogic leadership makes it possible to speak of a common perspective between the two, notwithstanding their differences on some of the other functions and notwithstanding the striking fact that the Founders were inveterate foes of parties while Van Buren was their ardent champion. Indeed, if one focuses on the Founders' objectives for the selection process rather than the institutional forms they established, and further if one takes into account the failures of their system and the new circumstances in America as of the 1820s, it can plausibly be argued that permanent party competition was the solution most compatible with the Founders' goals. Following this line of argument, the decisive break in the development of the selection process might be said to come not with the change from nonpartisanship to partisanship but rather with the change from traditional partisanship to the kind of "partisan" competition envisioned by Wilson under a plebiscitary system.

With Wilson's thought, we arrive at the heart of the contemporary view—and the contemporary confusion—about the role of parties and leadership in the selection process. Wilson, discounting or dismissing the dangers of popular leadership, wanted to strengthen it and make it the basis for choosing the president and even for governing. To accomplish this change, he sought to destroy traditional political parties and put an end to unreflective partisan voting. Yet Wilson's ideas for replacing the traditional party system led him in two different and contradictory directions. On the one hand, by the plebiscitary nominating system, he would remove the political party from all influence in choosing its nominee. On the other hand, to augment the executive's power, Wilson would establish under the old party labels a new kind of responsible party that would follow the president's initiatives in Congress and provide active support for the president with the electorate. In no way, however, would these powerful parties constrain or encumber the individual leader, whom Wilson hoped might ultimately attain a supreme transpartisan status. Wilson was thus at once the founder of the party-government school and its most formidable opponent. He portrays parties as strong when they can promote leadership but conveniently has them assume a weak and shadowy form when they might conflict with it. This kind of deception, however possible within the confines of a nicely written academic treatise, cannot pass the test of political reality. Parties must either constrain individual leadership or be undermined by it. This confusion—or ambivalence—about party and its relationship to leadership continue in the political thought of today.

38

After a long period of stability dating from the 1920s to the 1960s, a new selection system has begun to emerge. It has replaced the traditional "mixed" system which had combined in an uneasy but workable way elements of Martin Van Buren's theory of party dominance and Woodrow Wilson's theory of individual candidate supremacy. The former was "represented" in the power of the party organizations, the latter in the state primaries where the choice of delegates centered on their national candidate preference. The new system has upset this balance and moved to establish some variant of Wilson's model of individual candidate supremacy. Although the modern reformers most responsible for overturning the old system disclaim any debt to Wilson and the Progressives, the imprint of Progressive influence on their basic assumptions is unmistakable. Like Wilson, the modern reformers have attacked the role and legitimacy of the party organization in presidential selection by insisting on an "open" system with the focus on rank-and-file choice among national candidates; and they have denied any role to the selection system—criminal sanctions excepted—in restraining or directing political ambition. Reformers also follow Wilson in calling for stronger, more responsible parties even while the effect of their proposals has been to weaken the coherence and organizational unity of the party: they, too, have been unable to resolve, let alone acknowledge, the tension inherent in their dual commitment to party and individual leadership. Where reformers perhaps diverge most from Wilson is in the absence of any serious attempt to relate the selection system to presidential leadership. While one can certainly detect a desire for a pure, issue-oriented form of presidential leadership in some of the early reform doctrines when the "new politics" movement was at the forefront, as time went on reformers more and more seemed to adopt procedural goals as ends in themselves.

If the views of past theorists have any applicability to understanding the issues of selection today, they might suggest to us that the emerging system, by opening the selection process to the dominance of individual candidates, will also open it to the problems of "image" politics and demagogic leadership appeals. They might also forewarn us that the new system will remove a significant informal check on executive power at the same time that it provides the victorious candidate with a formidable claim to the possession of a personal mandate, a claim that he might be all the more disposed to employ to overcome his other weaknesses. What all this may suggest is the need to reestablish the political party as a restraining and moderating force on political power, but in such a way that it can pass the test of modern standards of republican legitimacy.

CHAPTER I

The Founders

THE recent crisis over presidential power has brought an increased respect for the Founding Fathers from virtually every segment of the populace. This includes even the highly educated, who for the past generation were brought up on a steady diet of the writings of Woodrow Wilson and Charles Beard—the former attacking the Founders' constitutional doctrines and the latter their personal motives. The ideas of these men appeared to be fully digested, and perhaps were, when the abuses of presidential power began. Upset by these events, many turned to the political thought of the Founders where convenient support could be found for many newly developed positions. As the educated came around to displays of public veneration for the Constitution, with society's opinion makers following closely behind, the Founders' stature grew rapidly and with it the prevailing opinion that no institutional problem could be intelligently discussed without first consulting their political thought.

No one, however, has been practicing what is preached when it comes to the question of presidential selection. Scholars writing on current selection problems have chosen to ignore the views of the Founders and to look elsewhere for their guiding principles. The reasons for this neglect seem obvious: how could a selection system predicated on non-partisan competition that made no provision for a distinct nominating stage be of any assistance in an era of partisan politics in which the major controversies center on the method of nomination? And how could a plan that did not explicitly provide for full popular participation in the election of the president, the very hallmark of our current system, be

41

sufficiently compatible with contemporary views to serve as a guide?

These objections are sound as far as they go. But it is not necessary to defend the Founders' institutional solution or assert its applicability today in order to benefit from their ideas on the selection process. In searching to answer the question of how to choose a powerful executive in an extended republic, the Founders were forced, virtually for the first time in history, to confront all the major issues and define the chief functions of the selection system. While their solution was flawed (as many of them soon realized), their deliberations constitute the most profound treatment of the topic in American political thought; and it is fortunate for our purposes here that the body of thought which appears first in this study is also the most comprehensive.

THE FOUNDERS' UNDERSTANDING OF POPULAR ELECTION

To the modern student, the Founders' theory of selection is deficient or incomplete on what is regarded today as the most critical question: how democratic is the method of choice? The Founders, it is fair to say, never provided a clear answer to this question. The Constitution, of course, carefully defines those who are immediately empowered to select: special electors are designated for the task; and in the event that they fail to give the requisite number of votes to any candidate, the election is then decided by the House, voting by states.[1] But the Constitution does not specify how the

[1] The complicated original provision is found in Article II, Section 2 of the Constitution, much of which has now been superceded by the Twelfth Amendment. The original plan called for the apportionment of electors to the states in accord with the combined total of their senators and representatives. Each elector had two votes, at least one of which had to be for a candidate from outside his own state. A majority of the electors (not of the electoral votes cast) would elect. In the event of a tie among candidates receiving more than a majority, the House would choose from among those tied; and in the event no candidate received more

electors themselves are to be chosen. This matter is left for each state legislature to decide. The different plausible alternatives under the Founders' system thus range from an essentially popular election, in which the electors would be selected by the people and instructed as to their choice, to an election twice removed from the people, in which the electors would be selected by the state legislatures and left free to make up their own minds.

How can one account for the Founders' failure to decide so fundamental an issue? Some have explained it by saying that the question of how democratic the election should be was of secondary importance at the time.[2] The principal nationalists at the Convention—men like James Madison, James Wilson, and Gouverneur Morris—all favored a strong and independent executive and were therefore willing to accept virtually any plan that did not involve the state governments or the Congress, no matter how democratic (or undemocratic) it might be. While this explanation has some merit, it breaks down if pushed to the extreme. The nationalists supported a strong and independent executive because of certain expectations they held about the attributes of the office. One such attribute—and a crucial one—was the ability of the president to withstand popular pressure when it conflicted with the public good. If the alternative to Congressional selection undermined this "conservative," i.e. nonpopulist, role for the presidency, it seems highly doubtful that the strong executive advocates could have supported it.

The mode of selection that one might think is most democratic in its effects, and hence most antithetical to the Founders' conception of the executive's role, is a direct vote

---

than a majority of electors, the House would vote by states, with each state having one vote and with a majority of all the states being required for election.

[2] See for example Paul Eidelberg, *The Philosophy of the American Constitution* (New York: Free Press, 1968), pp. 172-73 and Edward Stanwood, *A History of the Presidency from 1788 to 1897* (Boston: Houghton Mifflin, 1898), p. 3.

by the people. It is a striking fact, however, that the proponents of the strong executive all began the Convention
by advocating some form of popular election. Some have
suggested that they adopted this position merely for tactical
reasons, as a way of leading the Convention away from its
initial disposition in favor of a Congressional system and
toward some kind of indirect election by a special body. But
if they conceived of a popular election as a highly democratic
instrument likely to produce a "people's president," it is difficult to believe that they would ever have risked so dangerous
a tactic. The more plausible explanation, which will be developed at greater length below, is that the most influential
Founders thought of popular elections as a method that
would usually produce a "conservative" or moderate result.[3]

It is regrettable that so much of the scholarship on the
Founders has begun with an attempt to determine how
democratic (in form) the Framers intended the selection
system to be without first entertaining the possibility that they
understood popular election in very different terms than we
do today. The consequence of approaching the issue in this
manner has been that scholars have often based their interpretations on an assessment of how they believe the Founders
might have reacted to modern, i.e. partisan, elections. As one
might imagine, the positions that have been adopted on this
question have been colored by general views about the
Founders' intentions as a whole. The "democratic school"
of interpreters, partial to the notion that the Founders wanted
a democratic executive, has argued that the Founders favored
a direct popular election and stopped short of implementing
it only because of certain practical obstacles. Thus Martin
Diamond has written that "the Framers created a national
popularly elected Presidency with the best means available,

[3] Other accounts of the Founders' understanding of elections may
be found in Gordon Wood, *The Creation of the American Republic
1776-1787* (New York: W. W. Norton, 1969), pp. 511-18; and
Judith Best, *The Case Against the Direct Election of the President*
(Ithaca: Cornell University Press, 1975).

44

and with means wholly open to further democratic development"; and according to Lucius Wilmerding, "the electoral system was adopted only because it seemed the most practical way to give equal weights to equal masses of people where suffrage laws varied from state to state."[4] An "aristocratic school" of interpreters, on the other hand, holds that the Founders deliberately sought to make the election of the president indirect, not for practical reasons but out of a theoretical concern for limiting popular influence. The electors in this view would preferably be selected by the state legislatures, but in any case would make a choice which, in Sir Henry Maine's words, would be "the mature fruit of an independent exercise of judgment."[5]

It seems doubtful that this dispute will ever be resolved. The Constitutional provision governing selection will admit of either interpretation, and both sides can produce evidence in the Founders' works to support their positions. If the aristocratic school can cite Hamilton's argument that the people may be given too much to "heats and ferments" to decide the question on their own, the democratic school can counter with Madison's statement that the president "will be the choice of the people at large."[6]

Without denying the seriousness of their omission, it must nonetheless be pointed out that the Founders did not perceive the contrast between these two positions as being nearly as great as most of their subsequent interpreters. Because they thought that a direct nonpartisan election was basically

[4] Lucius Wilmerding, *The Electoral College* (New Brunswick, N.J.: Rutgers University Press, 1958), p. xi; Martin Diamond, Winston Mills Fisk, and Herbert Garfinkel, *The Democratic Republic* (Chicago: Rand McNally, 1966), p. 102.

[5] Sir Henry Maine, *Popular Government* (London: John Murray, 1885), p. 215.

[6] Alexander Hamilton, James Madison and John Jay, *The Federalist Papers*, ed. Clinton Rossiter (New York: New American Library, 1961), #68, p. 412; and Jonathan Elliott, ed., *The Debates in the Several State Conventions on the Adoption of the Federal Constitution*, 2nd ed., 5 vols. (Philadelphia, 1861), 3:487, 494.

45

a safe plan that would produce a moderate result, it follows that they would not have viewed the failure to specify exactly who should choose the president as a major deficiency. In particular, they would not have thought that electors popularly selected and instructed would normally be inclined to support a "people's candidate" in perennial conflict with an "aristocratic candidate" favored by electors chosen by an indirect method. Without a great disparity in results anticipated for these two systems, the Founders could justify their ambiguity about how the electors would be selected on the practical grounds that it might help secure the support of proponents of both methods.

Of course this leaves unanswered the question of exactly why the Founders changed from a direct election plan to the electoral method found in the Constitution. The reasons, as we shall see, were predominantly "practical," relating to the problems of differing suffrage requirements in the states and the question of how to count the slave population. Yet a theoretical distrust of popular elections was also partly at issue, at least for Hamilton, Jay, and in some measure Madison. The important point to observe, however, is that the objectives for selection favored by those having certain doubts about popular election were the same as those sought by the advocates of direct election.

This conception of the Founders' understanding of elections is likely to displease both their aristocratic and democratic interpreters. The former might object to the denial of any deep hostility on the Founders' part to the form of popular election, while the latter would probably take exception to the emphasis the Founders placed on its "conservative" results. To defend this view from the opposition of both these groups, it will be necessary to outline the Founders' general intention for the presidency, their understanding of the nature of a nonpartisan electoral process, and the relationship of their proposed selection system to the kind of presidential leadership they intended.

46

THE FOUNDERS' CONCEPTION OF THE EXECUTIVE

The Founders' understanding of the place of the executive in the American system cannot be understood apart from their general intention for the entire regime. Besides their well-known objection to the weakness of the existing confederal form of government, the Founders were reacting against two other basic problems in the society and government under the Articles. The first was the growing ascendancy in politics of the wrong type or "class" of persons. If one looks at the Founders' thought at the time of the Revolution, it is clear that one of their principal objectives was to overthrow a social structure based on artificial privilege deriving from royal favors. Their aim was not to level society but to erect a just order of social stratification with a hierarchy that reflected talent and merit. This order, they believed, would be able to win universal respect, and it followed that political leaders would be recruited from the higher rungs of society in which the most able would be found.[7]

But the Founders' expectations were disappointed. The creation of the new social hierarchy was met in the political realm not with respect but resentment. In state after state the Revolution spawned a conception of popular government in which it was held that only the "common man" or the "representative type" could be trusted to safeguard a republican form of government. Those at the top were excluded for their supposedly aristocratic leanings. From the viewpoint of many of the Founders, moreover, it was not the simple representative type who was succeeding, but rather a meaner kind of opportunist who made use of populist doctrines to advance in society. Public office, in the words of one Fed-

---

[7] Gordon Wood, *The Creation*, p. 393-429. I will be relying on Wood throughout this section and also on Bernard Bailyn, *The Ideological Origins of the American Revolution* (Cambridge: Harvard University Press, 1967), and Charles Thach, Jr., *The Creation of the Presidency, 1775-1789* (Baltimore: The Johns Hopkins Press, 1969).

eralist-minded tract of the time, was increasingly occupied by "demagogues of desperate fortunes, mere adventurers in fraud. . . ."[8] The disappointing replacements for colonial obsequiousness to the royal prerogative and contempt for the common man were flattery of the people and jealousy of merit. The kind of leadership the Founders had sought had escaped them under the Articles. In calling for a new system of government they were attempting to give the direction of public affairs to those who were called, either with bitterness or pride, the "better sorts."

The second problem against which the Founders were reacting was that of the distribution of power and the basis of political authority within most of the state governments. In some respects this problem was the institutional manifestation of the first, though it had separate roots in the radical Whig thought of the time. The pressure for a more direct expression in government of the will of the people led to the rise of the popular branch of the legislature as the supreme and unchecked sovereign in many states. As Gordon Wood notes, "the American legislatures, in particular the lower houses of the assemblies, were no longer to be merely adjuncts or checks to magisterial power, but were in fact to be the government. . . ."[9] Executive power, associated by many Whig theorists with monarchism no matter under what form it appeared, was distrusted and jealously circumscribed. Some of those who played a major role in establishing the Constitution had at one time sympathized with this position. But by 1787, those who took the lead in calling for the Constitutional Convention had rejected this view and adopted a decidedly more favorable attitude toward executive power. Moreover, they saw the unfettered ascendancy of the popular assembly as a symptom of yet a deeper problem: a reliance on popular authority. It was not just that the legislatures were supreme; it was that they based their power on a claim

[8] Edward Carrington to Jefferson, June 9, 1787 cited in Wood, *The Creation*, p. 498.
[9] Wood, *The Creation*, p. 163.

to immediate representation of the popular will. To the Founders this kind of government was the closest thing to a democracy, a term they reserved in a strict sense to refer to the direct rule by the people in what necessarily had to be a very small territory. The rule of the representatives in a larger territory on the (supposed) grounds of their expressing the people's wishes might then be called a "representative democracy." Like democracy itself, this form of government was very different from the regime the Founders wanted to establish. The Founders were seeking a regime of representative or constitutional government in which officials rested their power on the legally defined prerogatives of their offices and in which the claim to rule was based on the constituted authority of the institutions.

It was the ascendancy of these unanticipated popular doctrines with their prejudice against merit and their theories of unchecked legislative predominance that led many of the Founders to seek a new form of government. At stake for these men was not simply the well-being of a class nor even the prosperity of the community, but the fate of the entire republican enterprise. In the movement for the Constitution the leading Federalists sought to remove effective power in a number of crucial areas from the jurisdiction of the states, and hence from the influence of demagogues controlling the state legislatures, and place it in a new national government where it was considered more likely that the better sort of individuals would dominate. The regime would be a representative government, with a strong executive capable of restraining any tendencies toward popular authority. The intention was not to establish an aristocracy, though it was quite explicitly to institute a more moderate form of popular government than that which existed in many of the states.[10]

---

[10] This is most clear from their description of the type of men whom the Founders thought would serve in the most popular of all the institutions, the House. See especially *The Federalist* #35 and #36, where Hamilton argues that the representatives would consist primarily of proprietors of land, merchants, and members of the learned professions.

In making the case for this kind of government, the Founders naturally refused to concede the term republican to their opponents. The proposed government, they asserted, was rightly classified as republican because it "deriv[ed] all of its powers directly or indirectly from the great body of the people."[11] If this definition affirms that the Constitution as a whole is in the final analysis popular, it also acknowledges that its various parts might be more or less democratic. The House was clearly to be closest to and thus most representative of the democratic element, while the executive would be more partial to, and itself embody, certain aristocratic or monarchic elements. Thus both the democratic and the monarchic tendencies—which Jefferson and de Tocqueville considered the two natural and ineradicable "parties" in any body politic—were included and represented within the fabric of the Constitution, and this probably led many to believe that there was no need for political parties in the electoral realm.[12] But the implied identification of each of these institutions with certain societal forces was not to be understood literally or applied mechanically. No institution was tied directly to any particular group in society after the fashion of a representative of an estate; and every effort was made to enable each body to act independently and objectively. The Founders clearly understood that certain of the institutions would come closer than others to this goal. With the possible exception of the Court, their highest expectations in this regard were for the presidency. The presidency, they thought, could be so constituted as to reach beyond the partial and selfish interests of any group within society and consult the public interest as a whole. Indeed at one point during the Convention, Gouverneur Morris, one of the most conservative of all the Federalists, spoke of the Chief Magis-

[11] *The Federalist*, #39, p. 241.

[12] This idea is suggested by Harvey Mansfield, Jr., "Thomas Jefferson" in Morton J. Frisch and Richard G. Stevens, eds., *American Political Thought* (New York: Charles Scribner's Sons, 1971), p. 45.

trate as "the guardian of the lower classes . . . against the Great and Wealthy."[13] Nevertheless, in a popularly based regime, it was generally believed that the principal threat to constitutional government would come from the popular side—from disruptive currents of public opinion or from the House, in particular from certain demagogues who might win its confidence. It was ultimately for the president to make use of his independence to restrain these influences and to prevent constitutional government from dissolving into representative democracy.

The properties in the executive sought by the Founders can be summarized as follows. In negative terms, they wanted to prevent the president from defining himself and from being looked upon as a popular favorite. The president might earn the people's respect, but he was not to solicit their favor. In positive terms, the Founders looked to the president to lend "energy," i.e. firmness and competence, to the government and to provide a source of statesmanship. Statesmanship, meaning the exercise of personal judgment in accord with the dictates of political prudence, required in the Founders' view some distance or "protection" for the executive from the immediate pressures of public opinion, and hence a source of authority for the president in the prerogatives of the office itself. Finally, for the executive no less than for any other of the institutions, the Founders sought to ensure that power would not go unchecked. The two chief objectives of any sound constitution, according to Madison, were "first to obtain for rulers men who possess most wisdom to discern, and most virtue to pursue, the common good of society; and in the next place to take the most effective precautions for keeping them virtuous whilst they continue to hold their public trust." As much as the Founders hoped that the "best" or most virtuous would govern, they were

[13] James Madison, *Notes of Debates in the Federal Convention*, pp. 322-23 (July 19). The dates on which presidential selection was discussed were: June 1, 2, 9; July 17, 19, 24, 25, 27; August 24; and September 4, 5, 6, and 7.

aware that no institutional mechanism could ever assure that statesmen would "always be at the helm."[14] Nor did the Founders, for reasons that will shortly be seen, trust so much to virtue as to allow it to govern without restraints. In this respect the Founders differed decisively from the ancients and shared the modern idea that a constitution is defined even more by its institutional arrangements than by who rules.

Yet if all this expresses what the Founders wanted from the executive, it is quite another matter to explain how they hoped to attain it. Most scholars of the Founding have focused on the formal institutional properties such as the powers of the presidency, the duration in office, and the relationship between the executive and the Congress. But an important influence that has been all too often overlooked is the "electoral connection," the effect of the mode of selection on the character of the office.[15] The issue to be considered here, after looking at the Founders' general intentions from a slightly different perspective, is how they attempted to fashion the selection system to conform to their intentions for the executive.

The Problem of Popular Leadership

The Founders, we have said, were reacting not only against the idea of unchecked legislative supremacy, but against the claims of "popular authority" on which that power was based. The Founding, seen in the light of this problem, was an attempt to ensure that formal or constituted authority was not overwhelmed by informal or extraconstitutional authority, by power based on "charisma" or assertions of representation of the immediate popular will. The Founders were aware that claims to informal popular authority would inevitably play some role in the regime they

[14] *The Federalist*, #57, p. 350; #10, p. 80.
[15] The expression "electoral connection" comes from the title of David Mayhew's book, *Congress: The Electoral Connection* (New Haven: Yale University Press, 1974).

established. One cannot read *The Federalist* closely without noticing that the formal edifice of institutional authority is always in some sense constrained by the movement of public opinion. The intent of the Founders was to control or contain the influence of this informal authority, to carve out a realm of discretionary authority by creating a basic level of public opinion in support of the Constitution. The very present danger was that this fragile basis of constituted authority would disintegrate under the influence of a leader who would activate the raw force of popular sovereignty and transform it into the immediate source of political power. The potential for the exercise of this type of authority did serve one positive function. It deterred acts of sedition in the direction of oligarchy by one of the "unpopular" branches. Any such attempt, the Founders thought, could easily be foiled by a leader in the House who would sound the alarm among the people and if necessary claim authority for the legislature beyond its formal role.[16] This helps explain why the Founders never worried quite as much as the antifederalists about the threat of monarchism. They looked beyond the forms to the substance of the new regime and saw clearly that the preponderant power was with the people. But the corresponding danger was that a claim to popular authority would be employed by a leader not for defensive purposes, but, under that pretext, to throw off all constitutional restraint and achieve supreme power. To the Founders, informal popular authority would be the most probable source for what they called usurpation and for what we know today as institutional imperialism.

The theme of popular authority is treated in *The Federalist* mostly in relation to the House of Representatives. Urged on by its "leaders," the House was the institution most likely to attempt to "draw all power into its impetuous vortex . . . [to show] disgust at the least sign of opposition from any quarter . . . and act with such momentum as to make it difficult for any other members of the government to maintain the bal-

[16] *The Federalist*, #71, p. 433.

ance of the Constitution."[17] The House, of course, was best situated to make this claim because of its closeness to the people; but it bears emphasizing that it was not the House *per se* that the Founders distrusted, but the claim to informal popular authority. While *The Federalist* presents the executive for the most part as the Founders wanted it to be, it is clear from the debates at the Convention that the possibility of the president emerging as a "favorite" or a "demagogue" at some point in the future, after Washington had served and after the prejudice against executive power had weakened, was not dismissed. The picture of the executive in *The Federalist* is one that already assumes the "solution" to demagogic authority in the presidency, a solution that was based in large measure on the anticipated effects of the selection system. Even so, *The Federalist* contains occasional references to the possibility of a presidential "favorite," an indication that the Founders realized that their solution was not foolproof.[18]

Following the general terminology of the Founders, the general name we can give to this informal kind of authority is popular leadership. Popular refers to the source of the authority and leadership indicates its noninstitutional character. Although the Founders recognized the need for leadership in establishing the regime—twice they speak approvingly of the "leaders" of the revolution—elsewhere they use the term disparagingly.[19] (Indeed, the need for leadership at the time of the Revolution, when authority was not legally constituted, testifies to its extranomian character.) By giving authority an institutional basis in the Constitution, the Founders doubtless thought that there would be no further need for

[17] *The Federalist*, #48, p. 309; #71, p. 433.

[18] For the references to the president as a favorite, see #49, p. 317, #72, p. 440; and by way of denial, #64, pp. 390-91 and #68, p. 414. For the references to the demagogue, see #1, p. 35; and #85, p. 527.

[19] The positive use of the terms come in *The Federalist*, #14, p. 104 and #49, p. 315. I am indebted to Robert Eden for the observations on the use of the term "leader" in *The Federalist*.

leadership. Or, if they foresaw that it might be needed under some exceptional circumstances in the future, it would still be unwise—and perhaps impossible—to make any provisions for its institutionalization. No plan could be devised to accommodate it without at the same time encouraging it as a regular part of the constitutional order. Leadership, permanently instituted or approved, would lay the groundwork for institutional imperialism. Moreover, where authority is based on a leader's supposed representation of the people's will, competition for popular favor is bound to become the mode of soliciting office and with it the cultivation of whatever currents of opinion seem likely to provide a popular following. It is in this sense that leadership undermines the possibility of statesmanship, as that concept was understood by the Founders. Power generated by competition for public favor might well be formidable, more formidable than that which rests simply on institutional supports, but over the long run its scope and discretion are apt to become circumscribed. While appearing to direct the public, the leader may in fact be flattering and following it.

Besides being a claim to authority, popular leadership is a method of soliciting power. In this context, the Founders sometimes refer to it as the practice of "the popular arts."[20] The practice of the popular arts clearly helps to foster claims to informal authority by establishing a certain populist tone to politics, by generating expectations among the people in regard to how leaders should govern, and by "teaching" leaders the way in which they can win support. Furthermore, making the popular arts the usual basis of soliciting office has the effect of preselecting the candidates. Those skilled at the use of these arts are most likely to succeed, while others, perhaps better qualified in respect to their capacity to exercise power, may be deterred from making the race or even from entering politics.

The Founders identified two basic forms of the popular arts. One was the use of appeals that played up the personal

[20] *The Federalist*, #68, p. 414.

characteristics of contenders in such a way as to stimulate a fascination with dangerous or irrelevant aspects of character, methods which today we might call "image-building." Although the Founders, as we shall see, wanted considerations of character to govern the voters' (or electors') choice, they believed that it was possible to draw a rough distinction, applicable to the practice of politics, between character judgments based on qualities relevant to the performance of the potential officeholder and those influenced by strong emotions. The Founders expressed their disapproval of the latter type when Madison warned of the dangers of factions that form around persons whose fortunes have been "interesting to human passions" and when Jay spoke of the need to block "those brilliant appearances of genius and patriotism, which, like transient meteors, sometimes mislead as well as dazzle."[21]

The second form of the popular arts is issue arousal. Popular leadership here refers to the effort of an aspiring leader to win power by putting himself at the head of a broad movement based on some deeply felt issue or cause which he may have played a role in creating or arousing. It is associated with leaders who have established themselves as "friends" of the people—with men who give support to the idea that the immediate wishes of the people should have greater weight and who, in Hamilton's harsher view, commonly offer the "bait of popularity at the expense of the common good."[22] Demagoguery is a word sometimes employed to refer to this type of leadership and authority, but in common usage the term has such a pejorative connotation that its use will be restricted, as the Founders seem also to have done, to the most pathological form of popular leadership. So considered, demagoguery becomes very difficult to distinguish from the healthier forms of popular leadership. For V. O. Key and Allan Sindler in their studies of southern politics, demagoguery refers to two distinct though often related leadership

21 *The Federalist*, #10, p. 79; #64, p. 391.
22 *The Federalist*, #1, p. 35.

dimensions: one, a clowning, folksy, and friendly style irrelevant to the real substance of politics (though no worse perhaps than sophisticated image building); and the other— a more serious offense—the fomentation or arousal of a strong and divisive issue, based usually on a latent and deeply felt popular prejudice such as racial or class hatred.[23] Demagoguery in this last sense is characterized by the uniting of a constituency by means of opposing it to something else, be it an object within the community or another community altogether. The issue exploited to create the division must be based on a "bad" appeal, one that arouses dangerous passions. It is the "badness" of the appeal that distinguishes demagoguery as the pathological case from other kinds of popular leadership. As popular leadership becomes the predominant leadership style, charges and countercharges of demagoguery are bound to become a usual part of the prevailing political rhetoric. The great difficulty, as a practical matter, of preventing demagoguery where other forms of popular leadership are allowed may have been the one reason that led the Founders to attempt to discredit popular leadership generally and to search for a method of selection in which candidates would avoid campaigning by issue arousal.[24]

Popular leadership can be distinguished from two other

[23] Allan P. Sindler, *Political Parties in the United States* (New York: St. Martin's Press, 1966), p. 33, 34, and V. O. Key, *Southern Politics* (New York: Alfred A. Knopf, 1949), pp. 180-81 and 261-71.

[24] In addition, the demagogue is sometimes identified by reference to a certain motivational disposition. In its strongest and most sinister sense, a demagogue refers to a person of the highest and most warped ambition, who consciously employs the popular arts for the purpose of achieving a despotism or a tyranny. This is the sense in which Hamilton uses the term in the first and last numbers of *The Federalist*. When the person making the demagogic appeals is sincere, he may be less immoral than the other, but he is certainly meaner. The term "petty demagogue" seems to fit a leader of this type better, at least until he raises himself to the pinnacle of absolute power.

57

kinds of leadership suggested in *The Federalist*. The first is the leadership of the "politician" or broker—the one skilled in the art of mediating between various interest groups and welding together from these a coalition majority. This kind of leadership would seem to be essential in the House of Representatives because of the anticipated multiplicity of interests that would be represented in that body. Some combination of these would have to be forged from time to time into temporary coalitions to avoid continual deadlock, and for this the skilled broker would be required.[25] Leadership of this type would generally take place behind the scenes and would not normally be the source of a wide public reputation or great popular appeal. Though regarded as a positive function, it was certainly not envisioned as the distinguishing characteristic of either a candidate for the presidency or the president himself. The so-called "Madisonian system" of pluralism was never intended by Madison to extend beyond the legislature, and certainly not to the executive. The other form of leadership, which constituted the basis on which the Founders intended the presidency to be sought, may be labeled "nonpartisan" statesmanship. Under this form of leadership, the elevation of individuals to office should be the result of their having achieved a widespread reputation based on distinguished service to the state. The winner in such a process, no matter what his margin of victory, can in a sense legitimately assert the claim to be president of all the people,

[25] I am relying here on the interpretation of Martin Diamond who argues that the Founders expected that the response to the multiplicity of interests in Congress would be the formation of moderate coalitions (Diamond, Fisk, and Garfinkel, *The Democratic Republic*, p. 98). Hannah Pitkin, on the other hand, develops the idea that the multiplicity would lead to stalemate in the House; the House would then be forced to follow the lead of the other institutions. The "brokerage" function, in this view, would be considered undesirable and contrary to the intent of the Founders (*The Concept of Representation* [Berkeley: University of California Press, 1967], pp. 195 ff.).

since his selection would not divide the populace into strongly antagonistic parts.

The Founders held that popular leadership was most likely to arise under a direct democracy, and thus by extension in small republics. Under a direct democracy, as in ancient Athens, where the people met in one large assembly, it was possible for one man by his brilliant oratory and eloquence to rule "with as complete a sway as if a scepter had been placed in his single hand."[26] The small size and scope of these democracies allowed for clear and quick divisions which leaders could exploit and manipulate for their own ends. The Founders defined their regime in opposition to these qualities: all power is derived directly or indirectly from the people, but the people exercise none directly by themselves; and the extended territory of a commercial society would bring in a wide variety of interests, making a single, clear division less likely.[27] Finally, an extended republic, as distinct from a democracy, made direct communication between the leaders and the people more difficult. This was all to the advantage of a moderate form of politics, for it minimized the influence of popular rhetoric and thereby placed a higher premium on reputation.

But an extended republic, with its tendency toward moderate politics, was not a certain guarantee that the popular arts would never degenerate into the vicious or demagogic arts. The extended republic was only a partial solution to the prevention of a single-interest majority. The moderating effect deriving from the inclusion of a variety of interests applied particularly to the House, where election in separate

[26] *The Federalist*, #58, p. 360. The Founders evidence a distrust toward "mass" rhetoric, which was wholly in keeping with their opposition to popular leadership. Still, the Founders own use of rhetoric—see especially *Federalist* #14—attests to the necessity of such a practice in extraordinary circumstances.

[27] This definition combines the essential qualities of the two definitions given by the Founders in *The Federalist* #39, p. 241; and #63, p. 387.

districts guaranteed that different interests would be represented. The selection of the president, by contrast, took
place in a single constituency encompassing the entire nation. If popular leadership was permitted to dominate in
the presidential selection process, the Founders believed
that there was a very real possibility of stirring up national
divisions. Contrary to what some interpreters have implied,
the Founders did not hold that an extended republic guaranteed moderate national majorities in the case where aggregating a majority took place by issue arousal in a national election.[28] With a remarkable clarity, in fact, they identified in
1787 the very issues that caused the party disputes of the
next seventy-five years, even as they bent every effort to prevent them from coming to the surface. They were well aware
of the threat posed by slavery and sectionalism; and they
specifically worried about the emergence of populist doctrines that might charge either a usurpation of the rights of
the states by an all-powerful national government or an en-
croachment by a monarchic executive on the prerogatives of
the legislature.[29]

The last two concerns provide the occasion in *The Federalist* for the Founders' harshest attacks on demogagic leadership. They speak of those "influential characters" within the
states who, using the "bait" of separate confederacies, might
"seize the opportunity of some causal dissatisfaction among
the people . . . which perhaps they may themselves have
created"; and they allude to the possibility of someone within the House—"one of those leading characters on whom
everything depends in such bodies"—acting to expose the
alleged monarchism of the executive.[30] Neither of these statements, it is true, occurs in the context of a direct reference
to the presidency or presidential selection. Both, however,
indicate the basis on which a popular leader might attempt

[28] See James MacGregor Burns, *The Deadlock of Democracy*
(Englewood Cliffs, N.J.: Prentice Hall, 1963), pp. 1-7, 18-23.
[29] *The Federalist*, #49, pp. 316-17; #59, p. 366; #85, p. 521.
[30] *The Federalist*, #59, p. 366; #48, p. 309.

to build a national single-interest majority "below" the level of the interest-group politics depicted in *Federalist 10*; and it takes no great effort to imagine such a leader running for the presidency on either or both of these issues.[31] The possibility of a national demagogue was one of the greatest fears of the Founders and literally frames *The Federalist*, being mentioned in both the first and the last numbers. Hamilton identifies the source of the danger in a popular leader and warns of the need to be on guard against "a dangerous ambition lurk[ing] in the specious mask of zeal for the rights of the people. . . ." "History," he goes on, teaches that the "road to the introduction of despotism" usually comes from "those men who have begun their career by paying an obsequious court to the people, commencing demagogues and ending tyrants."[32]

[31] *The Federalist*, #49, pp. 316-17; #85, p. 521.

[32] *The Federalist*, #1, p. 35. This account is reminiscent of Hamilton's well-known attack on Jefferson in a letter to Edward Carrington, May 26, 1792 (*Works*, 9:535). In this letter Hamilton says that the easiest way in which to destroy the Constitution would be for a "demagogue . . . to mount the hobby-horse of popularity . . . cry out 'usurpation' 'danger to liberty' etc., etc., . . . and 'ride in the whirlwind and direct the storm.'" Though he stopped short of calling Jefferson a demagogue, he labeled him "'a man of profound ambition and violent passions.'" With Burr, however, he did not hesitate to use the term. See his letter to James Bayard, January 16, 1801, *The Works of Alexander Hamilton*, ed. H. C. Lodge, 12 vols. (New York: G. P. Putnam's Sons, 1904), 10:414.

Hamilton uses the term demagogue to refer to one who stirs up popular prejudices. What about one, however, who stirs up the feelings of the few and powerful by playing on their contempt for the common man? John Adams employed the term "aristocratic demagogue" for such a person and used it, coincidentally, to refer specifically to Hamilton: "There are many and as dangerous aristocratical demagogues as there are democratical. . . . Milo was as much an agitator for the patricians as Clodius for the plebians; and Hamilton as much a demagogue as Burr," *The Works of John Adams*, ed. Charles Francis Adams (Boston: Little Brown, 1850-56), 6:532. It is only slightly misleading to suggest that the first party division, which undermined the Founders' intended nonpartisan system, was over the issue of demagoguery.

The Problem of Political Ambition

The attempt to prevent popular leadership is related to another and more general theme in the Founders' theory of selection—the control of ambition. A cursory reading of *Federalist 68*, the paper in which presidential selection is discussed most extensively, might suggest that the direction of the Founders' solution to the problem of ambition is simply to screen out the ambitious, who are restricted to those who use the popular arts, and choose from among those "pre-eminent for ability and unspirited," the type of men who would never stoop to the practice of the popular arts. But this somewhat idealized picture (or impression) of presidential aspirants is belied by Hamilton's more candid discussion of the nature of political motivation that follows in the papers that deal with the presidency. In *Federalist 68*, it should be recalled, Hamilton is describing "almost the only part of the system of any consequence that has escaped without censure," and it would make no sense for him to introduce problems that the opponents of the Constitution did not bother to raise. Hamilton depicts the behavior of presidential aspirants here in the way he expected it might *appear* to the public, i.e. after the selection system had restrained the candidates from overt manifestations of ambition. Much as it was formerly the norm for aspirants in the nominating stage to wait for the party to confer its nomination without appearing to covet the honor, the Founders expected that their system would make candidates adopt a public posture of unconcern with their own success and appear only to be solicitous of the opportunity to serve their fellow citizens.

Yet this process would conceal, even as it controlled, the powerful ambitions of the candidates. Hamilton's chief objective for presidential selection was to attract men of great ability to the presidency, men capable of exercising the kind of positive statesmanship he envisioned. To accomplish this Hamilton argued that the presidency must offer the opportunity for individual fulfillment. The clear assumption Hamilton makes is that politicians, except in rare instances like George Washington, are fundamentally self-seeking and in search of the "reward" of political office.[33] Hamilton's conception of virtue, then, far from being an abnegating kind of self-sacrifice, is a striving for self-fulfillment that promotes—or, more precisely, that can be made to promote—the public good. The passion most likely to support this kind of virtue is "the love of fame, the ruling passion of the noblest minds"—a passion which in its concern for long-term reputation should be distinguished from the pathetic desire of some of our recent presidents, so openly expressed and shamelessly belabored, to sit well with the current generation of historical chroniclers. It is not clear whether this love of fame is so "elevated" as to preclude on its own any recourse to the popular arts; one suspects not. But in any case, Hamilton makes clear that most men in politics, including most of those likely to occupy the presidency, will not be dominated so much by a love of fame as by a driving and ceaseless ambition whose object would be the attainment of honors and power. Such persons, it is safe to assume, would not be above using the popular arts to satisfy their desire for power if it appeared that by such means they might best succeed. How to prevent men so motivated from undermining the regime and harness their energy on its behalf becomes one

[33] *The Federalist*, #72, p. 437; for other references to the man of ambition, see #72, pp. 438, 440; and #75, p. 451. Excepted from this description of mere ambition was George Washington, whose "true" virtue was a source of wonder and even awe to so many of his contemporaries. Washington was the perfect example of the "best" in power, and the Founders no doubt looked to him as a model for a republican executive. But they were also well aware that to expect to have a person of this type in power at all times was to ask too much of men and institutions. Herbert Storing shrewdly observes that the "Convention tried to take into account both the desirability of attracting men like Washington to the presidency and its unlikelihood" (Introduction to Charles Thach, Jr., *The Creation of the Presidency*, p. xi). Hamilton, we are suggesting, based his calculations for presidential selection on the prospect of the unlikelihood of "true" virtue.

of the critical problems of selection. The issue, it can be said, is how to transform ambition into virtue.

Hamilton's conception of the selection problem is at once broad and complex. One "part" of the selection system is the character of the presidential office itself. Its great power —as much as the nation could then accept—would serve as a magnet to attract individuals of ability into political life, something which the institutions of the selection process narrowly conceived could not accomplish. Yet making the office so attractive creates a problem of its own, for it stimulates the interest of the ambitious. It is at this point that the institutions of the selection process become critical. In one respect, the selection system would serve as a screening device, keeping out the petty kind of demagogue whose only means for achieving reknown is by stirring up public passions. But just as important, the selection system would channel and control the behavior of the able politicians. Since these men, too, would be ambitious, their behavior would adapt itself so as to maximize their chance for success. Hamilton's objective was to structure the selection system so as to promote actions on the part of the candidates that did not conflict with, and might even promote, the public good. The issue for Hamilton was not, as it is for many modern students, to find easy-going "democratic characters"—a goal he would probably have considered as undesirable as it was utopian; it was rather to induce or "train" politicians as we are apt to find them—which is to say, as decidedly "undemocratic" characters—to behave virtuously and serve democracy. The competition for office, as Hamilton envisioned it, would be intense, but it would assume the form not of a contest for immediate popular favor through issue appeals, but of a long-term striving to win a reputation for merit and virtue.

THE FOUNDERS' INSTITUTIONAL SOLUTION

In discussing the Founders' attempt to institutionalize their objectives, there is no need to belabor their reasons for rejecting the idea of Congressional selection. The issue here was clear cut, involving at bottom the question of the degree of executive independence. Spokesmen for the Whig theory of the executive, such as Roger Sherman, favored "appointment [of the president] by the legislature and for making him dependent on that body, as it was the will of that which was to be executed." For just the opposite reason the leading nationalists favored giving the president a base independent of the Congress. They feared that Congressional selection would make the executive, in Morris's words, "the tool of some leading demagogue in the Legislature."[34]

Once having rejected legislative selection, the Founders were faced with the problem of devising some alternative system that was consistent with their goals. Advocates of the strong executive at first endorsed a direct popular election, and even their final plan could allow for something approaching this kind of choice. The most interesting question is how the Founders could have thought that so democratic a plan could produce a "virtuous" president who would frequently serve as a counterpoise to popular demands. The general principle on which their solution was based, it has been said, was to make the outcome of a popular election turn on an assessment of character and not issue advocacy. Yet one wonders first how the Founders, who so deplored the kind of persons chosen for representatives to the state legislatures, could rely on the people's ability to choose a good person in a national election. While the Founders never denied the good intentions of the people, they would probably have agreed with de Tocqueville's assessment of the difficulties involved in popular judgments respecting the character of public officials:

> Consider the manifold considerations and the prolonged study involved in forming an exact notion of the character of a single man. There, where the greatest geniuses go astray, are the masses to succeed? The people . . . are bound to make hasty judgments and seize on the most

[34] Madison, *Notes*, p. 48 (June 1); p. 324 (July 19).

prominent characteristics. This is why charlatans of every sort so well understand the secret of pleasing them, whereas for the most part their real friends fail in this.[35]

The general problem, it seems, is that good character, however one defines it, is not immediately visible. Realizing this, the Founders in their practical deliberations did not, even when supporting a direct election, place full faith in the people's capacity to discern it. Their argument was different: if good character could not be directly "seen" by the people, some substitute for it could be. That substitute was an established reputation. The Founders did not hold that there was a perfect correlation between reputation and virtue, but they did think that prominence and competence would normally go together. Reputation was the closest visible approximation of merit. Thus the principle of the Founders' solution stated in practical terms was to have the field narrowed to those with preexisting reputations and to exclude those who sought to make their name during the campaign by issue arousal.

What institutional arrangement favored reputation? The Founders' first answer was simple: an election in a large district, a principle referred to by Hamilton as "the extension of the spheres of election."[36] The Founders proceeded to make their argument by contrasting the effects of elections in small districts, such as those employed in the case of state legislatures, with elections in the larger districts proposed for Congress and for the presidency. All elections, the Founders reasoned, pose a problem of name recognition in the sense that a viable candidate must at least become known to most of the voters. In a small district a candidate could gain familiarity with the voters by contacting them directly during the campaign and could easily make a reputation by issue arousal. Even the number of immediate personal acquaintances in a small constituency can be a signifi-

---

[35] De Tocqueville, *Democracy in America*, p. 198.
[36] *The Federalist*, #27, p. 174.

cant factor. But when the size of the district is increased, "impersonal" forces play a larger role. The Founders thought that this would make it more difficult for a candidate to make headway by personal contacts or electioneering techniques and would thus give a greater advantage to those possessing an established reputation. As Madison noted in comparing the size of the districts planned for the House with those used for the popular assemblies in the states:

> Large districts are manifestly favorable to the election of persons of general respectability and of probable attachment to the rights of property, over competitors depending on the personal solicitation practicable on a contracted theatre. And although an ambitious candidate of personal distinction might occasionally recommend himself to popular choice by espousing a popular though unjust object, it might happen rarely to many districts at the same time.[37]

Part of what is involved in this solution can be seen from contemporary analyses of elections in which the partisan element is weak or nonexistent, as in primaries and nonpartisan contests. The problem in these elections, as it has been identified by modern political scientists, is to determine which cues govern voter choice in the absence of party labels. The candidate factor, which includes name recognition and assessment of character, emerges as one of the most important influences. In the Founders' view, the salience of this factor would help ensure an advantage for the "blue-ribbon" can-

---

[37] James Madison, *The Writings of James Madison*, ed. Gaillard Hunt, 9 vols. (New York: G. P. Putnam's Sons, 1903), 4:126. A more "palatable" expression of this same argument is found in *Federalist* #10: ". . . as each representative will be chosen by a greater number of citizens . . . it will be more difficult for unworthy candidates to practice with success the vicious arts by which elections are too often carried; and the suffrages of the people being more free will be more likely to center on men who possess the most attractive merit and the most diffusive and established characters."

didate; and even today this result is sometimes cited as the benefit (or the defect) of nonpartisan elections.[38] But the changes that have taken place since the time of the Founding, in particular in communications, have made it much easier to build a constituency and win recognition during a campaign. This had led in modern times, at least in elections for presidency, to a form of competition in which preexisting reputation does not hold a decisive edge and in which it is possible for an "outsider" to capture public favor during the campaign. In respect to the use of the arts of popular leadership, it might be said that the modern national campaign, including the primaries, resembles more the character of what the Founders anticipated from small legislative districts than what they expected from a large constituency. On this basis, what one might expect under modern circumstances is the occasional triumph of personal merit accompanied by the continual agitation of candidates making use of the popular arts, either by manufacturing certain image appeals or building issue constituencies.[39]

[38] See Edward Banfield and James Q. Wilson, *City Politics* (New York: Vintage Books, 1963), pp. 159-61. Nonpartisan elections, it appears, also favor the incumbent, since the incumbent begins with an established reputation. See Austin Ranney, *Curing the Mischiefs of Faction* (Berkeley: University of California Press, 1975), pp. 127-28. It may have been that the Founders were relying on this influence as well to assist "established characters," assuming, of course, that persons of this sort won the office in the first place.

For the effects of direct elections in one state prior to the Convention, see Van Beck Hall, *Politics Without Parties, Massachusetts 1780-1791* (Pittsburgh: University of Pittsburgh Press, 1972). Hall's analysis tends to support the great role played by reputation in most of the gubernatorial elections. The possible exception, referred to by Gerry at the Convention on July 19 (*Notes*, p. 327), was the unseating of Governor Bowdoin by John Hancock. Hancock, while long prominent in his own right, adopted a popular appeal to defeat Bowdoin. (See Hall's *Politics*, pp. 235-36.)

[39] It should be noted that this statement of the nature of modern campaigns already assumes the reemergence of the *individual* as an important factor relative to the party. Where the party is strong and fully dominates electoral behavior, it is clear that the "im-

Since the Founders believed that elections in large legislative districts operated to discourage petty popular appeals
and favor men of reputation, it is not surprising that they
placed even greater confidence in the anticipated results of
a district that comprised the entire nation. Gouverneur Morris pressed this line of reasoning most vigorously at the Convention:

---

personal" element in elections that was noted above—that which
was to give the advantage to reputation in a nonpartisan scheme—
is taken over by the party label. The basis for this position is explained by Maurice Duverger in his well-known *Political Parties*
(New York: John Wiley and Sons, 1963), p. 357:

> The larger the constituency, the greater is party influence; the
> smaller the constituency, the more restricted is party interven-
> tion. . . . When the electoral division becomes larger personal
> contact between candidates and electors decreases; the electors
> no longer know the candidates personally. The political label
> becomes the essential element in the voting, whereas it remains
> secondary in small constituencies.

Simply substitute "reputation" for "party influence" and one has a
good statement of the influence that the Founders were relying on
to promote men of standing.

As parties emerged in state politics and assumed the role
formerly played by personal reputation, conservatives had second
thoughts about their preference for the larger district. Now the
larger district was controlled by the "fixed" majority that supported
the popular party, and individual merit had less influence. Thus we
find that the New York State Federalists supported placing more
authority in the hands of local powers in the debate on the new
state constitution in 1821 (see Nathaniel Carter and William Stone,
*Reports of the Proceedings and Debates of the New York State
Convention of 1821*, pp. 318-37). Though the small district was no
doubt still considered susceptible to the influence of the arts of
popular leadership, it also provided individual prominence with its
best chance for influencing election outcomes. At least personal
factors could play some role at the local level. This antipathy of
conservatives to elections at the center, which tend to be decided
by partisan leanings, has shown up again from time to time. But
conservatives obviously had to make their peace with partisan
politics, and have done so effectively, oftentimes in our history
being able to lead the largest party.

At the national level, too, party label came to play a great role

An election by the people at large throughout so great an extent of country could not be influenced by those little combinations and momentary lies which often decide popular elections within a narrow sphere. . . .

If the people should elect, they will never fail to prefer some man of distinguished character or services; some man if he might so speak, of continental reputation.

James Wilson agreed, stating that "the objects of [popular] choice . . . must be persons whose merits have general notoriety." Madison also concurred, though his support was qualified: "The people at large . . . was the fittest [source]. . . . The people generally could know and vote for some citizen whose merits had rendered him an object of general attention and esteem."[40]

Even though the direct election plan was not adopted, the Founders thought the beneficial effect of the "principle of the extended sphere" would operate under the Constitution's electoral system. Its influence would work on the electors, the stage legislators, and, to the extent that they participated, on the people. Hamilton summarized the operation of this principle as follows:

Talents for low intrigue, and the little acts of popularity, may alone suffice to elevate a man to the first honors in a

---

in dictating voter choice. The power of the "pull" of the party label has diminished greatly, however, since the highwater mark of party influence in the nineteenth century, and the importance of the individual candidate's characteristics or program has increased. Yet because the nineteenth-century parties were so closely balanced, and because the presidency is such a highly visible office, it was always the case that personal factors of the candidate were of some significance—hence the continuing search in the nineteenth century for the man of great personal stature, usually the military hero.

[40] Madison, *Notes*, p. 324 (July 19); p. 306 (July 17); p. 48 (June 1); p. 327 (July 19). It should be noted that Morris favored restricting the suffrage to "free-holders," but it is clear that the electorate would still have been a large one.

single state; but it will require other talents, and a different kind of merit to establish him in the esteem and confidence of the whole union, or so considerable a portion of it as would be necessary to make him a successful candidate for the distinguished office of President of the United States.[41]

It is important to point out that this principle had both a primary and a secondary effect. Its primary effect was to accord an advantage to aspirants possessing an established reputation over those making use of the popular arts. This effect worked through the influence it had on those choosing the president. The secondary effect operated on the candidates: men of ambition and ability, realizing that the attainment of a solid reputation offered the best chance of succeeding, would direct their energies toward establishing a distinguished record of service to the state.

But neither Hamilton nor Madison believed this solution to be foolproof. Although they both thought that a demagogue would be less likely to triumph in a large district, they feared that the type who might succeed would be of the most dangerous sort—not a petty rabble-rouser from the lower ranks but a skillful and attractive figure of great repute.[42] Auxiliary precautions to prevent such a Caesarist appeal were therefore needed. Accordingly, when the idea of a direct election was challenged at the Convention, chiefly on practical grounds, Hamilton and Madison were quite willing

[41] *The Federalist*, #68, p. 414. Hamilton's experience in New York, where he continually opposed George Clinton as governor, may well have been on his mind in his reference to elections in the states.

[42] Hamilton's reservations about the effect of a large district are contained in a note made to himself after hearing the discussion on this point. Hamilton observed that, "frequently small portions of large districts carry elections—An influential demagogue will give an impulse to the whole—Demagogues are not always inconsiderable persons—Patricians were frequently demagogues—." Max Farrand, ed., *The Records of the Federal Convention of 1787*, Revised edition (New Haven: Yale University Press, 1937), p. 147.

for theoretical reasons to abandon the plan in favor of an alternative that relied less directly on the people but still avoided selection by the Congress. What must be emphasized, however, is that their objective was not to limit the effective franchise to the propertied few in order to aid the cause of oligarchy; it was rather to decrease the chances that the office would be sought by the use of the popular arts. By making the choice of electors an event in its own right, the Founders were attempting to bring into play the interests of those wishing to be chosen for this role. The Founders hoped thereby to sever, or at least diminish, the connection between the contest for the electors and the choice of a national candidate. As Hamilton explained in *Federalist 68*, "The choice of *several* to form an intermediate body of electors will be much less apt to convulse the community with any extraordinary or violent movements than the choice of *one* who was himself to be the final object of the public wishes." The most significant aspect of the indirect plan was thus not the matter of who chose the electors, but the effect of an indirect selection on the character of the campaign. Because the people would not be choosing the president themselves, aspirants would have much less reason to cultivate popular favor.

In one respect, however, it is clear that the Founders wanted—and expected—that the wishes of the people would prevail. Up to this point the discussion has proceeded on the assumption that the major task of the selection process is to choose among "new" aspirants for the office. But this is not the case when an incumbent is seeking reelection. In these instances, elections have a somewhat different task. They serve principally as a referendum on the performance of the incumbent. Although the Founders did not envision that elections would perform the function of initiating "critical changes" emanating from popular movements, they did foresee a role for policy choice by the people in the form of a retrospective assessment of an incumbent's record. In his discussion of the advantages of a unitary executive, Hamilton makes clear that a president who has lost the public's confidence should not be returned; and he adds that the withdrawal or defeat of an incumbent "as the result of public choice" would naturally lead his successor to propose new policies on the reasonable grounds that "the dismission of his predecessor has proceeded from a dislike of his measures."[43]

The Founders' views on the function of choice and change in the selection process, though not well developed, are not very different from what has been observed to occur in "normal" elections, even allowing for the existence of political parties. Modern electoral analysis, under the influence of V. O. Key, has demonstrated that a significant portion of the electorate—and as it turns out usually the decisive one—bases its voting decision on retrospective assessments of presidential performance, which in a sense is a nonpartisan decision. For Key, this included not only a judgment on the incumbent himself, but also, through him, on his party, thus providing a retrospective dimension in voter decision-making for each election.[44] (With the parties now being weaker and with individual candidates sometimes running conspicuously against the record of their own party's incumbent, the prospect for continued party responsibility may have diminished.) For the Founders, responsibility would be borne by incumbents alone. But as they placed no restriction on reeligibility and seemed to think incumbents would ordinarily stand for reelection, they thought that the people would usually have the opportunity to pass judgment on how affairs had been conducted. Moreover, the Founders seemed to have in mind a purpose in this context that went beyond merely deciding the electoral fate of an incumbent president. Hamilton's analysis suggests that the people have a fundamental political need for someone to assume the burden of

[43] *The Federalist*, #70, pp. 427-29.

[44] V. O. Key, *The Responsible Electorate* (New York: Random House, 1966), p. 61. According to Key the electorate "judges retrospectively; it commands prospectively only insofar as it expresses either approval or disapproval of that which has happened before."

the nation's failures. By blaming an incumbent for reverses, whether justly or not, the people purge themselves of any feeling of frustration or responsibility and are able to look forward to the future with a more hopeful attitude.[45]

The final point to consider is the effect of the Founders' selection system on the power of the executive. Since the presidency of Woodrow Wilson, and perhaps even since the presidencies of Jefferson and Jackson, national elections have been viewed as power-generating events that supply the executive with the "energy" needed to govern. By contrast the Founders conceived the selection process to be neutral with respect to presidential power. Its purpose was to select a president, not to arm the executive with authority beyond that provided by the Constitution. Without any additional authority deriving from the selection process, the Founders believed that there was little to fear in the way of an imperial presidency. Indeed, the net effect of what one might call the informal or noninstitutional influences on the presidency, namely the selection process and the general public attitude toward the executive, was to restrain the president, at least when compared with the recent operation of these influences. The Founders' selection process did not add to the president's power, while the prevailing popular attitude toward the presidency was one of great suspicion. It is ironic that the Jeffersonian Republican Party, which attacked the scope of formal executive power, nevertheless provided the president with the weapon, in the form of a popular election, that eventually resulted in a constitutional imbalance. Of course this imbalance did not come about until very recently. It was prevented during the nineteenth century by the Democratic Party's limited view of the role of the national government and by the Whig party's mistrust of a "popular king."

[45] A discussion of this "function" of election may be found in Harvey C. Mansfield, Jr., "The Modern Doctrine of Executive Power," paper delivered at Midwest Regional Meeting of the American Society for Eighteenth-Century Studies, October 26, 1973, pp. 25-26.

In this century, until the Watergate crisis, these moderating influences were removed: Democrats became the champions of extensive federal involvement and an expanded role for the executive, while Republicans dropped their former suspicion of presidential power. What resulted was the doctrine of the powerful and popular executive backed by a popular mandate and unchecked by informal influences of any kind.

PROBLEMS OF LEGITIMACY

The legitimacy of the Founders' selection system was never seriously questioned during the ratification debates. The plan appeared to be sufficiently democratic to satisfy the opponents of the Constitution, and it was often the most democratic construction of the plan that the Founders emphasized. Despite general popular acceptance, however, there were two objections to the legitimacy of the system that arose at the Convention and that later played an important role in leading to its alteration. The first, made by two delegates who never endorsed the Constitution, Elbridge Gerry and George Mason, focused on the allegedly undemocratic effects of a direct nonpartisan election; the second, made by the Constitution's two greatest defenders, James Madison and Alexander Hamilton, concerned the undemocratic character of the auxiliary plan of selection by the House. In raising this objection, Madison and Hamilton also pointed out a problem regarding the system's capacity to promote legitimacy in the informal respect of securing a candidate with a broad national following.

The objection of Gerry and Mason to a nonpartisan election illustrates once again just how differently popular elections were understood at the time of the Founding. Gerry and Mason argued that while the form of a direct (or quasi-direct) election appeared democratic, its actual effect would be oligarchic. In a constituency the size of the entire nation, it was unlikely that the people would coalesce around a

75

single candidate. Rather, they would tend to disperse their votes among a number of candidates favorable to their interest. If under these circumstances an established national group could agree on a candidate, it would more often than not be able to control the outcome. Nonpartisan elections were not neutral but favored those who already were organized or who could most easily concert their efforts. This tendency would aid the oligarchic interest, and Gerry specifically had in mind the old Revolutionary War officers' organization, the Order of Cincinnati:

> The ignorance of the people would put it [the popular election] in the power of some one set of men dispersed through the Union and acting in concert to delude them into any appointment . . . such a society of men existed in the Order of Cincinnati. They are respectable, united, and influential. They will in fact elect the Chief Magistrate in every instance, if the election be referred to the people.[46]

What Gerry and Mason did not suggest, but what occurs to the modern reader, is the formation of a counterorganiza-

[46] Madison, *Notes*, p. 368 (July 25). See also p. 307 (July 17). John Mercer, speaking about the impact of popular elections, noted the unfair advantage they possessed in aiding the cities over the country: "The people in towns can unite their votes in favor of one favorite and by that means prevail over the people of the Country, who being dispersed will scatter their votes among a variety of candidates" (*Notes*, p. 405, August 7).

I can find no evidence, incidentally, to suggest that the Founders who promoted a nonpartisan election ever harbored any such secret plans. They believed simply that a nonpartisan system, either by a direct vote by the people or by their electors, would tend to elevate men of high standing. The Federalist Party did attempt to forge a connection with the Order between 1800 and 1804, though without much success. The Federalist Party, however, should not be considered the successor to the Founders; and in any case, by 1800 the nature of electoral competition bore little resemblance to what the Founders had envisioned. For a discussion of the Federalist Party's relationship to the Order, see *The Works of John Adams*, 6:543-44, and Roy F. Nichols, *The Invention of the American Political Parties* (New York: Free Press, 1967), p. 226.

tion to represent the interests of the broad mass of the people—in short, a mass-based political party. The original advocates of permanent political parties in the 1820s were
moved in part by just this kind of reasoning. Nonpartisan
elections, they argued, offered a decisive advantage to the
wealthy, who, because of their more frequent contacts and
greater political sophistication, would always find it easier to
concert their activities. To offset this advantage, it was necessary to make competition between organized political
bodies a fully legitimate part of the political system; this
would allow the people, meaning the common man or the
nonwealthy, to exert their proper influence in the electoral
process, since they could coalesce behind an ongoing organization whose fidelity to their long-term interest would
become apparent.

No such "radical" proposal, however, was suggested by
Gerry or Mason. A party solution, consisting of two parties
contending peacefully against each other in mutual tolerance
or forbearance, was a concept that the Founders never enter-
tained. Virtually all the Founders associated parties with
seditious bodies. To envision party competition would therefore be to concede in advance that their own party—the
party supporting the new Constitution—would fail. And even
if they had clearly foreseen the possibility of a nonseditious
form of organized competition, it seems certain that they
would have rejected it. To transform the presidency into an
object of competition among organized entities, with the
popular part usually predominating, would have undermined
the "conservative" function that national elections were supposed to promote. The best that Gerry and Mason could
offer, therefore, was to make the results of selection more
popular by making its form less popular. Both were advocates
of Congressional selection, in their case as much out of concern for protecting the popular cause as for limiting the independence of the executive. Their position was rejected, but
the problem they identified later became an important factor
in justifying the establishment of partisan competition.

The objection of Madison and Hamilton was quite different and focused not on the electoral plan but on the complicated and undemocratic auxiliary system of election by the House. Yet to understand this objection—including the reasons why Madison and Hamilton began to fear that the auxiliary system might be employed with some frequency—it is necessary to consider the entire electoral process and trace the Convention's deliberations on the issue of the emergence of "continental figures."

Large districts, most of the delegates agreed, favored men of elevated stature whose reputations could fill the constituency. But some delegates argued that there was a point in size beyond which individual reputations either would not exist or would not be felt with sufficient force. These delegates contended that the highest level at which individual reputations would normally be recognized by the people was the state or at best the region. The result, accordingly, of a national popular election would usually be a scattering of votes among a large number of favorite sons, none of whom would approach having the support of a majority of the voters. To declare any one of these the winner could be dangerous as the president might then be the choice of the people of a single state or region and lack the confidence of the people in the rest of the nation. The small-state delegates in particular tended to object to election by a simple plurality because of their fear that it would result in continual success of candidates from the larger states. According to Connecticut delegate Roger Sherman, "the people will never be sufficiently informed of characters and besides will never give a majority of votes to any one man. They will generally vote for some man in their own state, and the largest states will have the best chance for appointment." This issue was debated back and forth, with some delegates holding that men of national reputation would exist in the future and others contending that they would not. These arguments often reflected different assumptions about the future character of the union: those who envisioned a strong union with politics revolving about the center were more apt to accept the view that "continental characters would multiply as we more and more coalesce"; those who saw a union more confederate in character inclined toward the view that "the people will be sure to vote for some man in their own state." Despite the seriousness of this dispute, however, there was a realization that the issue would not have to be faced immediately. For the short term, there were, as Hugh Williamson observed in referring to George Washington, "distinguished characters . . . known to almost every man."[47]

One "practical" reason (though it is surely more than that) why the Founders adopted the electoral plan was to increase the chance of creating an acceptable national majority for one of the candidates. A number of factors entered into the Founders' calculations: the electors would possess more information than the people about national politicians; they could consult with each other, at least within each state, and thus perhaps avoid some of the scattering of a popular election; and they could each be given two votes, a measure that had been proposed for a direct election but rejected on the grounds that the voters would throw away their second choice on an unknown candidate so as not to detract from the chances of their preferred candidate. The two-vote plan, as the Founders expected it might work in practice, would permit the elector's "first" vote (perhaps the one on which he was instructed) to be given to a state favorite son. The "second" vote would then be at the elector's discretion and might represent his choice of a continental figure. The disposition for the elector to use his second vote seriously was strengthened by two considerations: first, the failure to achieve a majority for any candidate would take the election

[47] Madison, *Notes*, p. 306 (July 17); p. 578 (September 4); p. 309 (July 17). On the side seeing the evolution of national characters were apparently Madison (Va.), Morris (N.Y.), Wilson (Pa.), and Baldwin (Ga.); while on the other side were Williamson (N.C.), Sherman (Conn.), Mason (Va.), Gerry (Ma.), Pinkney (S.C.) and Dickenson (Del.).

away from the electors and give it to the House; and second, the runner-up would receive the office of the vice-presidency. Beyond this, the likelihood that the second vote would in fact be the elector's choice of a continental figure was increased by the requirement that only one of the elector's votes could be for a candidate from his own state. First preferences, going mostly to favorite sons, would decide the outcome. As Madison commented, "the second best man in this case would probably be the first, in fact."[48]

The electoral system was thus carefully designed to help promote what could be regarded as a legitimate national majority. There was, of course, something partly contrived in this arrangement. Each elector was given two votes but only a majority of the votes of all the electors was required for victory. This allowed election by what amounted to a plurality. Nevertheless, the plan was fair, ensured that the person chosen would have a broad base of support, and gave at least the appearance of protecting the democratic principle of decision by a majority.

But for all its ingenuity, the plan could not guarantee that a candidate would emerge with the minimum number of votes required for victory. This left the Convention with the choice of either accepting an election by a plurality of the electors or adopting a separate contingency process which would build a majority of a different kind. It was the latter alternative that was followed, and the result was the complicated House election scheme in which the representatives voted within their state delegations and each state was given a single vote. This plan was favored by the small-state advocates, many of whom believed that the election would often be decided in the House. These delegates therefore considered the adoption of the auxiliary plan a major victory. By contrast, some of the nationally minded delegates, including Morris and Wilson, felt that they were conceding very

[48] Madison, *Notes*, p. 368 (July 25). This comment was made in the context of the discussion over a two-vote plan under a direct election, but it applies equally to the electoral college system.

little. Believing from the first that "continental characters" would emerge on a steady basis, they doubted that the contingency process would often be needed and were therefore quite willing to make the concession.

Madison and Hamilton, however, felt differently and during the final days of the Convention strongly opposed the auxiliary system. Sensing the great strength of the states under the new system—much more than either had originally wanted—they began to express doubts that the electors could settle on a nationally prominent person, if indeed such persons would continue to emerge. The plan, moreover, was ill conceived. Not only did it introduce all of the problems of legislative selection back into the system, but it did so in an especially illogical and dangerous way. The arrangement, in Madison's view, allowed "the representatives of a *minority* of the people [to] reverse the choice of a *majority* of the states and of the *people*."[49] Madison and Hamilton accordingly sought to eliminate the plan altogether, or at least to reduce the frequency of its use. Madison proposed that a candidate should be eligible for selection with a plurality of one-third or more of the votes of all the electors; Hamilton favored a simple plurality. These suggestions, opposed by the small-state advocates and introduced at a point when the Convention, as Madison later recalled, "was not exempt from hurrying influence produced by fatigue and impatience," were quickly turned down.[50] Nor was this altogether unfortunate, for while Madison and Hamilton had identified a problem in the existing system, their proposed solutions also suffered from a major difficulty. They would have left unresolved the problem that had led the Convention to adopt the auxiliary system in the first place, namely the possibility that the president might be the choice of one state or region.

The adoption of the auxiliary plan and the well-known opposition of the principal Founders to legislative selection combined to produce a circumstance of major significance

---

[49] Madison, *Notes*, p. 595 (September 7).
[50] Madison, *Writings*, 9:147.

for the subsequent development of presidential selection. *The Federalist* naturally endorsed the full Constitutional plan, but it also made clear the Founders' support for a mode of selection independent of the legislature. Others went on record confirming the Convention's intent to avoid legislative selection. The elections of 1800 and 1824, in which the House decided the result, revealed to the satisfaction of nearly everyone how correct the Founders' sentiments had been. It accordingly became the accepted view, even of those partial to the states, that election by the House under the existing plan was a great evil—in Jefferson's words "the most dangerous blot in our Constitution."[51]

This tension between the known sentiments of the Founders and the actual operation of the legal machinery was later used to great advantage by the advocates of permanent party competition. The Founders, they argued, wished to avoid legislative selection while at the same time ensuring that there was an acceptable form of majority on behalf of some candidate. But they had not succeeded. The expectation that legislative selection would seldom be needed because of a steady emergence of national figures was too optimistic: there were either too few continental characters or too many. In either case, a national two-party system could solve the problem. Since each party held the allegiance of a large following among the people, it could "create" a national personage in the event none existed; and since together the two parties controlled the only gates to consideration for the presidency, they could limit the number of national personages in the event there were too many. Parties could therefore accomplish what the Founders had wanted but were unable to do, and what no foreseeable Constitutional amendment could do —virtually ensure that presidential elections were decided by the electors, without having to go to the House. This line of

[51] Thomas Jefferson, *The Works of Thomas Jefferson*, ed. Paul Leicester Ford, Federal Edition, 12 vols. (New York: G. P. Putnam's Sons, 1905), 12:303. Letter to George Hay, August 17, 1823.

reasoning became one of the chief instrumental justifications for the establishment of permanent national parties.

The Founders' Theory of Selection: Summary and Concluding Assessment

The Founders' views on the five functions of the selection system, all of which were implicitly or explicitly identified, may be quickly summarized: (1) *Controlling ambition*. The Founders feared the divisive and demeaning effect of the use of popular leadership in soliciting the presidency and sought to channel the ambitions of aspirants into constructive service to the state by foreclosing a campaign based on issue appeals. (2) *Presidential leadership and the power of the office*. The Founders wanted the president to be above the conflict of interests that characterized the "Madisonian Scheme" in the House and to be able to exercise independent discretion, often in opposition to immediate popular demands. Their selection system was calculated to safeguard these qualities by avoiding a contest in which the candidates would have to pose as "friends" of the people or make specific policy commitments. The Founders also wanted a powerful though not an unchecked executive, and executive authority that rested on the legal prerogatives of the office. Their selection system conformed with these objectives by denying the candidate any basis for informal authority as a popular leader possessing a mandate. (3) *Presidential character*. The Founders sought a distinguished and able executive who would have considerable political experience. The emphasis on reputation in the selection process would encourage the choice of those who were well known by their record of public service. The Founders were also in search of a "virtuous" character, but they were aware that most politicians are motivated by powerful and self-regarding passions. Their objective was to harness these passions and induce aspirants to contribute to the public good. (4) *Legiti-*

83

macy. The Founders' system was designed to be consistent with republican government, but they conceded no more to the democratic principle than they felt wise or prudent in light of the "demands" of the other functions. They also sought to devise a system that would help create an acceptable majority for a prominent candidate, although their system still presupposed in some degree an "automatic" emergence of continental figures. (5) *Choice and Change.* The Founders did not see elections as performing the role of instituting decisive changes in policy in response to popular demands. They did, however, recognize the need for a popular judgment of the performance of an incumbent, and the selection system was designed to be sufficiently democratic to register this kind of response.

It has often been argued that the Founders' theory of selection was totally unrealistic because of its failure to provide for the development of national party competition. But this criticism can hold, strictly speaking, only if it can be shown that sustained party competition was somehow a necessary outgrowth of the system of a popular (or quasi-popular) election. However much we have become accustomed to parties running the electoral process, a good deal of recent historical scholarship has suggested that the development of party competition was in no sense inevitable, but that it was the result in part of accident (the early national struggle between the Federalists and Republicans) and even more of design (the conscious intent of Martin Van Buren and a few others of the "party school" in the 1820s to establish permanent two-party competition).[52]

But if it cannot be readily concluded that the Founders were unrealistic in their failure to foresee permanent parties, what does seem somewhat unrealistic was their belief that a national competition could substantially exclude issue advocacy and take place on the basis primarily of individual reputation. Indeed, Hamilton himself seemed to sense an all

[52] See Richard Hofstadter, *The Idea of a Party System* (Berkeley: University of California Press, 1969).

84

too abstracted tone in much of the Convention's emphasis on reputation alone when at the last moment he spoke frankly of voter preferences being founded on "the different views of different states and of different regions. . . ."[53] In the Founders' defense, it can be said that they never believed that all considerations of issues and interests would be excluded, but only that these would be subordinated to reputation; and one should recall also that they did foresee a kind of "issue" evaluation taking place whenever an incumbent stood for reelection, which would be most of the time. Nevertheless, it still appears that the Founders did not realistically account for the role that public opinion and issues would have to play in a popular regime. Harry Jaffa's description of what many of the Founders had in mind for nonpartisan politics (not just for the presidency, but for all the institutions) serves best to indicate precisely what was problematic in their views:

An educational aristocracy, created out of the democratic principle of equality of opportunity, was the presupposition . . . of the idea of representative government. The bonds among the members of this class—the old school tie, American style—and the special allegiance its members would have to the union . . . would take the place subsequently taken by party loyalty. [Washington believed] that the holders of [high] office should, and could, work out their differences behind closed doors, as much as the Constitutional Convention had done, and then present to the country a standard to which the wise and good had already repaired, and which the rest of the country would certainly follow.[54]

This kind of politics, however desirable or undesirable one may find it, seems all too distant from the pressures of popu-

[53] Madison, *Notes*, p. 589 (September 6).

[54] Harry Jaffa, "The Nature and Origin of the American Party System," in Robert Goldwin, ed., *Political Parties U.S.A.* (Chicago: Rand McNally, 1964), pp. 80-81.

lar sentiment to endure for long under a genuinely republican system. In reacting against popular leadership, the Founders may have arrived at a conception of the presidency and presidential selection that was too detached and elevated.

Moreover, for all the attention they gave to the question of personal reputation, the Founders' thought remains vague on just how individuals would earn the "continental reputations" of which they spoke. Their view was that such reputations would naturally emerge in a regime in which national politics played a large, if not the dominant, role. The failure of persons possessing such reputations to emerge with regularity after the passing of the founding generation could be explained in part by the unexpectedly limited role of the federal government after the success of the Democratic Party. But this cannot account for the difficulty.

Considering the question of reputation in the most general terms, it can be said that there are three basic ways of attaining political prominence: through inheritance—being of the same family or, stretching the concept somewhat, being the designated heir of an already prominent figure—through the performance of great military or political deeds, or through popular leadership, i.e. advocacy of an issue or cause that divides the community. There was little mystery about how the reputations of the nationally prominent men at the time of the Foundings had been won. They had achieved their renown through great deeds, as military heroes or political advocates in the Revolutionary effort. But the Revolution was an exceptional event and therefore was not fully instructive about how reputations might be won in the future. The same could be said of the act to establish the new Constitution. Indeed, one delegate at the Convention argued that without events of a similar magnitude, no one would be able to attain a national reputation.[55]

But most of the Founders appeared to think that individual prominence could be obtained through the performance of

[55] Madison, *Notes*, p. 309 (July 17). The comment to this effect was made by Hugh Williamson.

normal—albeit distinguished—political activity. One wonders, however, whether a reputation achieved by this means
could provide sufficient renown, especially when competing
against reputations won by military heroics or perhaps even
popular leadership. The Founders' system was designed to
elevate a man who stood out from others on the basis of his
reputation for merit. This "bias" of the presidential selection
system continued in some degree even after the establishment
of permanent party competition. Yet, it did not always work
as the Founders envisioned. Individual prominence, it seems,
could just as easily be won outside of politics as through it.
Indeed, the parties often turned to candidates who had won
fame as military heroes, ignoring sometimes their political
qualifications. But this departure from the Founders' intentions, though significant, was less extreme than the one institutionalized in the current system: elevation by means of
popular leadership.

CHAPTER II

Presidential Selection in the Jeffersonian Era

THE nonpartisan selection system established by the Founders barely survived a decade. By the election of 1796, traces of partisanship were already clearly in evidence, and by 1800 the contest was being fought on strictly partisan lines. Each party in 1800 agreed on its candidates for president and vice-president in advance of the selection of the electors, and the electors were in turn chosen to act as instructed agents, not deliberative trustees. Contrary to the general line of argument followed in this study, the changes in the selection process in 1800 were not the product of a conscious plan to "legislate" a new electoral system. They emerged under the pressure of events, as partisans sought to win power in order to further their ideological goals. For the political actors in 1800, the question of the institutional character of the selection system was entirely subordinated to the larger issues involved in the partisan dispute of the day.

After 1800, however, theoretical concerns began again to play some role in influencing the development of electoral institutions. As passions cooled and the alignment of political forces became clearer, some politicians began to ask if the electoral procedures that had grown up in 1796 and 1800 were consistent with their long-range institutional goals. The central issue in nearly every discussion was whether parties (or a party) should be maintained. This issue can be broken down into at least three smaller questions: Was a system with parties more compatible with the basic requirements of republican government than a nonpartisan system? Would the existence of parties hinder or assist in the task of finding a "natural" majority on behalf of a candidate? And finally, what influence would a system of parties have on structuring the ambitions of presidential contenders? None of these questions was actually resolved during the so-called Jeffersonian Era (1800-24), and as late as 1836 many of the same issues were still being actively debated. But the practices and ideas of this period created a new set of circumstances and a new climate of opinion for later theorists and practitioners. It is important, therefore, to survey the major developments during this era. In keeping with the approach of this study, this will be done largely by tracing the thought of the politicians of the time, and in particular that of its dominant theorist and leading statesman, Thomas Jefferson.

THE ELECTION OF 1800 AND THE PREVAILING UNDERSTANDING OF POLITICAL PARTIES

"Had it not been for the firm and determined stand then made by a counter-party," Jefferson wrote in 1824, "no man can say what our government would have been to this day."[1] Jefferson was referring, of course, to the saving actions of the Republican Party at the turn of the century. For Republicans the victory of 1800 had rescued the nation from the threat of monarchic subversion. It had checked the atrophy of legislative power and guaranteed the existence of political liberty in a climate that was free of the unenlightened influence of ecclesiastical authority. To Republicans these achievements were sufficient to warrant designating this election as America's "second revolution."

Although this revolution had miraculously been accomplished without violence or direct violation of the law, it had clearly been achieved by means that were contrary to the spirit and intent of the Constitution. The election, in Jefferson's words, had been a "contest of opinion."[2] It served the

[1] Letter to William Short, January 8, 1824, *The Works of Thomas Jefferson*, ed. Paul Ford, 12 vols. (New York: G. P. Putnam's Sons, 1905), 12:396.

[2] James D. Richardson, ed., *A Compilation of the Messages and Papers of the Presidents*, 10 vols. (Washington, D.C.: Bureau of National Literature, 1897-1913), 1:322.

purpose of initiating a critical change in the character of the American political system, a function for elections which had not been contemplated by the Founders—or at least not on a recurring basis. What is most striking to those who have studied Jefferson's thought at the time, however, is that Jefferson, too, did not conceive of elections as regularly offering significant choice or providing for critical transformations on rare occasions. This must be considered all the more strange because Jefferson, unlike the Founders, often spoke of the need for periodic revisions of the constitutional system to keep pace with the "progress of the human mind" and with changes in opinions and manners.[3] Jefferson, it appears, had an abiding distrust of national elections and, except in the case of his own election, never regarded them as the proper forum for making decisive changes. Elections were suspect in performing this function because questions of policy changes were always mingled with the ambitions of political aspirants. Jefferson's belief in the need for change was more than matched by his fear of designing politicians. The function of "renewal" was best handled through the amendment process or by periodic Constitutional conventions, not by the presidential selection process.[4]

The paradox of Jefferson's election in 1800 was that while he was chosen for partisan reasons, he did not intend to institute a system of permanent party competition. In fact, all indications suggest that he held to the general view of the Founders and thought of the election of 1800 as a unique exception to the general rule. In his famous First Inaugural he proclaimed "we are all republicans; we are all federalists."[5] And while apparently meaning that all should be re-

[3] Letter to Samuel Kercheval, July 12, 1816 in *The Writings of Thomas Jefferson*, eds., Andrew A. Lipscomb and A. Ellery Bergh, 20 vols. (Washington, D.C., Thomas Jefferson Memorial Association 1905), 12:6-10.

[4] *Ibid.*; Jefferson, fearful of the consequences of democratic elections once expressed to Madison the view that they could be safer by making them more frequent (and thus less interesting). Letter to James Madison, December 20, 1787.

[5] Richardson, ed., *Messages and Papers*, 1:322.

publicans first, he intended this statement to signal an end to further partisanship and a return to nonpartisan competition, albeit on the foundation of a Republican interpretation of the Constitution.

Jefferson's understanding of the election of 1800 as a contest to end all further partisan contests reflected a doctrine about partisanship that he inherited from British political thought of the seventeenth and eighteenth centuries. It was a doctrine that was accepted by virtually all politicians of the founding generation. According to Richard Hofstadter, "the creators of the first party system on both sides, Federalists and Republicans, were men who looked upon parties as sores on the body politic."[6] To be more precise, the primary concern of theorists at the time was with major national parties. A major national party was understood to be an organization created to promote a view of the way in which society and government should be ordered; each party, then, had in mind a certain kind of constitution or regime. The American model for this kind of party is best illustrated by the Revolutionary War movement with its organized system of Committees of Correspondence. To a lesser degree, the organized efforts for and against the Constitution were also parties in this sense.

Given this view of parties, it stands to reason that once a regime has been established on a sound basis there can be no further need for parties, unless as a temporary instrument to rescue the regime from subversion. For anyone defending the existing constitutional system, the notion of allowing permanent party competition would be unthinkable. It would mean legitimizing a continual struggle between different views about the very foundation of the political order. Republicans and Federalists, as Hofstadter noted, both accepted

[6] Richard Hofstadter, *The Idea of a Party System* (Berkeley: University of California Press, 1969), p. 2. For the general interpretation of parties in this section I am following Hofstadter and Harvey C. Mansfield, Jr., "Thomas Jefferson" in Morton Frisch and Richard Stevens, eds., *American Political Thought* (New York: Charles Scribner's Sons, 1971).

this view. Where they differed was on the question of whether the Constitution was being maintained according to its true principles. To the Federalists it was, and they therefore saw the Republican Party as a seditious organization. To the Republicans, on the other hand, the Constitution was being subverted, and they therefore thought that a party was justified in order to restore republican government. Each party, then, saw the partisan struggle in terms of winning power with a view to returning the regime to nonpartisan competition. Sustained competition between groups espousing different but legitimate interpretations of the Constitution was an idea that neither side accepted.

Short of this ultimate reason for opposing parties, the thinkers of the founding generation had a number of other objections to partisan competition that would apply to parties, even where they did not begin with the intention of overturning the existing constitutional system. Where party competition is permitted, people will attach primary allegiance to their party and not directly to the regime. For republican government, which was not considered to be particularly strong or energetic, this loss of direct support could prove fatal. Parties, moreover, introduce a spirit of narrow partisanship into political life. They maintain themselves by attacking the opposition. This leads them to engage in such tactics as intentional distortion of the other party's positions, deliberate attempts to instill mistrust for its motives, and conscious efforts to embarrass its elected officials. The result of partisan competition is thus likely to be the creation of divisions far deeper and more serious than those which led the parties to form in the first place. Parties are a source of conflict, not just its result.[7]

Political thinkers of the time also opposed partisanship because it would interfere with the intended Constitutional role of legislators and the president. Parties, it was thought, might bind their members to preestablished positions. In the

[7] For the classic statement of this position, see Washington's Farewell Address, Richardson, ed., *Messages and Papers*, 1:205-16.

case of the legislature, this would conflict with the representative's obligation to deliberate, i.e. to weigh and balance the various considerations that are raised in legislative debates. As Madison observed in *The Federalist*, an atmosphere of heated partisanship is incompatible with a process of rational decision-making:

> When men exercise their reason coolly and freely on a variety of distinct questions, they inevitably fall into different opinions on some of them. When they are governed by a common passion, their opinions, if they are so to be called, will be the same.[8]

By a similar line of reasoning, when the president is chosen on partisan grounds, his ability to exercise discretion—the necessary prerequisite for statesmanship—would be restricted. The president's commitment to his party's program would act as a constraint on his decisions, making it more difficult for him to change policies in response to new information. Nor could a president chosen as a party leader avoid being considered as an "enemy" by the opposition and hence the object of partisan attacks. This would preclude the president from assuming his intended political and symbolic role as an independent force above the merely "political" squabbles of interests and factions. It is noteworthy that even with the general acceptance of parties today, the ambiguity in the president's role as party leader and chief executive remains a problem; no sooner does the victorious candidate reach office than he seeks to tone down his partisan image and without fully rejecting his role as party leader assumes the mantle of president of all the people.[9]

[8] *The Federalist*, #63, p. 384. For similar views expressed by Washington, see James Flexner, *George Washington: Anguish and Farewell* (Boston: Little Brown, 1969), p. 188.

[9] One of the foremost modern scholars of the presidency, James David Barber, has written at some length on the psychological need of Americans—or perhaps their conditioned response—for the president to serve as a truly national leader. "We elect a politician," writes Barber, "and insist that he also be a king." The president's

The Founders proposed two basic solutions for preventing the formation of national parties. The first, already discussed at length, was to make the selection of the president turn on individual reputation, not issue arousal. The second was to encourage the creation of a large number of minor parties, i.e. interest groups. This would make a virtue of necessity: since parties could not be suppressed and liberty maintained, parties should be allowed to multiply on a nonideological basis. In this way partisan energies would be channeled into a form in which they could be controlled. In *Federalist 10*, where this solution is spelled out, Madison lists four specific sources of parties or factions: religion, views about the form of government, attachment to contending politicians, and disputes over the distribution of property. Religious strife would be avoided in the national arena by the intended separation of Church and State, basic political divisions by the general acceptance of the Constitution, and personal factions by the presidential selection system. Conflicts over property, by contrast, should be tolerated, indeed must be, in any

---

role as party leader is one of the factors that conflicts with this "kingly" role, leading to the problems discussed above. (See "Man, Mood, and the Presidency," in Tugwell and Cronin, ed., *The Presidency Reappraised*, p. 205.) One recent method that has evolved to deal with this dilemma, according to Stephen Hess, is for the president to begin acting immediately as "Chief Magistrate of all the people" and to use his vice-president as the partisan leader. This practice seems to have been employed by both Eisenhower (using Nixon), and Nixon (using Agnew). See *Organizing the Presidency* (Washington: Brookings Institution, 1976), pp. 169-70.

There is, of course, the danger that too "elevated" a notion of independence confers too much authority on the executive and is incompatible with the spirit of republican government. Jefferson was no doubt correct in worrying about the particularly heroic aura which surrounded Washington, as much as this may have been needed to help establish the new government: "Such is the popularity of the President that the people will support him in whatever he will or will not do, without appealing to their own reason or to anything but their feelings towards him" (letter to Archibald Stuart, January 4, 1977, *Works*, 8:265).

modern "civilized" society. A commercial society, Madison argued, necessarily gives rise to different types of property, the protection and regulation of which form the "principal task of modern legislation."[10] If property interests, and only property interests, could be made to contend with each other on some basis other than the single and destructive division of rich and poor, the threat posed by parties could be contained. "Minor" parties based on matters of interest, as distinct from parties based either on class or fundamental political principle, would be made to compromise with each other, not out of a spirit of generosity but out of necessity. The very multiplicity of these parties, none of which would come close to representing a majority of the people, would supply the motive where a majority must decide.

These solutions were obviously not foolproof, and when national parties arose it became clear that the original consensus against them did not include an accepted doctrine about what should be done to deal with them. An important distinction existed between designing a system to avoid national parties and positive governmental action to discourage or suppress them. Given their respective positions in the 1790s—the Federalists holding power and the Republicans challenging from the outside—it was to be expected that they would divide on this issue. Republicans claimed that the government's actions in hindering or prohibiting an opposition amounted to a suppression of liberty. For this reason, Republicans adopted a more tolerant view of the right to opposition.[11] With their triumph in 1800, the legal right of a future organized opposition to form was thus established, even though most Republicans still held to the traditional

[10] The distinction between major and minor parties is implicit in Madison's argument in *Federalist 10*, though the terms major and minor are not used. Madison came closer to an explicit statement of this difference in his essay, "A Candid State of Parties," *The National Gazette*, September 26, 1972, to be found in James Madison, *The Writings of James Madison*, ed. Gaillard Hunt, 9 vols. (New York: G. P. Putnam's Sons, 1903), 6:106-20.

[11] See Hofstadter, *The Idea of a Party System*, pp. 111-21.

view respecting parties and presidential selection. In the future, elected officials might attempt to discourage parties by policy or through expressions of disapproval, but they could not suppress them by legal means.

THE CONSEQUENCES OF THE ELECTION
OF 1800 ON THE SELECTION SYSTEM

Despite the adherence of Republicans to the traditional understanding of partisanship and selection, their use of a party in 1800 together with their early recognition that it might be needed for some time had certain important consequences for the development of the selection system. Three points in particular stand out, the first two of which affect the selection system's function of influencing presidential leadership and executive power and the last its role in securing legitimacy in the accession. First, Republicans introduced and by their example helped to legitimize the idea of the candidate as a party leader. Second, they engrafted onto national elections a new function of using the electoral victory to supply energy for the president. Finally, they made some significant changes in the electoral institutions, including the creation of a nominating instrument in the form of the Congressional caucus and the adoption of the Twelfth Amendment which separated the electors' choices for president and vice-president.

The concept of the candidate as a party leader, meaning at the time a spokesman for a certain view of government rooted in a body of firm principles, emerged from the highly charged atmosphere of the initial phase of the partisan struggle. Each party represented a different view of government, and partisans looked to their leader to be an articulator of the party's principles. The ideological orthodoxy of the candidates thus became a decisive criterion for selection, while competence, virtue, and service to the state—the Founders' intended criteria—receded into the background. If one saw the opposition as advocating monarchism and consisting of "bigots" and "votaries," it would certainly be difficult to consider its leader, whoever he might be, a man "pre-eminent for virtue and ability." By the same token no "distinguished character" could lead a group committed to jacobinism and sedition, consisting of francophiles and petty demagogues. In turning down the entreaties of some Federalists to run again for the presidency in 1800, Washington summed up the new grounds for selection in the following terms: "There is no problem better defined in my mind than that principle, not men, is now and will be the chief object of competition . . . let the [opposition] party set up a broomstick and call it a true son of liberty and it will command their votes *in toto*."[12] Though Jefferson was not quite so insignificant a figure as this, his clean sweep in 1800, according to his foremost biographer Dumas Malone, was mainly attributable to his being perceived as a "symbol . . . identified with the freedom of individual human beings from tyranny or oppression. . . . He became a national leader less by his specific actions than by what he was and what he stood for."[13]

As principle came to predominate in the final election stage, the subordination of considerations of service to orthodoxy also became an important factor in the nominating stage. A candidate of capacity was of course wanted, but the strong partisan advocates also were searching for one firmly reliable and committed to their viewpoint. "Trimmers" were accordingly attacked. John Adams, a holdover from the days of nonpartisan politics, was opposed by many within the Federalist Party for his aloofness from partisan activities. Jefferson, on the other hand, assumed a clearly partisan role with his friends after 1796 and emerged as his party's undisputed leader. But dissension soon grew within the Republican fold as well. Parties whose chief motivating force is ideo-

[12] Letter to Jonathan Trumball, July 21, 1799, in Washington, *Writings*, 37:313.

[13] Dumas Malone, *Thomas Jefferson as Political Leader* (Berkeley: University of California Press, 1963), p. 11.

logical commitment are normally prone to bitter internal factionalism. Purists within their ranks object to any kind of compromises or any loose interpretation of the party's principles. This inevitably puts them in conflict with the party's office holders, who must seek support from a wider group. Purists may therefore oppose a moderate candidate, no matter what his claim in terms of merit, and advance someone more firm and trustworthy in his commitment. Jefferson's hand-picked successor, Madison, faced opposition from the Quid faction of the party on these grounds, while the Federalists experienced rifts throughout the period between the High Federalists and the moderate wing of the party.

As the leader of the first organized opposition in a presidential contest, Jefferson inevitably faced the charges, based on the traditional view of parties, that he was a demagogue engaged in an "unconstitutional" enterprise. To his prospective partisans, the answer was simple enough:

> Where the principle of difference is as substantial and as strongly pronounced as between the republicans and the Monocrats of our Country, I hold it as honorable to take a firm and decided part, and as immoral to pursue a middle line, as between the parties of Honest men, and Rogues into which every country is divided.[14]

But a justification of this kind would obviously carry no weight with those who prided themselves on taking a "disinterested" stance. For these people, Jefferson adopted a different defense in which he disavowed any personal desire to "govern men . . . or delight to ride the storm." His partisan stance could be explained by motives other than personal ambition in that he claimed to represent a point of view that was "natural" to political life. In fact, neither of the two parties could rightly be viewed as a trumped-up association designed merely to promote their leaders' personal aspirations. Each party stood for one side of a division that

---

[14] Letter to W. B. Giles, December 31, 1795, in Jefferson, *Works*, 7:43.

was coeval with politics itself: "The same political parties which now agitate the U.S. have existed through all time . . . in fact the terms Whig and Tory belong to natural as well as to civil history."[15] By asserting that both parties had a natural basis, Jefferson came close to legitimizing party competition and to distinguishing a party, understood as a body representing a "natural" and fundamental point of view, from a mere faction. On the basis of this "objective" standard he could distinguish his own leadership—and party leadership more generally—from any demagogic form of popular leadership. This element in Jefferson's thought later developed into a more explicit defense of party competition, though he never would quite settle on this as his final position.[16]

The candidate as a party leader creates certain difficulties not only in victory but in the campaign as well. The latter arise from the fact that many within the electorate are not fervent partisans; some decry partisan activity altogether, and others, though they might see some merit in the choice between principles, cherish an independent stance. Persons of this sort are apt to show an intense dislike for any candidate who displays what they consider to be signs of narrow partisanship—the pettiness, the exaggerated rhetoric, and the attitude which suggests that all should be subordinated to the good of the party. The candidate is thus left with the difficulty of satisfying the demands of partisans and of inde-

[15] Letter to Edward Rutledge, December 27, 1796, in Jefferson, *Works*, 7:94. But he did admit to having a "little spice of ambition . . . in my younger days" and to a concern with reknown preferring "posthumous" to "present fame" (letter to Madison, April 27, 1795). One wonders whether his preference for posthumous fame would not be an indication that he had a "little spice" of what Hamilton called "the ruling passion of the noblest minds."

[16] Thus he would write as late of 1823 that the Federalists were but a "faction" comprised of "sickly weakly timid" men. This reflected an earlier expressed view that the Republicans should not be considered a party but rather "the nation" (letter to William Duane, March 28, 1811, *Works*, 11:193).

pendents, both of whose support may be needed for victory. The seriousness of this problem naturally varies with the relative strength of antipartisan sentiment within the electorate. Antipartisanship was no doubt the dominant disposition of most people in the electorate after the Founding; it declined with the advent of the great conflict of 1800, though certainly not to the point where, as Washington self-deprecatingly remarked, "any other respectable Federal character would receive the same suffrages that I should";[17] it then rose again until the establishment of parties in the 1820s, after which it reached its nadir during the period of intense partisanship that followed the Civil War. In this century, as a result initially of the Progressive movement, the "spirit" of independence has again been increasing, and the point has now been reached where many leading students of electoral politics believe that we may be entering a "post-partisan era" in which partisan identification will play only a relatively minor role in determining voting behavior.[18]

How a candidate squares the demand of partisans that he be "a good party man" with the demand of a critical portion of the electorate that he be beyond mere partisanship is no simple matter. Political customs can help to ease his task. Nowadays, for example, allowance is made for a candidate to deliver what is labeled a "partisan speech" before a crowd of fellow party members, a practice which serves simultaneously to satisfy the candidate's partisan audience and to indicate to others that he is not usually so one-sided in his views. But no such customs existed in 1800, and Jefferson had to deal with the "candidate's dilemma" by the extraordinary means of keeping most of his partisan activities from the public view. His image in this respect was severely tar-

[17] Letter to Jonathan Trumball, July 21, 1799, Washington, *Writings*, 37:314.

[18] The phrase "post-partisan era" is taken from Nie, Verba and Petrocik's *The Changing American Voter* (Cambridge: Harvard University Press, 1976), p. 356. The literature on the decline of parties will be discussed at some length in chapters v and vi.

nished by the unintended publication in 1797 of a private letter containing an unseemly attack against George Washington.[19] After this Jefferson became more circumspect, urging his friends to conceal his involvement in certain projects. "Do not let my name be connected with the business" became his advice to his fellow partisans when proposing partisan activities.[20] Even his authorship of the Kentucky Resolution, a document with which he is now so closely identified, was then kept a secret and introduced under the names of others. Jefferson was doubtless motivated in his actions by his general distaste for partisanship and his desire ultimately to establish a new nonpartisan system, but his behavior also serves to illustrate the ambiguity contained in the candidate's—and president's—dual role as a party leader and a would-be leader of the entire nation. The office of the executive as outlined in the Constitution together with the nonpartisan norms that accompanied its development have served to counteract the emergence of a completely partisan system.

The initial experience with parties in America had a second major effect on the role of the selection system. It illustrated, though it did not permanently establish, a new function for national elections: providing the president with an additional source of energy and a new basis of authority. This function was the result of the simple fact that in a contest of clearly defined viewpoints one side emerges as the victor and can claim the backing of the final sovereign authority—the majority. This more active role for the majority, under which it lends direction to government, involved a break with the earlier view that the ultimate sovereign would actively "rule" only in the making of fundamental law—that is, in passing on the Constitution and in pos-

[19] Letter to Philip Mazzei, April 24, 1796, Jefferson, *Works*, 7:72-78. The incident is discussed in detail in Dumas Malone, *Jefferson and the Ordeal of Liberty* (Boston: Little Brown, 1962), pp. 261-72.

[20] Letter to James Monroe, February 11, 1799, in Jefferson, *Works*, 9:36.

sibly amending it by means of conventions, as outlined in Article v. For the Founders, popular participation in the selection process had been designed to provide the victor with a legitimate claim to the office and a measure of the people's confidence, not to arm the president with a new source of power.

Whether Jefferson had this new function in mind as a permanent institutional feature is not known. That he made use of it himself in 1800, however, is clear. In his First Inaugural he pronounced what amounted to a Republican program for reformation, including a strictly limited role for the federal government, economy in public expenditures, and the encouragement of agriculture over commerce. Jefferson clearly implied that this program should command allegiance because of its endorsement by the people in the national election. The First Inaugural makes no less than three references to majority rule that envision a role for it which, if not antithetical to the views of the Founders, is nevertheless decidedly more active than they ever contemplated. Jefferson called for "a jealous care of the right of election by the people" and "absolute acquiescence in the decisions of the majority."[21] Whatever Jefferson's intentions may have been for the long-term relation of the selection process to executive power, it soon became clear that this new source of authority was one which Republican presidents sorely needed. By weakening the presidential office in comparison with the original Constitutional design, and certainly in comparison with the status it held under Washington and Adams, the Republicans had brought about the situation in which energy, if it were to come from the executive, would have to rely on a noninstitutional source. Ironically, however, the very success of the Republicans in the electoral sphere undermined this source of authority. With the decline of the Federalists as a nationally competitive party, Republican candidates faced election campaigns without a clear division that could stir popular enthusiasm or provide a vindi-

[21] Richardson, ed., *Messages and Papers*, 1:323.

cation for a platform presented during the contest. "Energy," as it derives from an electoral campaign, requires the existence of a credible opponent. Of the three Republican presidents, only Jefferson benefited from the advantages of a heated partisan contest. After Jefferson, the presidency began to lose authority, shrinking to its limited Constitutional role as prescribed by orthodox Republican doctrine. While the personalities of these presidents played some part in this change, the decline in partisan competition with its attendant implications for a loss of presidential energy was probably the decisive factor.[22]

The third consequence of the first party division was a series of changes in the institutions of the selection system. As the parties began nominating their candidates in caucuses of their Congressional delegations, the electors lost control of the "preselection" or nominating process. Even after competition ceased between the two parties and the nominating machinery of the Republican Party lost effectiveness, the practice continued of choosing electors to act as instructed agents. Party competition also had the effect of encouraging the use of winner-take-all systems for selecting electors. Once a party won a majority within a given state legislature, it had an incentive to maximize its influence by enacting legislation that would transform the slimmest plurality into full support for its candidate. When this practice was adopted in some states, others felt strongly pressured to go along, initially to deny the other party an advantage, and later, as

[22] James Sterling Young, *The Washington Community, 1800-1828* (New York: Harcourt, Brace and World, 1966), pp. 193-210 and pp. 229-49. It should be noted, in connection with Jefferson's claim to an endorsement of his program by public opinion, that while only five states chose their electors by popular vote in 1800, Jefferson nonetheless believed that there was a clear basis for concluding where the majority sentiment lay. Moreover, the Congressional elections of the same year gave the Republicans a significant victory. It was not until 1816 that the number of states choosing by popular vote exceeded the number of states choosing by indirect means. By 1828, all but two of the states were selecting their electors by popular vote.

national party competition subsided, to ensure the maximum electoral weight for each state in the national election.

Perhaps the most significant institutional change—although one that has received only a modest amount of attention—was the passage of the Twelfth Amendment. The original electoral scheme, it will be recalled, allowed for two votes for each elector. This system had been adopted to help produce a "majority" for one candidate at the electoral stage. It was designed so that the acts of nominating and electing would take place at the same time. The system was predicated on a nonpartisan form of competition in which the electors would use both of their choices to promote their favored presidential candidates. (The selection of the vice-president as the runner-up under this system was hardly discussed at the Convention but was nevertheless a fully workable arrangement; the vice-president would be the "second" best person, and there was no reason under a nonpartisan system for supposing any ideological incompatibility between the president and vice-president.) But when electors became bound in their choices by political parties, this system lost its original rationale and created a number of serious problems. Nomination was now seen to be a party function, and the idea that electors should possess discretion was rejected as undemocratic. This meant that there could no longer be any legitimacy in a majority "created" by the electors. Under a partisan system, moreover, electors would make use of their "second" ballot to vote for their party's vice-presidential candidate. This created the possibility of a tie between the presidential and vice-presidential candidates, throwing the election into the House where the opposition party might hold a majority. More dangerous (and likely) was the possibility that the defeated party might give its electoral votes to the vice-presidential nominee of the victorious party, thus making him the president. Clearly this system needed to be changed. Jefferson proposed separating the electors' votes for president and vice-president and allowing only one vote for each office. This proposal was adopted in the Twelfth Amendment in 1804, in time for Jefferson's own reelection.

The Congressional debates on this amendment reveal a great deal of confusion about the future role of parties in the selection process and, more generally, about the "informal" problem of securing national support for the candidates. The proponents of the amendment, without seeking to ratify the existence of party competition, nevertheless seemed to think that groups of some sort would form to designate slates for presidential and vice-presidential candidates. In their view it was only reasonable to separate the choices for the two offices. But opponents could legitimately wonder about the provision to reduce the number of electoral votes for each office from two to one, for in the absence of national parties this would greatly increase the chance that the election would be decided in the House. Under the original system a candidate could be chosen if he received more votes than a majority of the electors; this requirement was maintained under the Twelfth Amendment, but since only half as many electoral votes would now be cast in the presidential voting, a majority would be much more difficult to obtain. And one might add that the diminished role for national politics which Republicans envisioned would lessen the likelihood of the emergence of continental figures. At the very least, nothing in Republican theory made it any more likely that the difficulty of creating a national majority for a candidate could now be resolved under a truly nonpartisan system.

In the final analysis, then, the Twelfth Amendment seemed to require parties—or a party—to perform the task of concentrating national support behind a candidate, even though most Republicans were reluctant to admit this. One Congressman, however, clearly recognized this need and foreshadowed the position that Jefferson later would adopt:

> While the country is divided into two great political parties . . . each party will endeavor to select the most prominent character, whose political sentiments are in

105

unison with their own, and place him in the Presidential chair, without any regard to local situation. His politics will be the criterion by which he will be judged, without any reference to his being an inhabitant of the Eastern, Middle, or Southern sections of the Union.[23]

If parties began to disintegrate, the Twelfth Amendment had thus inadvertently provided a powerful new justification for recreating them. Short of another amendment to the Constitution, parties were the only means to accomplish one of the major objectives for which the Twelfth Amendment had been enacted—keeping the presidential election out of the House.

JEFFERSON'S LATER VIEWS ON THE PRESIDENTIAL SELECTION SYSTEM

After returning to Monticello at the end of his second term, Jefferson began to reflect at greater length on the selection problem. His thoughts took a number of turns, moving from his original position of nonpartisanship to the advocacy of a one-party system and finally to the temporary support for two-party competition. His shift from nonpartisanship to support for the continued and perhaps even permanent existence of the Republican Party can be traced back to his early position that a national election could be used as a protective device for preventing the government from coming under the influence of an oligarchic faction. Originally he seemed to think that this protective act could be accomplished by a single electoral victory, but his failure to achieve consensus after 1800 made him change his mind. There were also certain structural features to a nonpartisan system that led Jefferson to think it was harmful to the Republican cause. As early as 1795, in a set of notes he made to himself on the

[23] *Annals of Congress*, vol. 13, p. 704. Comment by Representative Gregg, December 8, 1803.

origin of parties, Jefferson indicated why the antirepublican interest might always be formidable in any "open" electoral system:

> Trifling as are the numbers of the Anti-republican party, there are circumstances which give them an appearance of strength and numbers . . . their wealth is . . . greatly superior. . . . They all live in cities, together, and can act in a body reality and at all times. . . . The agricultural interest is dispersed over a great extent of country [and] have little means of communication with each other. . . .[24]

Of course Jefferson was referring in these notes to the "old" nonpartisan system as it existed prior to the Republican victory of 1800. But there was no reason why these same advantages should not reassert themselves under any nonpartisan scheme. The objections Jefferson made in 1795 were in fact very similar to those that had been raised at the Convention by Mason and Gerry against the idea of a direct nonpartisan election: nonpartisanship was advantageous to that element in society which because of wealth, capacity, and location was in a better position to concert its efforts. These advantages, Jefferson had concluded by 1816, were rooted in the structure of a system without parties, and he therefore began to oppose his own original plan for amalgamating the two parties. Monroe, who as President pursued a policy of amalgamation, now became the indirect target of Jefferson's criticisms. In Jefferson's view the death of the Federalist Party and its absorption by Monroe into the Republican Party posed a new threat to the Republican interest. The Federalists, shedding their support for monarchism and adopting "the next ground, the consolidation of government," had insinuated themselves into the ranks of the Republicans and thus managed to avoid the stigma of the Federalist label: "Like the fox pursued by the dog, they

[24] Notes on Professor Ebeling's letter of July 30, 1795, Jefferson, *Works*, 8:210.

take shelter in the midst of the sheep."[25] Only by maintaining a separate identity and concerting their efforts behind a single nominee could Republicans avoid falling prey to the Federalists' schemes.

Jefferson's recognition that the Federalist interest could not be totally defeated led him for a time to advocate a return to open party competition. As Jefferson saw it, leaders of the oligarchic interest, once they discovered that they could not be successful in appealing openly to their party's principles, would turn instead to popular issues that had strong momentary appeal. They would drop their antidemocratic posture and campaign as popular leaders. Madison had pointed out this possibility as early as 1792 in an essay in the *National Gazette* on the current state of parties:

> It will be equally their true policy to weaken their opponents by reviving exploded parties, and taking advantage of all prejudices, local, political, and occupational, that may prevent or disturb a general coalition of sentiments.[26]

Jefferson took up this argument on a larger scale in 1820, when he charged that the old Federalist leadership was deliberately exploiting the slavery issue, using the Missouri statehood issue as its vehicle:

> The Missouri question is a mere party trick. . . . The leaders of Federalism . . . have . . . changed their tact and thrown out another barrel to the whale. They are taking advantage of the virtuous feelings of the people to effect a division of parties by geographical lines.
>
> On the eclipse of Federalism with us, although not its extinction, its leaders got up the Missouri question, under

[25] Letter to William Short, January 8, 1824, Jefferson, *Works*, 12:396; letter to Marquis de Lafayette, October 28, 1822, Jefferson, *Works*, 12:260. See also Jefferson's letters to William Johnson, October 27, 1822, and June 12, 1823, and to Albert Gallatin, August 2, 1823.

[26] Madison, "A Candid State of Parties" in *Writings*, 6:119.

the false front of lessening the measure of slavery, but with the real view of producing a geographical division of parties, which might insure them the next President.[27]

For Jefferson, then, it was the conservative interest playing on popular sentiments that was the most likely source of irresponsible popular leadership and demagoguery.

Jefferson's views on popular leadership as they appear in this context merit further consideration for what they reveal about the general character of democratic appeals. The anti-slavery position of the northern Federalists exploited none of the ugly passions usually associated with demagoguery, such as fear, hatred, or appeals to "closed" or tribal instincts. Indeed, Jefferson conceded that these leaders had inspired in their following "virtuous feelings . . . [and] a zeal truly moral and laudable."[28] He nevertheless condemned these leaders because they were arousing expectations which could not be practicably satisfied. It might even be said that for Jefferson an appeal of this sort was more insidious than the more common demagogic appeal. By hiding the motive for political gain behind a mask of rectitude, clever popular leaders could disarm sensitive and enlightened people and either ensnare them in their cause or at least render their disapproval half-hearted. While one might well question Jefferson's application of this argument in this instance, his general point makes one wonder about the adequacy of distinguishing demagoguery from moral leadership on the sole grounds that the one incites fear while the other fosters hope.

[27] Letter to Charles Pinckney, September 30, 1820, *Works*, 12:165; letter to Marquis de Lafayette, November 4, 1823, *Works*, 12:323. See also Madison's letter to William Bland Lee, August 5, 1819: "Political parties intermingled throughout the community unite as well as divide every section of it. Parties founded on local distinctions and fixed peculiarities, which separate the whole into great conflicting masses, are far more to be dreaded in their tendency" (*Letters and Other Writings of James Madison*, 4 vols. [Philadelphia: J. B. Lippincott and Co., 1865], 3:142).

[28] Letter to Charles Pinckney, Jefferson, *Works*, 12:165.

But having himself once raised a popular party and having employed a form of popular leadership to do it, on what basis could Jefferson now oppose this new popular cause and its leaders? Neither the charge of ambitious motive nor the assertion of dangerous consequence was an adequate public grounds for preventing such evils. Jefferson's own experience with the attacks of the Federalist opposition at the turn of the century must have taught him the ease with which such "subjective" arguments could be dismissed in a partisan-charged atmosphere. What was required to exclude irresponsible popular leadership was an objective "rule," i.e. a constitutional doctrine capable of simple application and institutionalization. For the Founders, as we have seen, this rule had been to oppose popular leadership and national parties altogether. For Jefferson, who earlier hoped for a similar solution within a reformed republican regime, a new solution was now needed. Party competition should be instituted, but restricted to the division between the two "natural" parties. A concession would thus be made to an inevitable partisanship. More importantly, partisan energies would be channeled in a way that would bind political leaders—and Jefferson had specifically in mind the leaders of the opposition—to more or less responsible positions. In 1822 Jefferson wrote William Barry: "I consider that party division of Whig and Tory the most wholesome which can exist in any government and well worthy of being nourished to keep out those of a more dangerous character."[29] Under this solution popular leadership on behalf of both "natural" parties would be accepted, while in the case of other parties, where it was apt to be irresponsible, it would be regarded suspiciously.

[29] Letter to William Barry, July 2, 1822, in Jefferson, *Writings*, 15:388. In his letter to William Short of January 8, 1824, Jefferson called the division between Whig and Tory or republican and federal "the most salutary of all divisions, and ought, therefore, to be fostered instead of being amalgamated." This was written after the election of 1824.

This solution, it is apparent, could not be enacted by a law mandating two-party competition but had to be based on the propagation of a norm that recognized its desirability.[30]

Although Jefferson is well known for the confidence he placed in the people, he should not be classified with later theorists of selection, such as the Progressives or some of the current party reformers, who see no need for institutional restraint within the electoral process. Jefferson was explicit in his belief that the people could be led astray by designing popular leaders. Some safeguard beyond a reliance on the people's good intentions was therefore necessary. If somewhat more reluctantly, Jefferson like the Founders distinguished between the people's preferences and their true interest and sought an institutional solution that would discourage leadership from pandering to the one while allowing it to serve the other. His recommendation was two-fold: to secure a norm supporting a restricted kind of political division, and to inculcate a long-term trust among the people for the one party having their interest at heart. On both of these counts Jefferson's views contrast with the unfettered, free-floating, and present-oriented electorate envisioned by the Progressives.

---

[30] The "Tory" party under this solution would have to abandon its defense of monarchism—which the Federalists had already done—and take its stand on the principle of greater national power. While seeming here to admit the legitimacy of the Federalists' position, Jefferson in fact could never quite reconcile himself to this view. Just one year later he declared that "consolidation" was the "premier pas to monarchy" (letter to Albert Gallatin, August 2, 1823, *Works*, 12:300). Fully legitimated party competition, it will later be seen, required the additional step of conceding at least a possible compatibility between one's opponent's position and the basic principles of the regime. It is noteworthy that while Jefferson termed the Whig-Tory conflict the most wholesome that could exist, he qualified his support by maintaining that it was valuable only for suppressing more dangerous divisions, suggesting perhaps that it was needed only as a short-term solution.

111

Parties and the Nominating Process, 1808-1824

Jefferson's conclusion that at least the Republican Party had to be maintained led him further and further from the norms of the Founders and embroiled him in disputes not only with the Federalists but with many who espoused Republican principles. The idea of maintaining the Republican Party was attacked by the party's Quid faction which adopted the Founders' arguments in part from conviction and in part for tactical reasons, and even by some of the moderate Republicans who considered themselves to be following orthodox Jeffersonianism by seeking a complete amalgamation of the parties. These attacks all weakened support for parties, and by the end of the Jeffersonian era in 1824 both the doctrine of permanent parties and the use of partisan nominating instruments had been discredited at the national level.

In defending the Republican Party, Jefferson had to support the institution of the Congressional nominating caucus and a new ethic for political action. According to this ethic, a party member had to be willing to sacrifice his own judgment "on men or measures" in order to promote the well-being of the party. Party "regularity" would substitute for the traditional norm of independence. In regard to presidential selection this meant setting aside one's opinions about the best person or the best interpretation of republican doctrine in order to present a united front to the opposition. In regard to the behavior of legislators, it meant reaching a consensus within the party and acting in concert on the floor. In defending this new ethic, Jefferson wrote:

> Some [Congressmen] . . . think that independence requires them to follow always their own opinion without respect for that of others. This has never been my opinion. . . . The want of this spirit of compromise, or of self-distrust, proudly, but falsely called independence, is what gives the federalists victories which they could never obtain. . . .

Leave the President free to choose his own co-adjutors, to pursue his own measures, and support him and them, even if we think we are wiser than they, honester than they are, or possessing more enlarged information of the state of things. If we move in mass, be it ever so circuitously, we shall obtain our object; but if we break into squads, everyone pursuing the path he thinks most direct, we become an easy conquest. . . . We ought not to schematize on either men or measures.[31]

Jefferson's support for the caucus and the idea of party regularity drew fire first on the expected grounds that it would sacrifice men's independent judgment to the tyranny of party opinion. This argument was seized upon by Quid Republicans in preparation for the election of 1808. John Randolph, the self-proclaimed leader of the Quid faction, published an open letter in which he asserted that "the people ought to exercise their right of election without any undue bias." Only when necessity demanded, i.e. when the opposition was strong and could win the election, could a caucus be justified. No such necessity existed in 1808, for the Federalists were "comparatively few in number and form but a feeble party. . . ."[32] The second line of attack directed against the caucus was again advanced in the "spirit" of the Constitution. The Founders, as was noted, had wanted the election to be decided by electors for the express purpose of avoiding selection by the Congress. Under one party rule, however, the nomination of the president by the Congressional caucus had in fact turned the effective decision over presidential selection to the Congress. Not only did this violate the doctrine of separation of powers, but it was extremely undemocratic. In a reversal that must have annoyed many

[31] Letter to William Duane, April 30, 1811, *Works*, 2:196; letter to William Duane, March 28, 1811, *Works*, 2:193.

[32] John Randolph, "Public Letter of Protest Against the Caucus," March 7, 1808, cited in Arthur M. Schlesinger, Jr. and Fred Israel, eds., *History of American Presidential Elections 1789-1968*, 4 vols. (New York: Chelsea House, 1971), 1:230.

Republicans, opponents labeled the institution "King Caucus" and contrasted its oligarchic tendencies with the democratic intent of the Founders' nonpartisan system. Any form of party machinery, it was said, constituted an unwarranted interference with the democratic process. As one Congressman argued during one of the many debates on the caucus system:

> . . . this whole proceeding appears to be monstrous. It must be corrected, or the character of this Government is fundamentally changed . . . the Chief Magistrate of the nation owes his office principally to *aristocratic* intrigue, cabal, and management. Preexisting bodies of men, and not the people, make the appointment. . . . On every side these leaders are accessible to the assaults of corruption. . . . Thus, in practice, do we find all the advantages frustrated which, in the choice of a President, the Convention so anxiously sought to secure, and all the evils realized against which barriers were so sedulously erected.[33]

The proponents of party regularity were not without responses to these arguments. They denied, at least through 1816, that the Federalists were helpless and argued that even if the Federalists could not win an election they might be able to dictate which Republican candidate would be chosen. After 1816, they shifted ground and contended that in the absence of a caucus, a Federalist might be able to win by posing as a faithful Republican. As to the assertion that the caucus violated the separation of powers, its supporters responded by distinguishing between Congressional participation in the nominating and the election stages. In the former, the Congressmen were said merely to be acting in their capacity as private citizens making a recommendation to the public. In no way did this interfere with the final election decision, which remained entirely that of the people, the state legislators, and the electors. Candor, however, obliged

[33] *Annals of Congress*, vol. 26, pp. 842-43, comment by Representative Gaston, January 3, 1814.

the proponents of the caucus to admit that if the caucus's "recommendations" were always accepted, which was clearly the intent, there was indeed a sense in which the separation of powers was being undermined. But judged by the very same criterion, they argued, the alternative would be much worse, for under a nonpartisan system the final election would normally be decided in the House. As Jefferson remarked, "Would we rather the choice should be made by the legislature voting in Congress by states; or in caucus *per capita*? The remedy [the Caucus] is indeed bad, but the disease is worse."[34]

The debates on the caucus system that took place during this period proceeded on the assumption that the caucus was in fact an effective agency in disciplining the behavior of Republican leaders and voters. How much influence the caucus actually had, however, has recently become the subject of a good deal of scholarly interest.[35] To decide this matter, one would have to determine first the extent to which elites—potential candidates, elected party officials, and party opinion leaders—respected the decision of the caucus, and second, the extent to which those selecting the electors—the people or the state legislators—felt bound by its recommendations. Such an analysis would have to proceed by placing the nominating arrangements of this period on a continuum that indicated the degree to which a party system, consisting usually of two or more parties but in this case of only one, dominated the preselection process and monopolized the function of presenting candidates. At one end of the continuum would be a fully nonpartisan system in which candidates are presented as individuals and in which party sup-

[34] Letter to George Hay, August 17, 1823, Jefferson, *Works*, 12:303.

[35] See James Chase, *Emergence of the Presidential Nominating Convention* (Urbana: University of Illinois Press, 1973); James Sterling Young, *The Washington Community*; Theodore Lowi, "Party Policy and Constitution in America," in William Chambers and Walter Burnham, eds., *The American Party Systems*, 2nd ed. (New York: Oxford University Press), pp. 245-50.

port is either excluded or inconsequential. Close to this would be a different kind of nonpartisan system in which candidates are presented by *ad hoc* groups or organizations of the candidates' own making; under this arrangement no preexisting electoral organizations would retain permanent control over the presentation of candidates. At the opposite end of the spectrum there would be a fully partisan system in which established parties are widely accepted as the legitimate agents for nomination. Without the backing of a party, no candidate could hope for success. In the strongest instance of this case, parties would possess the widest latitude over their choices and could—if they so desired—pass over prominent men within their ranks. Between these poles of nonpartisanship and partisanship are other possible nominating circumstances. There is the situation in which persons of prominence are able to run on their own but find the backing of a party helpful. This roughly was the state of affairs in 1828 and 1832, when Jackson accepted the help of the Democratic Party but could clearly have made a run on his own. There is also the situation in which candidates of individual prominence would not be able to run without a party's backing, but in which they command so great a personal following that the party has little choice but to select them or lose vital support. A candidate so chosen is more properly considered "invested" than nominated.[36] In certain cases, the prominence of a candidate may be such that all parties vie for his acceptance, as occurred in Eisenhower's case. Though maintaining the form of partisan control, nominations in these cases, if only for the time-being, represent the substance of nonpartisan selection.

In looking at the responses of elites during the Jeffersonian era, the evidence suggests that the control of the caucus over the preselection function was far from absolute. The caucus was under attack by Republicans as an institution al-

[36] For this point and a discussion of what nomination means, see Maurice Duverger, *Political Parties*, trans. by Barbara and Robert North (New York: John Wiley and Sons, 1963).

most from its inception. From 1808 on, supporters of the unsuccessful candidates in the caucus either challenged its legitimacy or held renegade caucuses. James Young has compiled evidence indicating that for all the caucuses after 1804, the attendance at the "official" meeting never exceeded seventy-five percent of the party's Congressional delegation.[37] In addition, agencies besides the caucus, most notably some of the state legislatures and state legislative caucuses, continued to make "nominations" on their own. While in some cases these were designed to influence the decision of the Congressional caucus, in others they acted independently and were intended as an alternative avenue for preselection. Finally, the presidential aspirants themselves did not always accept the caucus's verdict. Although active campaigning for the office did not take place, making the candidates' intentions unclear, efforts on behalf of Monroe and George Clinton in 1808 and De Witt Clinton in 1812 continued after the caucus had made its decision.[38] William Crawford withdrew after being defeated in the caucus meeting of 1816, but apparently in exchange for a promise from certain Monroe supporters to back him in the succession of 1824. This bespoke more an arrangement among prominent men than an example of full party control.

The impact of the caucus's decisions on those who chose the electors—in some cases the people and in others the state legislators—is more difficult to determine. For a time scholarly opinion seemed to accept the view that the caucus was decisive in "biasing" electoral decisions, and the obvious fact can be cited that from 1800 through 1816 its choice always prevailed in the general election. But this last fact must be treated with considerable caution, since it can-

[37] Young, *The Washington Community*, pp. 113-17.

[38] De Witt Clinton, a Republican, had Federalist backing in 1817. Never having very much of a chance with the caucus, he relied from the beginning on other means of presentation. He ran "the first active campaign for a presidential nomination in American history," according to Roy F. Nichols, *The Invention of the American Political Parties* (New York: Free Press, 1967), p. 240.

117

not be known if the caucus's decision was the reason for the candidate's success. The famous party historian Moise Ostrogorski, who did much to establish the view that the caucus exercised great influence, nevertheless conceded that "the personages raised to the presidency by the caucus were not so much its creatures as men designated beforehand by public opinion, or by a considerable section of it, owing to their great services and their character."[39] It would be possible to interpret this as elevation on personal grounds, with the party nominating machinery merely acquiescing to an already established fact. One modern student of the institutions of this era, James Chase, asserts this conclusion unequivocally: "As the acid test of party regularity, the caucus failed. Far more effective in unifying the party was the transcendent popularity of its presidential nominees."[40] Without a good deal more evidence, however, one should be wary of accepting so sweeping an assertion of the ineffectiveness of the caucus. This conclusion could be tested only if the caucus had put its prestige on the line and passed over one of these prominent persons. Its "failure" to do so could perhaps be interpreted as the result of an unwillingness on the part of caucus participants to risk the institution's power. But it is equally plausible that the prominence of the candidates was a natural source of their support within the party. Perhaps the most that can be said, then, is that the caucus did not possess a monopoly of influence either with elites or the electorate. Parties did not win this kind of authority until 1840.

To say that the caucus did not monopolize the preselection function, however, is quite different from claiming that it possessed no prestige or that it was disdained by presidential

[39] Moise Ostrogorski, "The Rise and Fall of the Nominating Caucus, Legislative and Congressional," *American Historical Review*, 2 (December 1899): 281. For other treatments of the caucus, see William G. Morgan, "The Origin and Development of the Congressional Nominating Caucus," *Proceedings of the American Philosophical Society* (April 1969), 113:184-96, and Charles Thompson, *The Rise and Fall of the Nominating Caucus* (New Haven, 1902).

[40] Chase, *Emergence*, p. 28.

aspirants. The contrary, in fact, is suggested by the eagerness with which most of the candidates sought its endorsement and the vigor with which it was attacked by the supporters of those whom it had turned down. Moreover, if the question is not how influential in fact was the caucus nomination, but rather how the ambition of presidential aspirants was structured, it is the candidates' perception of the system that is the crucial factor to consider. And on this point, enough first-hand evidence exists to indicate that most of the candidates directed their initial efforts at winning the caucus's approval.[41] Though the option existed for a candidate defeated in the caucus to carry his campaign directly to the people and the state legislators, the caucus was still clearly a very important factor in affecting the character of presidential candidates until 1824.

The campaign strategy dictated by the caucus system was for the candidates to attempt to win the backing of a large constituency within Congress. With many of the aspirants in this period coming from the cabinet, one of the principal effects of this system was a weakening of the president's hold on his own officials.[42] Ambitious cabinet secretaries had greater reason to please a Congressional group than their own president; and as several secretaries were involved, the consequence was to undermine the unity of the Administration in its dealings with the Congress. As John Quincy Adams ruefully remarked in 1819:

> The only possible chance for a head of Department to attain the Presidency is by ingratiating himself personally with the members of Congress; and, as many of them have

[41] Despite his comments about the lack of support for the caucus, Young's discussion of campaign strategies reveals the importance of the system for the strategies of the candidates. See pp. 240-49.

[42] The period being referred to in particular lasted from 1814 until 1823. By 1824, it became clear that the caucus endorsement would be worth very little. A partial countervailing influence to Congressional dominance was the president's ability to "designate" a successor, especially by his appointment to the post of secretary of state. Only in Jefferson's case of the appointment of Madison, however, did this presidential "nod" appear to have been very important.

119

objects of their own to obtain, the temptation is immense to corrupt coalitions.[43]

Such a system was hardly conducive to the "unity" and "energy" in the executive branch that Hamilton had sought. And if in certain instances the struggle among cabinet secretaries led to good policy—as Ernest May argues was the case in the creation of the Monroe Doctrine—it cannot be said that as a general rule it structured ambitions in a way that promoted effective policy-making or sound administration.[44]

It is important to point out, however, that the weakness of the presidency insofar as it resulted from the selection system was not caused by the caucus alone. The caucus gave Congressmen control over the nominating process but not over the final election. The caucus endorsement became tantamount to election only because of the existence of a one-party system. Hence the party system rather than the nominating system could be viewed as the chief factor denying the president an independent constituency in the electorate. When the advocates of two-party competition such as Martin Van Buren proposed maintaining the caucus system in 1824, they did not intend to weaken the presidency but on the contrary to strengthen it, at least in comparison to its status under one-party rule. Whatever difficulties the caucus system presented, it nevertheless served to discourage popular leadership in the selection process by focusing the ambitions of contenders on winning the initial support of an "elite" group.

But as the election of 1824 approached, it became clear that the caucus nomination would no longer count and that one could just as easily run against it as with it. This gave

[43] John Quincy Adams, *The Memoirs of John Quincy Adams*, ed. Charles Francis Adams, 12 vols. (Philadelphia: J. B. Lippincott, 1875), 4:242. Adams noted as well the caucus's effort on an incumbent president seeking reelection; the practice "places the President in a state of undue subserviency to the members of the legislature."

[44] Ernest May, *The Making of the Monroe Doctrine* (Cambridge: Harvard University Press, 1975), p. 255.

rise to the four-cornered nonpartisan race of 1824. Nonpartisanship, as far as one could then make out, represented the future form of presidential selection. But under the changed circumstances of the second decade of the nineteenth century, and without a deliberative electoral system, nonpartisan competition could scarcely be expected to assume the form that the Founders had intended. The more likely result, as Martin Van Buren feared, would be the ascendancy of a destructive popular leadership.

Jefferson on the Five Functions of Selection

On the question of selection, as in so many other areas, Jefferson never expounded a consistent theory. Yet he offered some important suggestions and in the course of justifying his own political actions established a number of highly influential doctrines. His views on the five functions of selection may be summarized as follows: (1) *Controlling ambition.* Jefferson undermined the Founders' nonpartisan selection system by making issue advocacy rather than reputation the chief criterion for presidential selection. Once having done so, however, he feared the consequences of his own precedent, especially in the case of opposition leaders campaigning by demagogic means, and proposed (for a time) establishing party competition to contain leadership appeals. (2) *Presidential leadership and executive power.* Jefferson used a party but with the object of ending partisan conflict. He understood presidential leadership to be partisan while performing its temporary task of restoring republican government, but its "normal" role, once the restoration had taken place, was nonpartisan. In a matter unrelated to the selection process, Jefferson espoused a limited view of the executive's formal powers. But the formal authority of the president would be supplemented by his potential claim to represent the majority's policy preferences as determined in the selection process. This claim to authority, however, was undermined by the emergence of a one-party system; and the presi-

121

dent's power was further eroded by the partial control of the nomination (and election) by the Congressional caucus. (3) *Presidential character*. Jefferson advocated no discernible change from the Founders' general emphasis on virtue in presidential candidates. But unlike Hamilton, he never recognized a positive role for ambition and indeed appeared to view it as only a dangerous force. (4) *Legitimacy*. Jefferson's emphasis on majority rule along with the rise of parties helped to undermine any discretionary role for the electors. The formation of national support for candidates was thus implicitly pushed back to an earlier phase in the selection process and to some new—though for a time unspecified—institution. Jefferson sought to end the dangerous possibility of a deal between the vice-presidential candidate of the victorious party and the electors of the defeated party; and he wanted also to keep the election from going to the House. The Twelfth Amendment was adopted to serve both of these ends. It was successful in accomplishing the first; but it actually increased the likelihood of a House election, at least under a nonpartisan system. This result compelled Jefferson on practical grounds to support the Republican Party caucus, perhaps in spite of his theoretical opposition to political parties. (5) *Choice and Change*. Jefferson used the presidential selection process to effect a major change in the American political system, and this precedent was perhaps as important as any theoretical doctrine he expressed. But it is nevertheless important to observe that he never favored using national elections to perform this function on a regular basis, largely because he feared the possibility of demagogic leadership appeals prompted by personal ambitions. The institution he proposed for periodic "renewal" of the system was a constitutional convention once each generation.

CHAPTER III

Martin Van Buren and the Case for Electoral Restraint

IF ANY one individual can be accorded the distinction of establishing permanent party competition in the United States, it is Martin Van Buren. Van Buren's accomplishment was of both a theoretical and a practical nature. He defined and promoted a new doctrine for the role of party competition, and he took the lead in founding the Democratic Party, which in turn forced the opposition to organize in response. Although Van Buren himself was a strong partisan, his success depended on his ability to view parties in an impartial and detached light. Party competition, he contended, was required for the good of the nation as a whole to resolve an emerging crisis in the presidential selection process. Van Buren viewed party competition as a new "institution" in the constitutional system that could help eliminate personal factionalism, manage electoral conflict, and prevent presidential elections from being decided by the House under the widely distrusted auxiliary plan. On the basis of this understanding of party competition, it can be said that national parties in America were "legislated" into existence as part of a deliberate constitutional change rather than merely evolving, as most interpretations would have it, in response to the quest of different groups for political power.[1]

When Van Buren arrived in Washington in 1821 as a

[1] For the works placing emphasis on the role of ideas in the development of party competition, see Robert Remini, *Martin Van Buren and the Democratic Party* (New York: Columbia University Press, 1959), Richard Hofstadter, *The Idea of a Party System* (Berkeley: University of California Press, 1969), and Michael Wallace, "Changing Concepts of Party in the United States: New York 1815-1828," *American Historical Review* 74 (December 1968): 453-91. I have relied extensively on all these sources for the idea

senator from New York, he found the prevailing attitude in the capital to be highly unfavorable to the idea of reestablishing party competition. The nation's leading political figures opposed parties, having as their justification not only the old eighteenth-century theories that the Founders had relied on but their own experience with the bitter partisan disputes of the previous two decades. President Monroe called parties the "curse of the country" and rejoiced that they had "cooled down or rather disappeared."[2] Monroe himself had followed an active policy of attempting to rid the nation of the vestiges of partisan sentiment, sometimes by making symbolic gestures of national unity and sometimes by offering tangible benefits in the form of administrative posts to tractable Federalists. Van Buren was especially upset by this last policy, and in publicly objecting to one such appointment he first became aware of the strength of antipartisan sentiment that existed among most national leaders. In his *Autobiography*, Van Buren recalled how his views about parties brought upon him the "odium . . . [of] the White House and most circles, political and social, of Washington." Van Buren's reception must indeed have been chilly, for it prompted one of his few attempts at irony in eight hundred pages of often painfully sober but nevertheless highly instructive narrative. "The noisy revels of bacchanalians in the Inner Sanctuary," he wrote, "could not be more unwelcome sounds to devout worshippers than was [my] peal of the party toscin in the ears of those who glorified the 'Era of Good Feeling.'"[3]

---

that the establishment of party competition was a deliberate, "rational" act. In none of these sources, however, is a similar emphasis placed on the crucial role of the breakdown in presidential selection and the need to control the ambitions of the candidates in their pursuit of the office.

[2] Letter to Madison, May 10, 1822, *The Writings of James Monroe*, ed. S. M. Hamilton, 7 vols. (New York: G. P. Putnam's Sons, 1902), 6:284-91.

[3] Martin Van Buren, *The Autobiography of Martin Van Buren*, ed. John C. Fitzpatrick (Annual Report of the American Historical Association, 1918), p. 126. In Van Buren's view, Monroe deviated

Monroe's successor in the White House, John Quincy Adams, was an even more ardent opponent of political parties. Before assuming office he revealed that "My great object will be to break up the remnant of old party distinction and bring the whole people together in sentiment as much as possible."[4] His goal was to free selection from partisan influences and reinstitute the Founders' ideal under which the choice of the executive would be based on an assessment of the candidates' merit and virtue. In his First Inaugural, in which he made antipartisanship one of the major themes, Adams asked his fellow countrymen to join him in "discarding every remnant of rancor against each other . . . and yielding to talent and virtue alone that confidence which in times of contention for principles was bestowed only upon those who bore the badge of party communion."[5] Adams's plan to return to the earlier view of leadership and selection represented more than a pious hope or a cold patriot's disdain for partisanship. It had factual support in the events of his own election. Adams was the first president of the century to be chosen without the nomination or backing of a political party; and his election witnessed the collapse of all party machinery which, in the aftermath of the widespread attacks on "King Caucus," was widely regarded as an oligarchic intrusion into the presidential selection process.

---

completely from the policies of Jefferson and Madison: "[he] took the ground openly, and maintained it against all remonstrances, that no difference should be made by the Government in the distribution of its patronage and confidence on account of the political opinions and course of applicants" (p. 124, see also p. 303).

[4] Quoted in Harry V. Jaffa, "The Nature and Origin of the American Party System" in Robert A. Goldwin, ed., *Political Parties U.S.A.* (Chicago: Rand McNally, 1964), p. 65. Van Buren assessed Adam's intentions in the following terms: "He [Adams] therefore embraced with avidity and supported with zeal the project of Mr. Monroe to obliterate the inauspicious party divisions of the past and to bury the recollection of their causes and effects in a sepulchre proposed by himself—to wit in 'the receptacle of things lost on earth' " (*Autobiography*, p. 193).

[5] Cited in Van Buren, *Autobiography*, pp. 192-93.

Such was the hostile atmosphere, then, in which Van Buren operated. His own initial preference for parties can probably be explained as almost an instinctive response. Van Buren was a product of the very strong partisan system in New York and had learned there that party competition was the only means by which men of little reputation or stature could contend against the "great names" of New York politics. On his arrival in Washington, accordingly, he began to urge a "radical reform in the feeling of this place . . . a general resuscitation of the old Democratic Party."[6] But a defense of partisan competition at the level of national politics demanded something more than a simple application of the ideas derived from the conduct of politics in a single state. It required a new and broader theoretical justification, and Van Buren seems to have had some assistance in this task from a familiar quarter. In the spring of 1823, Van Buren made a trip to Monticello where for the first and only time he met with Jefferson, his *"beau ideal* of thorough patriotism and accomplished statesmanship."[7] During the ensuing two-day seminar on republicanism, Van Buren must have taken up the question of presidential selection, which was then uppermost in his mind, and learned from Jefferson his revised thoughts on the advisability of maintaining party machinery and renewing party competition.[8] Van Buren's subsequent defense of parties, in any case, owes a good deal to Jefferson's post-Missouri views, although Van Buren expanded on the ideas of his mentor by abandoning the charge

[6] Letter to Charles Dudley, January 10, 1822, in Catharine Bonney, *A Legacy of Historical Gleanings* (Albany: J. Munsell, 1875), pp. 382-84. Van Buren is also reported to have told a friend before leaving for Washington of his intention "to revive the old contest between federals and antifederals and build up a party for himself on that." Cited in Remini, *Martin Van Buren and the Democratic Party,* p. 15.

[7] Van Buren, *Autobiography,* p. 188.

[8] Van Buren does not mention that this came up specifically in his recounting of his discussions with Jefferson (*Autobiography,* pp. 185-88), but he soon wrote Jefferson on the subject after leaving Monticello. Jefferson's reply (June 19, 1824) was taken by Van Buren as an endorsement of his plan to reinstitute party competition.

126

of illegitimacy against his opponents and by broadening the defense of parties to include a much more general treatment of their potential role in controlling the ambition of presidential aspirants.

If Van Buren needed the help of Jefferson in devising his theoretical case, he also required the assistance of Jackson in carrying out his practical plans. The election of 1824 convinced Van Buren that neither the argument for party competition on its merits nor an appeal to partisan sentiment was sufficient to bring parties into being. A stronger and more immediate galvanizing force was required. For this Van Buren turned to Andrew Jackson, seeking to link his personal popularity with the Democratic Party and the antipathy toward him with the opposition. Van Buren realized that a division formed on such personal lines was in tension with his long-term goal of competition based on party competition. As long, therefore, as Jackson was on the scene, it could not be certain that a lasting partisan division had taken root. The status of party competition was not finally decided until the election of 1836, in which Van Buren appropriately enough was the Democratic candidate and in which the opposition, by refusing to nominate a single candidate, once again raised the entire question of the legitimacy of political parties. The Democrats were thus forced to make the case for partisan competition as a key element in the campaign, and they went to the nation with many of the theoretical arguments made by Van Buren a decade earlier. In defeating the opposition in 1836, Van Buren not only fulfilled his private ambition of becoming president but also attained his constitutional objective of establishing party competition. After 1836, the idea of partisan nominations was never again seriously challenged; it became part of the living constitution.

VAN BUREN'S CASE FOR TWO-PARTY COMPETITION

Van Buren's defense of party competition proceeded on two different levels, one of which can be called partisan and the other constitutional. From the perspective of a partisan,

127

Van Buren argued that party competition would be beneficial for his own party, and from the perspective of a constitutional legislator that it would promote the good of the regime. Van Buren blended these two levels of argument, emphasizing one or the other depending on which audience he was addressing. Van Buren used the partisan appeal to persuade those of a political disposition similar to his own that there were distinct advantages to be derived from organizing in a separate party; and he used the constitutional defense to justify his proposed change to the general public, as well as to overcome any doubts among his fellow partisans that party activity was somehow harmful or unpatriotic.

To understand Van Buren's approach, it will be helpful to elaborate in a general way the distinction between these two levels of argument. A partisan defense urges persons who share some common aim or interest to concert their actions in order to advance their goal. To defend party from a partisan posture is in the first instance to promote the well-being of *one* party, one's own party, and not political parties or party competition in general. In fact, there would seem to be a tension between the advocacy of a partisan cause and the idea of party competition. The objective of the pure partisan is for his own party to win, always and decisively; and how could this goal better be attained than by having his own party totally displace the opposition and become the only party? Such a presumption against party competition could be reversed, however, if the partisan could be convinced that party competition served a partisan interest. On the demonstration of this fact, the partisan might be willing to concede the existence of another party and even to check the excesses of his own partisan zeal in order to promote the goal of party competition.

A constitutional defense of party, by contrast, consists of a detached advocacy of a particular kind of party *system* on the grounds of its contribution to the common good. Under a constitutional defense, the doctrine of party competition is discussed in much the same manner as any other "neutral" constitutional doctrine, such as separation of powers or federalism.[9] The questions asked are whether and how party competition serves the public interest. Virtually all scholars of political parties today defend the idea of party competition, though they differ considerably about the types of parties and party competition that are most desirable. These differences reflect alternative preferences about the meaning of popular government, as the party system is usually considered one of the most important factors affecting the character of the political system as a whole. Efforts to change the type of party system are therefore often more important than attempts to change the stances of particular parties within any given system. A change in the character of the party system constitutes a constitutional change, and any movement that advocates such a change, whether it calls itself a party or poses as a nonpartisan reform movement, in effect qualifies as a "party" in the eighteenth-century meaning of the term, i.e. as an organized movement to change the character of the constitutional system. It is curious, therefore, that it is accepted practice within the political science discipline today to be a "partisan" on behalf of a particular kind of party system but not, *qua* political scientist, the advocate of a particular party.

With partisanship in this sense barred from most contemporary defenses of party competition, one might wonder what modern theorists expect will fuel the actual partisan division. In fact, this matter is all too often overlooked, and the assumption is made that once the best type of party system has been discovered in the abstract, the proper kind and amount of partisanship will be forthcoming. That the requirements of creating and sustaining party organizations might impose certain constraints on the types of parties and the nature of the

---

[9] A constitutional defense is identified here with a system having party competition, i.e. two or more parties. Of course, constitutional defenses have been made for one-party systems, often in the case of developing nations, but in all developed liberal democracies competition between two or more parties is assumed.

party system are considerations that have apparently escaped many theorists.[10] There is, nevertheless, some rationale to the constitutional theorist's downplaying of partisan fervor, for when all is said and done the constitutional theorist cannot afford to have partisans hold their views in an absolute way. Underlying almost every constitutional defense is the belief that which partisan view triumphs is less important than that the party system should survive. And as the survival of the party system is usually thought to depend on an alternation of power between the parties, the constitutional defender must grant the benefit of a party turnover even when it works to the detriment of his preferred party. While one could conceive of a constitutional defense based on the idea that a party system is best maintained when partisans blindly follow their partisans instincts, most political scientists have no faith in the operation of any such invisible political hand. The usual position is that a well-functioning system of party competition requires party leaders to accept the view that the well-being of the party system is as important as the well-being of their own party. At this point, party conflict becomes something of a game, and it can be demanded that it should be played according to the rules.

Van Buren's defense of party is unique because it includes both a constitutional and a partisan dimension. He was a political scientist and a partisan, and for that reason neither one in the purest sense. His adoption of both of these roles was necessitated by the circumstances he faced. Party competition had ceased during the Era of Good Feeling because of the pervasiveness of the view that partisanship was prejudicial to the public interest and because of the absence of a set of safe issues of sufficient prominence to generate and sustain a partisan division. As a political scientist, Van Buren presented a general argument on behalf of parties, asking that people "recognize their necessity and give them the credit

---

[10] This criticism will be made in subsequent chapters in reference to the views of Woodrow Wilson, certain proponents of the modern party government school, and many modern party reformers.

they deserve." In the same vein, addressing this time not the proponents of antipartisanship but the potential proponents of a pure partisanship, he expressed his "repugnance to a species of cant against parties in which too many are apt to indulge when their own side is out of power and to forget when they come in." To distinguish himself from this kind of partisan, Van Buren declared, "I never could bring myself for party purposes to deprecate their existence." As a party man, however, Van Buren took the lead in finding and accentuating a set of partisan issues, calling on his fellow Democrats to "devote ourselves to improve and elevate the principles of our own [party] and to support it ingenuously and faithfully."[11] As the party man, too, he sought to make Democrats see that their only hope for maintaining the purity of their own principles was to admit the existence of an opposing party. Regardless of their natural partisan inclinations, Democrats had to understand that any attempt to end party conflict, even if in the name of their own principles, would aid the opposition, since the opposition, unlike the Democrats, "found no difficulty in uniting wherever union promised success."[12] Thus these two postures, that of the political scientist and the partisan, reinforced one another: the doctrine of party competition was necessary to justify a partisan stance, and a partisan stance was necessary to create the Democratic Party and ultimately two-party competition.

Van Buren's Constitutional Defense of Party Competition

In attempting to discover the major benefits that Van Buren and members of his party school were seeking, care must be taken not to look only for those points that correspond to the modern understanding of party competition. The modern case, which derives from the school alternately

[11] Van Buren, *Autobiography*, p. 125.

[12] Martin Van Buren, *Inquiry into the Origin and Course of Political Parties in the United States* (New York: Hurd and Houghton, 1867), p. 6. Hereafter cited as *Political Parties*.

known as party government or responsible political parties, is a product of late nineteenth- and twentieth-century scholarship in America. Its central propositions are that: (1) the abuse of governmental power is best prevented by the check supplied by an opposition party and by periodic alternation of power between the parties; (2) democratic participation is aided or assured by parties at least one of which will have an incentive to broaden the electorate; (3) mass democracy depends on party competition which alone can provide the means by which citizens determine the direction of public policy.[13] These propositions have become so embedded in the minds of modern scholars that many seem to regard them as the only possible defenses of parties. But if one looks with an open mind to the thought of the 1820s and 1830s, it is clear that while these points were occasionally mentioned, they did not form the core of the defense of party competition. The concern of the party advocates at that time was less with such abstract considerations of democratic theory than with certain immediate problems in the presidential selection process.

Van Buren began his analysis of the existing selection process by claiming that the quality of presidential campaigns had begun to deteriorate. The cause was a nonpartisan system which led to personal candidate factions and unchecked popular leadership. The system allowed a large number of candidates to enter the contest without doing anything to channel their ambitions. As early as 1822, Van Buren observed that the contenders for the presidency, already aware that nomination by the Congressional caucus might not be a factor, had begun to campaign for office on their own initiative. The results were dismaying:

> In Congress Messrs. Crawford and Adams and Calhoun have each decided and have active friends; every day produces some resolution aimed at the one or the other of the departments they represent. These resolutions are dis-

[13] These elements of the party government school are summarized in Hofstadter, *The Idea of a Party System*, pp. 1-9.

cussed with great bitterness. Every good man deplores the state of things which has grown and is growing out of it, and would hail with gratitude any measure having a tendency to avert the evils it must produce.[14]

Van Buren considered the open commencement of the campaign so far in advance of the election to be a "premature" intrusion of electoral politics into the normal processes of governing.[15] Again, he believed, this was a direct consequence of the nonpartisan system, and it is noteworthy that a later historian of the development of parties identified the campaigns of this era as the longest of the nineteenth century.[16]

The system under which the candidates sought office in 1824 led them to cast about for an issue that would allow them to raise a popular constituency. Following Madison and Jefferson, Van Buren argued that this method of soliciting office could already be seen in nascent form in the election of 1820. The "moving springs" of the conflict over the Missouri question, he charged, were at least in part "political rather than philanthropical. . . ."[17] For the election of 1824,

[14] Letter to Dudley, January 10, 1822, in Bonney, *A Legacy*, pp. 382-84.

[15] *Ibid.*

[16] S. R. Gammon, Jr., *The Presidential Campaign of 1832* (Baltimore: Johns Hopkins Press, 1922), p. vii. The campaigns in question were those from 1824 through 1836. Parties, of course, existed in nascent form in 1828 and 1832, but the full development and acceptance of partisanship and party nominating agencies had yet to take root. Gammon writes:

> . . . the presidential campaign of the period [was] never an affair of less than two years' duration. That such was the case is shown by the fact that the campaign of 1824 was well under way before the close of 1822, that of 1828 began as soon as its predecessor closed, and the opening of that of 1832, by no stretch of the imagination, can be put later than July 4, 1830. . . .

Today, with party organizations having lost much of their control over the nomination process to the people, one finds the length of the open canvass rivaling that of the prepartisan era.

[17] Van Buren, *Autobiography*, p. 140. See his full discussion of this issue on pp. 138-141.

the two major issues were internal improvements and a protective tariff. They were treated by the contenders as "shuttlecocks" and "tossed backward and forward according to the feelings and exigencies of the moment." The effect of this was to take the task of establishing the agenda of national debate out of the hands of the executive and allow it to be set by the claimants for the office. Although Van Buren never extensively discussed the nature of executive power and its connection with the selection system, in this instance he showed a deep concern for the debilitating effect of the campaign on presidential leadership. By encouraging some of the most prominent politicians to find issues and keep them before the public, the selection system had interfered with what he believed was an important presidential prerogative. While Monroe was partly to blame because of his own shortcomings as a leader, Van Buren believed that the problem was also institutional in character. "Neither of these great issues," he wrote, "originated with the Administration or were regarded as administration measures; they found their origin in other sources and were called into existence by other considerations than those of Executive recommendation." Nor could anything be said in favor of allowing the agenda to be set by the selection process rather than by constituted authority. The objective of a candidate in finding an issue was to make sure that it was *not* settled, gratitude in politics being less important than the ability to bestow future benefits:

> Hence the continued agitation of all these questions [internal improvements and tariffs] from near the beginning to the end of Mr. Monroe's Administration—leaving them at its close as unsettled as they were at any stage of their discussion and as it was expedient to Presidential aspirants that they should be.[18]

When Van Buren looked back on this election more reflectively in one of his later works, he argued that this de-

[18] *Ibid.*, pp. 309, 115, 116.

plorable condition was directly attributable to the absence of political parties. "In the place of two great parties arrayed against each other in a fair and open contest for the establishment of principles in the administration of government," there were "personal factions . . . having few higher motives for the selection of their candidates or stronger incentives to action than individual preference or antipathies. . . ." These factions overran the country and "moved the bitter waters of political agitation to their lowest depths."[19] In contrast to the Founders, Van Buren made a clear distinction between a "party" and a "faction," his purpose evidently being to build up the one and denigrate the other. A party was a body committed to some general principle and therefore tended to persist for some time. A faction was of short duration, usually existing to promote the ends of some one individual or interest and having no genuine foundation in principle.[20] Had parties existed in the 1820s, Van Buren argued, they could have restrained the candidates from their early and open indulgences, compelled them to adhere to general principles, and removed the incentive to raise a personal following by building new issue constituencies.

The more one studies Van Buren's analysis of presidential politics, the more it becomes evident that his central concern was controlling political ambition. Left to itself and unguided by institutions, political ambition led men to act at odds with the public good. Politicians had to be restrained, both in the pursuit and exercise of power. Unlike Jefferson, Van Buren did not have in mind only Federalists masquerading as favorites of some popular cause, but men of his own political persuasion. The problem was general, not partisan. Controlling ambition and deflecting it from its excesses were the most important tasks of the constitution maker. Van Buren, it seems, was prepared to sacrifice the heights politics might attain in order to check "the disposition to abuse power, so deeply planted in the human heart."[21] He speaks little about

[19] Van Buren, *Political Parties*, pp. 3-4.
[20] *Ibid.*, p. 10, and *Autobiography*, pp. 123-24.
[21] Van Buren, *Autobiography*, p. 125.

presidential excellence or the possibilities of statesmanship. In this, it might be said that he turned his back on the Founders and showed himself to be a thoroughgoing Republican, being concerned first and foremost with restraining power. But Van Buren might well have countered that the Founders' system, which was designed both to restrain popular leadership and to promote excellence, had not worked. The existing nonpartisan arrangement that was being defended in their name had failed to produce the restraint they sought and in fact became the principal cause of personal factionalism and a demagogic style of politics. If a larger price had now to be paid for the suppression of these evils, who is to say that the Founders, faced with the same choice, would not have resolved the issue in the same way?

It must be added, moreover, that the nonpartisan system that Van Buren attacked in the 1820s bore little resemblance to the one that the Founders had intended. The crucial difference was that direct popular appeals by the candidates had become an accepted element of the campaign, a change that resulted from the precedent of the election of 1800 and from the transformation of the elector from a discretionary trustee to a bound agent. Unless some means could be found to prevent campaigning by the "popular arts" under the nonpartisan system emerging in the 1820s, a call for a return to a nonpartisan system, such as Adams made, was not in reality a true restoration of the Founders' system. If popular leadership was now an accepted and legitimate part of the selection process, the new challenge was somehow to distinguish its healthy from its unhealthy expressions and to devise some institutional means to admit the former while excluding the latter. In proposing party competition to solve this problem, it may well have been that Van Buren, and not Adams, was the truer heir to the Founders' intentions.

Van Buren presented his case against nonpartisanship to a large number of his contemporaries in letters and conversations. The task of disseminating these views to the public he left largely to others. One such person was Thomas Ritchie,

136

editor of the *Richmond Enquirer*. Van Buren met Ritchie on his second trip to the Old Dominion in 1823 and formed a friendship that would last for many years. Following Van Buren's visit, and intermittently throughout the next year, Ritchie wrote a series of editorials defending the existence of political parties, though not yet emphasizing the merits of party competition. What is of particular interest here is Ritchie's treatment of the relationship between party and the control of political ambition. Ritchie began his series with a clear statement of the general problem: "Ambitious struggles for power, with the bitter uncontrollable passions which they inevitably engender, are the most formidable evils which threaten free governments, and wise people will never cease to guard against and mitigate their consequences." This was especially the case in the struggle for the presidency, for it placed in jeopardy the safety of the entire nation. Ritchie hoped the nation would never see, even as it was then on the verge of seeing, "the spectacle of five or six candidates for the Presidency, traversing this continent and chaffering for votes." Such a system would tend to exclude the best men, who would not stoop to such a level, leaving the field to those who had no hesitancy about "travelling through the country, courting support, . . . and assiduously practicing all the low arts of popularity. . . ." What the nation needed was an instrument to nominate candidates, thus avoiding the personal solicitations that existed under a nonpartisan system. Such a system would also promote more "energy" in government by preventing factions from needlessly redoubling their efforts against one another and undermining the administration. The existence of party machinery would tend "to blunt the edge of disappointed ambition, and to disarm the rage of maddened factions."[22]

[22] *The Virginia Enquirer*, editions of December 23, 1823; January 3, 1824; January 1, 1824. Since Ritchie was writing these editorials before 1824, his defense was of the existing caucus system under one-party rule, and it reads very much like the Founders' justification of the electoral college. The caucus, he argued, would

If the issues of internal improvements and tariffs had been the "shuttle-cocks" of 1824, Van Buren feared that the more dangerous issue of sectionalism might become the source of dispute in the future. Sectional feeling, Van Buren saw, was the most readily available "bait" that a candidate could throw out. Writing to Ritchie in 1827, Van Buren reflected on the need for reconstituting the old party division to counteract this possibility:

> If the old ones [party feelings] are suppressed, geographical divisions founded on local interests or, what is worse, prejudices between free and slaveholding states will inevitably take their place. Party attachment in former times furnished a complete antidote for sectional prejudices by producing counteracting feelings.[23]

Though this problem was avoided in 1828 and 1832 because of the existence of party competition, it arose again in 1836 when the Whigs, in part from design and in part from disunity, adopted a strategy of antipartisanship and allowed the "nomination" of three different candidates, each with a special sectional appeal. Hugh White was the candidate in the south, William Henry Harrison in the midwest, and Daniel Webster in the east. Whig spokesmen attacked political parties in speeches and editorials, decrying their selfishness and their practice of enforcing unity on their members at the expense of considerations of truth and justice. Typical of the

---

allow a candidate only to "repose himself upon the public confidence in his qualifications and the republican simplicity of his character, and be content to be designated by the public voice. . . ." When it became clear that one party could not be maintained without having a second, Ritchie, like Van Buren, saw that such a complete exclusion of popular leadership was no longer possible and that the best solution was to limit it to two safe standards. And he joined Van Buren in calling for—and defending—the convention system. For an account of Thomas Ritchie's career, see Charles Ambler, *Thomas Ritchie* (Richmond: Bell Books Stationery Co., 1913).

[23] Letter to Ritchie, January 13, 1827, *Martin Van Buren Papers* (Library of Congress).

Whig's view was Tennessee Congressman John Bell's speech before a Nashville audience in 1835, in which he declared that "party is the only source whence destruction awaits our system."[24] The Democrats responded in a lengthy document written by an officially appointed campaign committee of the 1836 Democratic convention. Following closely the views of Van Buren, the committee cited the dangers of sectional division inherent in the nonpartisan system:

> Hence, it is, that in different parts of our country we see mischievous and misguided men attempting to weaken the bond of union . . . [sectionalism] is ever a ready and fruitful subject, to create these jealousies and dissensions. . . . It cannot be concealed from you that many of our opponents, both in the North and the South, under different names and denominations, are playing into each others hands, by creating geographical parties, kindling sectional animosities, stirring up local jealousies, and arousing all the angry passions.[25]

The victory of the Democratic Party in 1836 convinced the Whigs of the necessity for party solidarity, and the principle of partisan competition thereafter became an established part of the American political system. Van Buren had won his point—or rather one half of it. If the principle of partisan competition was now safe, the basis on which that partisan division would take place remained at issue. The supposedly "natural" division between Whig and Tory proposed by Jefferson and Van Buren was continually challenged by the division it was designed to suppress, and in the end the ques-

---

[24] Cited in Joel H. Silbey, "Election of 1836" in Arthur Schlesinger, Jr., ed., *History of American Presidential Elections*, 4 vols. (New York: Chelsea House, 1971), 1:639. Silbey's highly informative essay quotes from a number of Whigs who attacked party organization. See pp. 585-86.

[25] Andrew Stevenson, Silas Wright, *et al.*, "Statement by Democratic Republicans of the United States" in Schlesinger, ed., *History of American Presidential Elections*, 1:623 and 625.

tion of freedom and slavery proved more fundamental than that of national consolidation and limited federal powers.

That the sectional division finally became the line of partisan cleavage by the 1850s does not deny the significance of Van Buren's constitutional perspective. Nor does it disprove his contention that the party system in its relationship to the divisions of the electorate can serve in some degree as an independent influence. Van Buren himself understood that his perspective, though significant, was only partial. He considered the avoidance of a direct division on slavery for so many years as a "wonder more surprising than [the] dissolution of the union." It was something that could only be explained, he believed, by the "single fact that there have always been neutralizing considerations of sufficient force to maintain party cohesions between men of the free and the slave states."[26] Yet Van Buren was aware of the precarious nature of the "neutralizing" force of parties and was not surprised by the final emergence of a sectional division, nor, as will be seen momentarily, entirely "blameless" in its occurrence.

To treat the issue involved here in general terms, it can be said that parties in the American system play—or can play—two different roles: they are instruments for winning power in the name of some view or principle, "radical" perhaps in its relation to the *status quo*; and they are electoral institutions, which, according to how they are organized, affect differently the behavior of candidates and influence, up to a point, the issues permitted to arise in an electoral contest. They serve, at different moments, as conveyors of some new sentiment, and thus as agents that begin "outside" the normal institutional structure, and as established institutions which are very nearly parts of the formal system of government. Established parties in this second sense become the generally recognized agencies for nominating candidates

[26] Letter to Moses Y. Tilden, September 1, 1856, Samuel J. Tilden Papers (New York Public Library). This letter was kindly brought to my attention by Michael Holt.

and thus may stand "over" the raw electoral cleavages, possessing some leeway or discretion about which potential issues and electoral divisions will be emphasized and which will be suppressed or kept at the fringes. This discretion is exercised according to the interests of the organizations and the judgment of their leaders. But it is important to bear in mind that the degree of this discretion is limited, the most important reason being that parties are not formally established and maintained by Constitutional sanction. Their discretion is always threatened or held in check by the possibility that they might be displaced by a new party having as its goal the advancement of a certain policy (or by an insurgent movement from within the party having the same objective). When a sufficiently powerful and enduring issue exists, an impartial reading of American party history suggests that the party system in the end will have to respond to it, regardless of how the established parties initially react. To this extent, the institutional perspective on parties cannot comprehend the whole of the study of parties. On the other hand, issues of a magnitude that force themselves on the party system in spite of the stand of the established parties are rare. In the absence of such issues or until they mature, the parties maintain a significant potential to "manage" the issues. Because legislators cannot control with any certainty the kind of issues that arise, but can shape the form of the institutions, it is quite proper that they should concern themselves with this aspect of parties.

The normative question of whether a party system should be so constituted as to allow or encourage parties to exercise this discretion has long been a topic of debate by democratic theorists. Some contend that any such limitation on the people's wishes is an affront to the very meaning of democracy: the function of the party system must be to allow as quick and as accurate an expression of the raw cleavages as possible. Others would grant such discretion on the demonstration that it would tend to be used responsibly. This was Van Buren's position. Moreover, as Van Buren believed that no electoral system was actually neutral with respect to the issue divisions it expressed, the real choice was among alternative systems of influence. The people do not simply decide in a vacuum but are strongly affected by those who present the issues. In the supposedly neutral and open nonpartisan system which Van Buren opposed, the formative agents would be the individual aspirants acting under competitive circumstances that would tend to drive them to adopt dangerous popular appeals.

Van Buren's support for a two-party system that promoted consensus did not, however, preclude him from accepting the presidential nomination of the Free Soil Party in 1848 and thereby injecting the issue of slavery into a national election. In taking this dramatic step, Van Buren was not directly contradicting himself, though he was exposing the limits of his own position. Nor can it be said that he ever fully resolved the apparent tension, although he made some tentative steps in this direction, and some of his followers proceeded to a more direct confrontation of the issue. The kind of resolution toward which they were moving could be described in the following terms. A consensual two-party system was Van Buren's preference for the normal institutional arrangement of the electoral system; but there may be certain occasions when following normal institutional procedures cannot meet the exigencies of political action. Just as the Founders and Jefferson made allowance for the use of a party even though they were opposed to party competition, so it might be said that Van Buren permitted the creation of a third party even though he subscribed to the doctrine of two-party competition. In both cases, extraordinary circumstances would justify a departure from normal institutional practices. In Van Buren's case, this departure would seem to be less extreme, however, since the electoral system he favored did not officially bar third parties or even identify them as being outside of the political system. A third party was exceptional, but not in any sense illegitimate.

Still, it was exceptional; and at a time when two-party

competition was just becoming established, it inevitably threatened that system. Van Buren, one may assume, did not take such a step lightly, for he must have known, as he later confided to a friend, that the election of 1848 "produced impressions which neither you nor I will live to see eradicated."[27] Van Buren and his followers took this risk not merely to settle a score with those who denied him the nomination in 1844, but, as Eric Foner has shown, for more substantial reasons.[28] The Democratic Party, they felt, had fallen into the hands of southerners whose guiding principle was the extension of slavery. This represented a change from Van Buren's view that slavery should be left where it was and on that basis kept outside the scope of direct partisan conflict. But as long as the control of the party remained in the hands of southerners, northern Democrats seeking the presidency would trim their doctrines to fit their presidential aspirations. Party, the device that Van Buren had established for channeling ambition in a safe direction, was now channeling it along undesirable lines. On this basis a third party could be justified, if not to replace the Democratic Party then at least, by denying it victory, to restore it to its former position. A success in this sense, in David Wilmot's words, might teach, "the ambitious and aspiring . . . that they cannot reach the Presidency by a base bowing down to the power of slavery."[29]

In addition to his constitutional defense of party competition as an institution that would prevent personal factionalism and avoid dangerous divisions, Van Buren argued that it would perform a third function of ensuring the legitimacy of the system by keeping the election from going to the House. The House system, mistrusted since the nearly catastrophic experience of 1800, was again being discussed in the early 1820s, as it became clear that the presidential choice

[27] Letter to John A. Dix, July 14, 1848, from John A. Dix Papers, cited in Eric Foner, *Free Soil, Free Labor, Free Men* (New York: Oxford University Press, 1970), p. 154.

[28] Foner, *Free Soil*, p. 151.

[29] Cited in Foner, *Free Soil*, p. 153.

143

might again have to be made by that body. Madison, reiterating his earlier criticisms, labeled the existing system of election in the House "a departure from the republican principle of numerical equality . . . and pregnant with a mischievous tendency in practice. . . ."[30] Van Buren made similar criticisms during a Congressional debate on the issue before the election of 1824.[31] The validity of these criticisms became even more apparent after the election had taken place. Jackson, proclaimed by his supporters to be the people's real choice, charged that the election had been stolen from him by a corrupt bargain made while the outcome was being considered before the House. Notwithstanding the falseness of this charge, it succeeded in creating doubts in the minds of many about the fairness of the existing system. Though the immediate problem was with the House method, it was necessary to consider the selection process in its entirety, because it had been a breakdown in the nominating process that caused the election to go to the House in 1824.

There were two basic approaches to solving this difficulty. One was to change the Constitution so as to reduce—or in some proposals even to eliminate—the need for a Congressional decision. Under this approach, the formal institutions would have to bear the full burden of deciding on and legitimating a choice from what might well be a large field of candidates.[32] The other and simpler solution was to reinstitute

[30] Letter to George Hay, August 23, 1823, *The Writings of James Madison*, ed. Gaillard Hunt, 9 vols. (New York: W. W. Norton), 3:333. In this letter Madison seemed to be opposed to a renewal of two-party competition and suggested instead a Constitutional amendment that would give the electors two votes in the choice of the president.

[31] Van Buren, *Autobiography*, p. 118. Van Buren here refers to the "inadequacy of the provisions of the Constitution and laws for the government of Congress in canvassing the votes for President and Vice President. . . ."

[32] Such an approach was being widely discussed in 1823 and came up for consideration in Congress. The issues included not only keeping the election from the House, but also the mode of selecting the

party competition, thus saving the Constitution from its own defect by an "informal" means. As the difficulty of agreeing on a Constitutional amendment became clear, the renewal of party competition moved into the forefront as the only realistic solution. It was this theme that Van Buren's followers stressed in defending parties against their nonpartisan detractors.

Perhaps the frankest statement of this position appeared in the circular of the Democratic Campaign Committee of 1836. The Committee had no doubts about the gravity of the House election scheme: "One of the greatest evils which can threaten public liberty and our happy system, next to revolution and disunion, *is an election of President by the House of Representatives.*" The Founders put the House scheme in the Constitution, but "they never imagined the occasion would arise when its exercise would be required." Clearly they had been mistaken. But their intent could now be realized through instituting party competition, which, at a minimum, could be regarded as a *de facto* amendment to the Constitution:

> It matters not how strong the objections to a Convention, the enquiry must still be, is there not less danger to be apprehended from them, than a Congressional Election? Is it not a thousand times better that the evils of a Convention, whatever they may be, should be borne, than that we should be exposed to the calamities of an election by the House of Representatives, the Pandora Box of our whole system? This is the only true issue. If, however, any better mode can be devised, gladly, we doubt not, would the nation bless the amending hand. But until some amendment of the Constitution shall be adopted to cut off the possibility of an election by the House of Representatives,

electors. Some now proposed that the "winner-take-all" system within each state be abolished and that the electors be selected by the people within the Congressional districts. See Madison's letter to George Kay, August 23, 1823.

145

and cause the will of the people to be respected in the choice of their Chief Magistrate, it should be the duty of the Republican Party . . . to concentrate their power and produce harmony and union among their friends.[33]

The corollary to the question of the formal legitimacy of the electoral system is the problem of securing a president with a broad national following so that his selection appears to be a natural and not a forced or manufactured result. Many of the Founders, it may be recalled, believed that the increased focus on national politics under the Constitution would ensure a steady supply of continental characters, one of whom would either be preferred by the people or else chosen by the electors when employing their second ballot. In the unlikely event that no such person existed or if there was a split among a number of continental figures, the House would be faced with the task of forging a consensus for one of the contenders. The advocates of party competition were much less confident than the Founders about the automatic emergence of such continental figures. What was needed, in their view, was an instrument to ensure a supply of candidates who had a broad national backing, thus saving the formal Constitutional machinery from the task of performing a very delicate function which experience had already suggested it could not perform well. Their intent was to institutionalize the creation of candidates with a continental backing by removing this matter from the realm of chance and making it subject to human control. The solution they proposed was two-party competition in which each party would have a continental constituency. By conferring the nomination on its standard-bearer, whether he possessed a continental reputation on his own or not, each party would immediately produce a candidate with a national following. The nation did not need continental characters, only continental parties.

In his defense of parties in 1823, Thomas Ritchie outlined

[33] Silbey, "The Election of 1836," pp. 618-19, 620-21.

146

the kind of nomination process that this solution required. The choice of a candidate who could command the support of a continental following was a difficult task, for it required not only an appreciation of the people's preferences but an assessment as well of the intensity of those preferences. The notion that a direct nonpartisan election could produce the people's "true" choice seemed to Ritchie quite implausible— and the same could be said for a national primary. The usual effect of such a process would be a distortion of the people's wishes because second choices could not be taken into account. What the electoral process required was a body that would be able to meet and deliberate about the choice of the nominee. This was Ritchie's defense of a discretionary power for politicians in the nomination stage:

> Vain is any expectation founded upon the spontaneous movement of the great mass of the people in favor of any particular individual, the elements of this great community are multifarious and conflicting, and require to be skill-fully combined, to be made harmonious and powerful. Their action, to be salutary, must be the result of enlight-ened deliberation, and he who would distract the councils of the people, must design to breed confusion and dis-order, and to profit by their dissentions.[34]

The persons within the party who should be given this deliberate authority was not to Ritchie or Van Buren a ques-tion of the first order of importance, at least not when com-pared with the more general objective of establishing the legitimacy of a party nomination. Originally Van Buren wanted to retain the caucus, which until 1824 was the only known mechanism for making presidential nominations. When it became clear to him, however, that the caucus sys-tem had lost credibility, he abandoned it and proposed to Ritchie in 1827 that the Republicans consider a national convention as "the best and probably the only practicable

[34] Thomas Ritchie, "Congressional Caucus No. 3," *Richmond En-quirer*, January 2, 1824.

mode . . . of effecting . . . the substantial reorganization of the Old Republican Party."[35]

Many scholars have recently discussed the significance of the shift from the caucus to the convention, the most prominent among them being James Sterling Young. Young argues that the change to a nominating agency outside of the Congress was the critical institutional development in reinvigorating the power of the president, for it gave him a base of support outside of Congress.[36] Van Buren neither supported nor denied this proposition. But his general indifference to this matter and his relegation of it to the status of a tactical concern suggests that for him the primary question was not the mode of nomination but the absence of party competition. With party competition the victorious party would be able to derive the added "energy" that comes from a contested national election—even with the caucus.[37] Without party competition, this would have been impossible. While there is surely some merit to Young's argument, it is questionable whether he correctly identified the crucial variable. This issue will probably never be resolved to everyone's satisfaction. It would require one to disentangle the effects of the nominating system from those of the character of the party system, which is nearly impossible because the caucus method was used during the period of one-party rule and the convention system arose at about the same time as the reestablishment of two-party competition.

Perhaps the major significance of the shift from the caucus to the convention system, then, did not involve the question of presidential power but rather the question of the relative weight of national and state politicians, i.e. the issue of federalism. According to Roy F. Nichols, the proponents of the convention system in the Democratic Party, Van Buren

[35] Letter to Ritchie, January 13, 1827.

[36] James Sterling Young, *The Washington Community 1800-1828* (New York: Harcourt, Brace, and World), pp. 245-49.

[37] This point is hinted at in Van Buren's discussion of Monroe's failures, *Autobiography*, pp. 115-16.

being the foremost among them, thought of the convention as merely a substitute for the caucus in which instructions would continue to be handed out from Washington.[38] But they soon discovered the federalizing influence of the new institution, an influence that exceeded even their own republican principle of limiting the powers of the Washington establishment. Under the convention system the power of choosing the nominees came increasingly into the hands of state and local politicians, men who may have been less inclined than Congressmen to view problems from a national perspective and more disposed, at least in the long-run, to introduce narrow considerations of local patronage into the selection process.

Van Buren's Partisan Defense

Van Buren wrote his lengthy treatise, *An Inquiry into the Origin and Course of Political Parties in the United States*, with the express intention of providing the first full account of the development of parties in America that was untainted by the bias of partisan feelings. In this impartial account, however, was contained a teaching that was of greater partisan value to the Democrats than to the Whigs, and Van Buren did not consider it inconsistent with his general purpose to emphasize this theme. Democrats, he contended, often accepted the plausible view that "what was good for one party must be good for another," i.e. that the existence or absence of party organizations was equally advantageous or disadvantageous to both. But this was quite untrue. The party organization of the Federalists and their Whig successors "did not stand as much in need of extraneous means to secure harmony in its ranks as did that of their opponents." Accordingly, opposition leaders, who stood to gain a relative advantage from a nonpartisan system, "have always

[38] Roy F. Nichols, "Adaptation *versus* Invention as Elements in Historical Analysis," *American Philosophical Society Proceedings*, vol. 108, no. 5, 1964, p. 408. See also his *Invention of the American Political Parties* (New York: Free Press), pp. 359-81.

been desirous to bring every usage of party into disrepute with the people. . . ."[39] Oblivious to this advantage, Democrats, according to Van Buren, were always in danger of being taken in by the high-toned appeals of their opponents that called on both sides to abandon partisan instruments and dedicate themselves unselfishly to the public good.

Van Buren proposed in his work to go to the bottom of this issue and treat the puzzling question of why a system of open party nominations "is in fact so much less necessary to one [party] than to the other."[40] The answer, which is never clearly spelled out in this unfinished manuscript, is explored in his *Autobiography* and in the statement of his campaign committee in the 1836 election.[41] The argument follows along the same lines as the one made by Madison and Jefferson in the 1790s and suggested even earlier by Gerry and Mason at the Constitutional Convention. It is an argument that touches on the issue of legitimacy by exposing the actual unfairness of procedures which on their face seem unassailable. An election that seems perfectly democratic—as a direct nonpartisan election does—may nevertheless work undemocratically in practice. Behavioral effects as well as formal procedures must be taken into account. Because the "party" of the wealthy possesses the relative advantage in those resources that can most readily be employed in nonpartisan politics—money, intellectual power, and informal organizations—it always fares better under this system than the "party" of the people:

[39] Van Buren, *Political Parties*, pp. 5-6. In providing an impartial account of party origins, Van Buren contrasted his treatment with that of John Quincy Adams, which he claimed showed evidence of the "rage of party spirit" (p. 9). Adams's views, which are discussed briefly below in the text, were given most fully in his Jubilee Address of 1839 and can be found in his book, *Parties in the United States* (New York: Greenberg, 1941).

[40] *Ibid.*, p. 6.

[41] Van Buren's views on the opposition's advantage in monetary resources can be found in his discussion of electoral corruption, *Autobiography*, pp. 222-24.

The opposition is a smaller body and has more bonds of union. In their system of corporations and exclusive privileges; in the partial legislation of the States as well as of the United States which enable the rich to become richer and render the poor poorer, its members have a common interest which will generally induce them to act together. If to the power of union of wealth and general intelligence, they are enabled to add the advantage of division among the Democrats, they are certain to run the country. . . .[42]

The strength of the popular interest lay potentially in its numbers. But this strength was all too easily dissipated by the people's lack of awareness of their own interest. What the people needed, according to Van Buren, was "an extraneous means to secure harmony in its ranks."[43] It needed the device of a party.

Van Buren felt that Republicans began to learn their lesson about the disadvantages of nonpartisanship after the election of 1824. The new president, though nominally a Republican, quickly showed himself to have Federalist views, a fact that "soon satisfied those who had yielded to the idea of the extinction of party of their delusion—a conviction mingled with self-reproach."[44] The occasion for this recognition was Adams's First Annual Address to the Congress in which he proposed the extensive use of federal power to stimulate economic development and support scientific research. The old division over the use of federal power, Adams contended, should be laid to rest. As long as the use of federal power was directed by the proper persons and used for the proper ends "every speculative scruple [would be] solved by practical public blessings."[45] In further support of this view, Adams argued that the issue of federal power had not been at the root of the conflict between the two original parties. Rather, the division had arisen from dif-

[42] Silbey, "Election of 1836," pp. 222-23.
[43] Van Buren, *Political Parties*, p. 5.
[44] Van Buren, *Autobiography*, p. 193.
[45] Richardson, ed., *Messages and Papers*, pp. 299-317.

ferences over the conduct of foreign policy, differences which had long since been resolved.[46]

In Adams's program Van Buren saw the perfect opportunity for rekindling partisan sentiments. The issue would be the principle of national power. Adams would be identified as a Federalist posing as a Republican—an archetype of the wolf in sheep's clothing—and sacrificed to the opposition. But to justify this call to partisan arms, Van Buren had to counter Adams's interpretation of the origin of parties. For Van Buren the original party division had its genesis not in differences over foreign affairs but in a fundamental dispute about the nature of popular government, and the extent of federal involvement in domestic policy-making was a crucial element in that dispute. The old issue was thus still alive in the current debate and neither could, nor should, be buried.

Van Buren's thesis that a direct connection existed between the past and the present division undoubtedly reflected his honest assessment of the history of American parties. But it is impossible not to observe how well this historical assessment fitted with his constitutional plan to reestablish party competition. By forging a connection between past and present, Van Buren hoped to infuse the present controversy with some of the much needed partisan feelings of yesteryear. To bring about a new realignment, he believed, would be impossible under existing circumstances, except on the basis of a dangerous appeal to sectional prejudices. There was every reason, therefore, to invoke the old line of division. Writing to Ritchie in 1827, Van Buren took the pragmatic position that "we must always have party distinctions and the old ones are the best of which the nature of the case admits. . . . It would take longer than our lives (even if it were practicable) to create new party feelings to keep these masses together."[47] To express this point in contemporary

[46] See Van Buren, *Autobiography*, pp. 193-95; John Quincy Adams, *Parties*, pp. 14-16.

[47] Letter to Thomas Ritchie, January 13, 1827. Van Buren's views

terms, Van Buren wished to reinforce the latent partisan alignment without provoking any new cross-cutting cleavages or disrupting old or transmitted partisan identities. This "surrender" of the electorate to the bonds of the past would later become one of the chief objections of the Progressives to Van Buren's model of electoral behavior.

Van Buren's View of Partisan Conflict

Van Buren's defense of party competition rested on the premise that conflict would take place within certain boundaries. Elections should not involve disputes over the basic form of government, but neither should they degenerate into contests for mere material or personal benefits. In attempting to locate more precisely Van Buren's views on the range of acceptable conflict, it may be helpful first to indicate the general categories into which many scholars now place the different forms of party competition.[48] First, there is conflict between "great parties," parties which hold opposing views about the way the political system or society should be ordered. At the extreme, conflict at this level convulses society and may lead to civil war. It was chiefly for this reason that the Founders, who identified parties with "great" parties, opposed partisan conflict. Second, there is the conflict between what some call "Burkean parties." Such parties are formed to promote significant principles, but principles that are not incompatible

---

on the inheritance of partisan identification are strikingly "modern," as illustrated by the following passage from *Political Parties* (p. 7):

> The two great parties of this country, with occasional changes in their names only, have, for the principle part of a century, occupied antagonistic positions upon all important political questions. . . . Sons have generally followed in the footsteps of their fathers, and families originally differing have in regular succession received, maintained, and transmitted this opposition.

[48] This typology is implicit in Richard Hofstadter's treatment of parties in *The Idea of a Party System*. The use of the terms "great" and "small" parties that follows is taken from de Tocqueville's discussion in *Democracy in America*, ed. J. P. Mayer, trans. George Lawrence (New York: Doubleday), p. 175.

with the existing framework of government. The conflict between these parties may be intense and elevated, but it need not exceed the level of a spirited contest that takes place under mutually respected rules. Such is the type of conflict envisioned by advocates of the party-government school. Finally, there is the agitation of "small parties"—parties that compete under a dim banner of principle, but which in reality have no other goal than the acquisition of power. When the desire for power is shared throughout a large organization and when the objective of that organization is to hold office and distribute the jobs that keep it in being, we have America's special breed of small party, the mass-based patronage party.

If one had to place Van Buren's model of party conflict into one of these three categories, it would be the second. Yet the fit would be far from perfect, for Van Buren's parties allowed for a greater degree of interest than is envisioned under the so-called Burkean model. Thus Van Buren's parties would seem to be a hybrid falling between the second and the third categories noted above. This would suggest either some confusion on Van Buren's part or a problem in the scheme of categorization. While Van Buren did not discuss parties in terms of this scheme, one can be almost certain that he would have thought it inadequate. His general position suggests that a "pure" Burkean party system is not a viable option as an institutional solution for mass electoral parties. The only workable middle position is that of parties which mix principle and interest.

To understand Van Buren's view on this question, one must begin with his attitude toward great parties. In defending the doctrine of partisan competition against the prevailing hostility to it, Van Buren was in some measure compelled to present the original partisan division in a more favorable light than most of his contemporaries. One finds, accordingly, that he often praises the purity of motive and even the intensity of commitment of the original partisans. Yet he conceded, perhaps referring to the bitter moments of the original conflict, that wherever parties exist "excesses frequently attend them and produce many evils."[49]

Van Buren's attempt to moderate these excesses and reduce the level of conflict assumed three forms. First was his espousal of the doctrine of party competition as an institutional norm. Unlike the attitude of earlier partisans, Van Buren asked the present-day partisans to look at parties "in a sincerer and wiser spirit" and accept the benefits of party competition.[50] The realization of these benefits, he foresaw, would itself tend to moderate political extremes, as partisans would be less likely to endanger the party system by pushing their zealousness to the point of an all-or-nothing struggle. Next, Van Buren proposed a new ethic of partisan behavior, offering his own actions in this respect as a model for others to emulate. Though committed in his partisan views, he nonetheless took great pride in not being "rancorous in my party prejudices" and in maintaining close personal friendships with many of his political adversaries.[51] This attitude was a far cry from the one that prevailed in 1797 when, as Jefferson described, "men who have been intimate all their lives cross the streets to avoid meeting, and turn their heads another way, lest they should be obliged to touch their hats."[52] Finally, Van Buren offered as the content of the new party division a conflict that was more moderate than the original one. The new conflict, though based on the same lines of electoral division as the original one, would not go to the heart of that controversy and involve the bitter charges of monarchism on the one hand and radical democracy on the other. It was to remain more on the surface, dealing at the extreme with the question of consolidation versus limited government. Here for Van Buren was a source of division that was significant yet involved something less than ultimate principle, one over which the parties could honorably con-

---

[49] Van Buren, *Autobiography*, p. 125.
[50] *Ibid.*
[51] *Ibid.*
[52] Cited in Hofstadter, *The Idea of a Party System*, p. 90.

tend, yet one not so vital that neither side could live with the other.

While a division of this sort seems to be entirely "Burkean," Van Buren went on to show that the practical task of building and maintaining party organizations required the introduction of further incentives based on self-interest. Van Buren rejected the idea that one could ordinarily find the perfect "pitch" of conflict at which the principled incentive to participate was sufficient to maintain party organizations but not so great as to threaten the underlying consensus in the regime. While in theory the Burkean ideal might represent the perfect solution, Van Buren's position suggests that it is inconsistent with the constraints imposed by practical politics. Specifically, it failed to take into account the incentives that motivate men to take part in politics: "great parties" could rely on principle to motivate their members, but parties standing for a lesser order of conflict, except in rare instances, would have to make up by spoils what they inevitably would lose in purposive dedication.[53]

Beyond this, Van Buren had in mind what for him was a positive reason for introducing spoils. By allowing men who possessed neither wealth nor name to dedicate themselves to politics as a profession, spoils performed a democratic function: it opened the doors of politics to a less privileged group. The democratizing influence of the party was twofold. The party organization sustained politicians while they advanced themselves, and the party label enabled men of little personal reputation to compete in electoral politics. By making politics into a profession of its own, Van Buren sought to break the direct link between social and political

---

[53] In comparing Burke's treatment of parties with that of Van Buren, it must be borne in mind that Burke was referring to parties organized chiefly within the legislature while Van Buren was speaking of mass electoral parties. It would stand to reason that a mass party would require a greater degree of incentive based on interest to motivate its organizational cadre.

156

elites that was contemplated under the original constitutional scheme.[54]

More, perhaps, than anything else, it was the introduction of the "professional" and the professional motivation into politics that caused criticism of Van Buren's constitutional transformation. While Van Buren envisioned a mix in which principle would dominate interest, others, alarmed over the emphasis he placed on spoils and over the type of men this seemed to bring into politics, saw the change to this new form of party in a very different light. Objections were voiced that national politics would fall to a level of meanness and self-interest never before seen and that the emergence of statesmen would be blocked by organizations run by petty and unprincipled men. For John Calhoun, who voiced these criticisms with remarkable prescience at the time, the alternative suggested was a new form of nonpartisanship—the concurrent majority—and the control of politics by "distinguished" men—in his case virtual oligarchs.[55] For Woodrow Wilson, who followed in a long line of reformist antiparty critics, the alternative was a new and ostensibly more complete majoritarianism based on a new kind of party moved and dominated by respected and able public opinion leaders.

Van Buren's View of Political Leadership

Van Buren's model of political leadership seems to have derived in the first instance not from his view of the kind of executive he wanted but from the evils he sought to avoid in the selection process. The solution to the crisis in the se-

[54] See Marvin Meyers, *The Jacksonian Persuasion, Politics and Belief* (Stanford: Stanford University Press, 1960), p. 242. Meyers cites Van Buren's comments at the New York State Convention of 1821. See also *Autobiography*, pp. 124, 193, 223.

[55] John C. Calhoun, *A Disquisition on Government* (Indianapolis: Bobbs Merrill, 1953), p. 32.

lection process required parties, and thus the ideal leader had to be the party leader. Since Van Buren understood a party to be a body of persons dedicated to certain general principles but differing widely on matters of substance beneath these broad generalities, the chief task of the party leader was to maintain consensus in the party. His virtue would be to forge compromises and placate men never fully satisfied with any bargain. Van Buren's ideal leader can thus be described as a broker or a skilled politician, a kind of leader that is very different from both the elevated statesman envisioned by the Founders and the principled partisan represented by Jefferson.

Although the requirement of controlling ambition was the most important concern to Van Buren, it does not follow that he believed that the quality of executive leadership would have to be sacrificed in the process. Others, certainly, would have disagreed. By admitting partisanship in the form of a coalitional party into the selection process, it could be said the presidency was being pulled down from its pedestal of independence above the contending factions. The Madisonian pluralist scheme was being extended from the Congress to the presidency, where Madison never intended it should go. Indeed, Van Buren himself seemed to have acknowledged that a kind of lowering of the tone of presidential leadership was about to take place. But he saw this as inevitable, as the effect not of his proposed change to partisanship but of the passing of the leaders of the Revolutionary generation: "Mr. Monroe was universally regarded as the last class of statesman to which the country had invariably theretofore looked for Presidential candidates."[56] There were no more continental figures whose reputation had been earned in such a way as to bring a natural deference to them from the populace. Without this special status, it was no longer possible (or safe) for a president to be at once independent, i.e. free of party, and effective at the same time.

[56] Van Buren, *Autobiography*, p. 125.

Indeed, Monroe, the least able of these statesman and the last to earn his reputation in the Revolutionary War or the Founding, had already lost the capacity to govern energetically. To restore a medium of executive effectiveness, the president would have to "descend" to the level of partisanship and perform the tasks that were necessary to cement the allegiance of a partisan following.

There was, of course, one conspicuous exception to Van Buren's claim that continental figures no longer existed: Andrew Jackson. Van Buren was aware of this exception, but he was quite correct in not placing Jackson in the same category as the "class of statesmen" of former times. The men of the Revolutionary generation had come to have reputations for their statesmanlike qualities and possessed a kind of universal respect. Jackson's reputation was based on his military heroism, and he was more popular than respected. Yet it is well known that Van Buren supported Jackson in 1828, and to correct the possible impression that Van Buren's model of political leadership was that of the popular hero rather than the broker, it is necessary to explore Van Buren's complex assessment of a Jackson candidacy in 1828.

For Van Buren, Jackson's candidacy in 1828 represented both a threat and an opportunity. As a threat, Jackson's great personal popularity gave him a chance to win the next election without the support of a party. A Jackson victory on this basis would postpone, if not entirely undermine, Van Buren's plan to renew party competition. On the other hand, if Jackson's personal popularity could be tied to the cause of the Old Republican Party, then the chances for its revivification, and along with it the restoration of competition between the parties, would be considerably enhanced. This was the opportunity. "I have long been satisfied," Van Buren wrote to Thomas Ritchie, "that we can only get rid of the present and restore a better state of things by combining General Jackson's personal popularity with the portion of

159

old party feelings yet remaining." Van Buren closed this fascinating letter with a statement of the "Jacksonian dilemma":

> His election as the result of his military services without reference to party and so far as he alone is concerned, scarcely to principle, would be one thing. His election as the result of a combined and concerted effort of a political party, holding in the main to certain tenets and opposed to certain prevailing principles, might be another and far different thing.[57]

The dilemma was compounded by Jackson's own previously expressed opposition to partisanship. Jackson had shared the "end of party" sentiments of Monroe; and even after he tacitly accepted the help of the Old Republicans in 1828, he proposed to change the presidential selection process to make it accord with his own view of a fully democratic choice among a variety of *individual* aspirants. In his first message to the Congress after becoming President, he urged a Constitutional amendment providing for direct election of the president and for a run-off between the top two in the event no candidate received an absolute majority in the first election.[58]

---

[57] Letter to Ritchie, January 13, 1827. See also, *Autobiography*, p. 198.

[58] In that speech, given on December 8, 1829, Jackson argued as follows:

> To the People belongs the right of electing their Chief Magistrate: it was never designed that their choice should, in any case, be defeated, either by the intervention of electoral colleges, or by the agency confided, under certain contingencies, to the House of Representatives. . . .

> The number of aspirants to the Presidency, and the diversity of the interests which may influence their claims leave little reason to expect a choice in the first instance. . . .

> I would therefore recommend such an amendment of the Constitution as may remove all intermediate agency in the election of President and Vice President. The mode may be so regulated

If Van Buren's proposal to connect the Democratic Party's fortunes to Jackson seems too expedient for one who claimed to be an orthodox Republican, it must be noted that he felt he had little choice in the matter. Either he could attach his party to Jackson and succeed, or else lose all. His support for Jackson accordingly should not obscure the deep suspicion he harbored toward a personal form of popularity, at least as it existed independent of a party commitment. His general objective was to "substitute party principle for personal preference."[59] Personal popularity was the democratic equivalent of the "name" politics that characterized the politics of earlier nonpartisanship. Van Buren accordingly insisted that Jackson must commit himself to party principle as the condition for the party's support; only then, he wrote, will our success "be worth something."[60]

For all his reservations about Jackson in 1827, Van Buren felt that he possessed a "positive" attribute for leadership— his lack of a firm stand on many of the pressing issues of the day. Jackson could thus be positioned in a way most advan-

---

as to preserve to each State its present relative weight in the election; and a failure in the first attempt may be provided for, by confining the second to a choice between the two highest candidates (*Senate Documents* I, 1829-30).

Jackson's earlier hostility to partisanship was expressed in a letter of support to Monroe on October 23, 1816, in John Spencer Bassett, *Correspondence of Andrew Jackson*, 2 vols. (Washington, D.C.: Carnegie Institution, 1927), 2:262.

[59] Letter to Ritchie, January 13, 1827.

[60] Letter to P. N. Nicholas, November, 1826, quoted in Remini, *Martin Van Buren and the Democratic Party*, p. 120. Van Buren insisted on some commitment from Jackson, but whether Jackson fully gave such assurances is not certain. For the relationship between Van Buren and Jackson on this point, see Remini, pp. 123-26. In his *Autobiography*, Van Buren reports how he attempted to modify the anxieties of some Republicans by arguing that Jackson "was at an earlier period well-grounded in the principles of our party, and that we must trust to good fortune and to the affects of favorable associations for the removal of the dust they have contracted. . . ," (p. 198).

tageous for his victory: "General Jackson has been so little in public life that it will not be difficult to contrast his opinion in great questions with those of Mr. Adams."[61] This freedom from strong issue identification, it may be suggested, was critical for a candidate's acceptance within a coalitional party. Yet in emphasizing this as a positive element in Jackson's appeal, Van Buren exposed a weakness in his own plans for political leadership. The function of "brokering" among the interests within the party was not one that a candidate himself had to perform in any active sense; it was one which, given the candidate with the proper degree of elevation, could be performed by others working "underneath" him. The formal leader, in other words, did not need to be the skilled politician but could be one with a certain general reputation.

In a highly critical assessment of American presidential selection after the creation of permanent parties, Lord Bryce characterized the pre-Civil War Presidents—and he implied the same for the parties' nominees—in the following terms:

> . . . from Jackson till the outbreak of the Civil War in 1860, the Presidents were either mere politicians such as Van Buren, Polk or Buchanan, or else successful soldiers, such as Harrison or Taylor, whom their party found useful as figure-heads.[62]

In the case of both types, the politician and the figurehead, one finds the needed quality of issue flexibility—the one occupying a middle ground on the issues and the other maintaining a distance from political issues altogether. This dichotomy between the politician and the figurehead roughly parallels the two types of candidates most suited to perform the new leadership task. The first was the broker typified best by Martin Van Buren, whom Horace Creely once characterized as "the reconciler of the estranged, the harmonizer

---

[61] Letter to Ritchie, January 13, 1827.

[62] James Bryce, *The American Commonwealth*, 2 vols. (London: MacMillan, 1889), 1:80.

162

of those who were at feud among his fellow partisans."[63] The second was the hero, a man of actual or reputed military achievement, who could be presented as a popular figure around which his party could unite. The basis for this unification inhered in the fact that the hero's reputation transcended politics, which was the reason why such men had to be recruited from outside of politics. In the choice of a candidate for his capacity as a broker, one finds the recognition of a considerable political skill, though certainly of a different and less elevated character than that which the Founders had envisioned for the presidency. In the selection of the figurehead, on the other hand, one sees something of the "independence" of the continental character that the Founders sought, but at the same time a dissociation of presidential selection from the requirement of political excellence of any sort. If a statesman arose by this means, it would depend to a larger extent on good fortune than the Founders had anticipated.

Van Buren's preference, as already noted, was for the skilled politician. But from his own very calculated reasons for backing Jackson in 1827, including the fact that he believed Jackson could be well positioned on the issues, one can appreciate how other party politicians might have learned from Van Buren how to overlook candidate quality when an advantage could be gained. The urge merely to win for the sake of spoils was strong, and in an era of closely balanced partisan strength the small advantage that a "hero" might bring could spell the margin of victory. Although Van Buren had grounds for viewing Jackson's candidacy in 1827 as a necessary exception to the "system" he planned to develop, his own lack of emphasis on the issue of candidate quality makes it reasonable to blame him at least in part for his failure to establish his own objective of exclusive rule by skilled politicians.

Van Buren also miscalculated in underestimating the ex-

[63] Schlesinger, ed., *History of American Presidential Elections*, 1:580.

tent to which the people themselves would look beyond party considerations in viewing the presidency. Established in a nonpartisan era, the executive as an institution did not require party and thus continued even in a partisan era to maintain certain transpartisan characteristics. At the very least, there was likely to be some distaste for the mere party politician with whom the broker or skilled politician was inevitably associated. The talents of the skilled politician were exercised behind the scenes and failed to give him that element of stature which the people preferred. Van Buren himself sensed this "nonrational" aspect to public opinion: "in this matter of personal popularity the working of the public mind is often inscrutable . . . feeling has of course more to do with it than reason. . . ." Van Buren felt the people reacted according to their view of the motives of public men, giving to those who adopted their cause with sincerity every benefit of the doubt; but when they suspected that a public man took the popular side "from motives of policy, their hearts seemed closed against him, they look upon his wisest measures with distrust and are apt to give him up at the first turn of affairs. . . ."[64] Van Buren did not mean this to apply to the "politician," but it is perhaps the best explanation for why many people had second thoughts about this kind of candidate. Although we have no hard contemporary evidence of the public reaction to candidate image, one study of the assessment of the era's media men (the campaign biographers) observes:

> The word "politician" was not freighted with derogatory implications before 1840. . . . It is difficult to fix the date when the term "politician" begins to take on a sinister character. . . . By 1844 there can be little doubt that henceforth to use the term without some qualifying adjective was to damn utterly. . . . From 1844 onward whenever it is an unavoidable fact that a candidate has

[64] Van Buren, *Autobiography*, p. 168.

been a politician, great care is taken to assure the voter-reader that he has never been a "mere politician."[65]

The politician thus ended up moving to share the presidency with the military hero. Yet the differences between these two should not obscure the important element they had in common: both were democratic alternatives to the meritocratic leadership the Founders had envisioned. This quality was in accord with the "spirit" of the times, bred at least in part by the decline in the respectability of old Federalist views. As Marvin Meyers has written: "When the rich, the well-born and the able lost touch with their community, the fluent, agile, self-taught law-abiding party lawyer, aided by the local editor and some prospective farmers and small businessmen, took the main responsibility for ordering public life."[66] Aided by the change to popular election of the electors in most states, presidential politics after 1824 increasingly stressed the idea of the "commonness" of the leader—his identity in manners, origin, and life style with the common man. Liberal democracy, which hitherto had left a place for "excellence" in political life, now was construed to require leadership of a more representative type. In the case of the politician, the connection with the common man was direct: the politician was like the common man, working his way up in society through his own profession of politics. In the case of the hero, the connection was only slightly less direct. The hero was indeed exceptional, but in no way did his prominence set him apart in style or bearing from his democratic peers. He was prominent without being aristocratic. The closer and more popular relationship was most revealingly indicated by the use of affectionate nicknames for presidential hopefuls, such as "Old Hickory" and "Old Tip." The new view of leadership at first favored the popular party, but the successor of the "aristocratic" party,

---

[65] William Brown, *The People's Choice, The Presidential Image in the Campaign Biography* (Baton Rouge: Louisiana State University, 1960), pp. 104-5.

[66] Meyers, *The Jacksonian Persuasion*, p. 246.

the Whigs, demonstrated in the log cabin and cider barrel campaign of 1840 that it could more than compete with its rival in playing on the democratic theme. If Van Buren had not envisioned or been entirely responsible for all these changes, he nevertheless suggested that the era of the "statesman" was at an end and that the political party was desirable precisely because it offered a means to counteract the aristocratic influence of family name.

VAN BUREN'S LEGACY

Whether the new kind of leadership appeared in the form of the skilled politician, as Van Buren hoped, or in the form of the manufactured popular hero, it could not meet with the approval of the traditional defenders of the elevated standards of "talent and virtue." Writing in 1840, the most famous spokesman for this viewpoint, John Quincy Adams, complained that the new system of partisan competition brought the triumph of demagogic politics:

> Would not the retrospect furnish as practical principle in the operation of the Constitution—1. that the direct and infallible path to the Presidency is military service coupled with demagoguery policy; 2. that, in the absence of military service, demagogue policy is the first and most indispensable element of success, and the art of party drilling the second; 3. that the drill consists in combining southern interest in domestic slavery with northern riotous democracy. . . .[67]

In one respect, Adams' criticism may have had a certain validity. Insofar as demagoguery can be identified with the celebration of a friendly and familiar attitude on the part of a leader toward the people, it was certainly not discouraged by party competition. Although a populist style of leadership

[67] John Quincy Adams, *The Memoirs of John Quincy Adams*, ed., Charles Francis Adams, 12 vols. (Philadelphia: J. P. Lippincott, 1876), 10:182.

preceded the rise of permanent parties and would almost certainly have persisted under any form of popular non-partisan competition, it is nonetheless true that party competition was defended mainly as a democratic change. Furthermore, the parties became tremendous "advertising" agents, often extolling their nominees for their "common" qualities. To the Founders, this emphasis on friendliness and empathy would probably have been seen as destructive of the tone of politics needed to support constitutional government.

In another and more important respect, however, Adams's criticism was wide of the mark. In the stronger meaning of the term, demagoguery refers to a powerful form of leadership that achieves power by stirring up dangerous passions. The demagogue, when enjoying success, will own a strong personal following which is the product of his seizing upon a major issue or deep prejudice and splitting the community into antagonistic parts. This kind of leadership, which Van Buren sought expressly to prevent, was characteristic neither of the military heroes after Jackson, who were chosen because of their distance from political issues, nor the politicians. Arousing a new and volatile mass constituency, which is the distinguishing feature of popular leadership, was antithetical to the requirements of the parties Van Buren had founded. What in fact came to characterize nineteenth-century politics—omitting the great events of the Civil War with their accompanying new parties and popular leaders—was the strength of the "party-drill" and the *weakness* of the individual candidates. These two features were intimately connected. Given the coalitional aspect of the parties, their continued strength required candidates who could be flexibly placed on the major practical issues of the day. As long as such strong but fragile parties dominated the scene, the emergence of demagoguery was discouraged, though perhaps at the price of a strong candidate of any sort. Lord Bryce's description of the effects of candidate selection of the nineteenth-century party remains the best statement of the problem:

167

Party feeling, strong enough to carry in on its back a man without conspicuous merits is not always strong enough to procure forgiveness for a man with positive faults . . . party loyalty and party organization have been so perfect that any one put forward by the party will get the full party vote if his character is good and his "record," as they call it, unstained.[68]

Adam's critique of the emerging party system, which he more or less offered in the spirit of his interpretation of the Founders, raises the general question of the relationship of his opponent, Martin Van Buren, to the Founding. In establishing the new "institution" of party competition, did Van Buren intend to alter dramatically the character of the Constitution, making it, in particular, more democratic, or did he have in mind "merely" correcting some of its major defects? Unfortunately, Van Buren never posed this question in his own writings; and if we attempt to impute an intention to him by looking at his proposal, the matter is in no way simplified, for party competition at one and the same time seems to correct certain defects and to lead to certain constitutional changes. Given the nature of Van Buren's solution, these two effects were inseparable, and the most one can do is note the ways in which Van Buren's transformation fulfilled and altered the objectives of the original Constitutional design. In line with the Founders' aims, party competition would prevent personal factionalism and control popular leadership; discourage sectional divisions and encourage moderate, coalitional majorities; ensure the existence of candidates with broad national support and thus avoid the evils of Congressional selection; undo any unjust advantage to the oligarchic party deriving from unforeseen electoral influences; and restore at least a modicum of energy to the executive. But these objectives, to the extent that they were attained, extracted a certain price in terms of the Founders' ends. A coalitional style of politics went outside the legislature to the nation at

[68] Bryce, *The American Commonwealth*, pp. 74-75.

large and extended its influence to the executive, thus "lowering" the presidency from an independent to a brokering institution. The use of partisan organizations which corrected an unanticipated oligarchic advantage also served to give a distinct edge to the people's party and more generally to democratize the tone of the presidential campaign and American politics. And finally, the attempt to bind leadership to established principles reduced the discretion of presidential leadership and diminished the capacity of the formal institutions to initiate changes from the top.

CHAPTER IV

Woodrow Wilson and the Origin of the Modern View of Presidential Selection

WOODROW WILSON published his first article on American politics in 1879, when the selection system established by Martin Van Buren had achieved complete dominance. Party organizations were as powerful as they ever would be, and nearly all of the voters felt a strong sense of partisan attachment.[1] Wilson never spoke directly about Martin Van Buren's theory of presidential selection, nor is there any indication that he was aware that permanent party competition had been founded as a deliberate act. His own views nevertheless read like a point by point response to the theories of the nineteenth-century party school, as if he and Van Buren were engaged in a direct dialogue. Whereas Van Buren wanted to limit and control the electoral appeals of individual aspirants for fear of their dangerous effects, Wilson encouraged a selection process that would foster popular leadership as an aid to establishing a powerful democratic presidency. And whereas Van Buren favored a partisan-minded electorate and nomination by party leaders, Wilson sought to free the voters from the grip of habitual partisanship and make them directly responsible for choosing the nominees. For Wilson, the party was almost a complete opposite of its nineteenth-century counterpart. The name "party" would be maintained, but its role and function would be completely transformed. Instead of constraining its leader, it would now form around him and adopt his program or "vision" as its own.

Yet it was not the nineteenth-century party system that

---

[1] See Walter Dean Burnham, *Critical Elections and the Mainsprings of American Politics* (New York: W. W. Norton, 1970), pp. 72-73.

170

bore the direct brunt of Wilson's criticism, but rather the Constitution. For Wilson the old parties had been almost a natural outgrowth—and certainly a necessary one—of the Founders' scheme. Parties managed to provide a degree of cohesion in a formal system in which power had been dangerously fragmented. But though parties partially offset this fragmentation, they could not, as presently constituted, overcome it. Indeed, they remained more a reflection of this defect than a correction. The central problem of the American system continued to be the absence of a unitary source of vitality and direction that could arouse and move the nation. Wilson called this condition "Leaderless Government" and held that it was producing a dangerous sense of drift that threatened the future of republican government in America.[2]

Wilson believed that nothing less than a complete transformation of the political system could save representative government in America. As a first step in this transformation, it was necessary to undermine the reverence Americans felt for the Constitution and the Founders. Wilson sought to expose the outmoded "Newtonian" theory of static checks that had informed the Founders' thought, contrasting it with the modern "Darwinian" theory that recognized the need for growth and change. This was a prelude to his plan for a new institutional arrangement that would embody the proper understanding of representative government. Although Wilson changed his mind about which form of government was best, shifting from a proposal for cabinet government to a plan of presidential dominance, his basic objectives remained the same: to establish a greater capacity in the government for change through dynamic leadership and to make the relationship between the leader and public opinion the focal point of the new system. Thus the two functions of selection that Wilson emphasized were the relation of the selection

---

[2] Woodrow Wilson, "Leaderless Government" in *College and State*, ed. Ray Stannard Baker and William E. Dodd, 2 vols. (New York: Harper Brothers, 1925), 1:339. Except where otherwise noted, all articles by Wilson cited in this chapter are from *College and State*.

system to executive leadership and power and the role of the selection process in encouraging the proper degree of political change. To attain his goals, Wilson sought a selection system that would assist in the concentration of political power in the presidency by an able and distinguished "popular statesman" and that would force a public discussion of new principles and programs.[3]

Under Wilson's original plan of locating the source of leadership in the House, the executive power would in effect have been lodged in the Speaker, while the president's role would have been reduced to that of a "mere administrator" holding office, like other civil servants, for life.[4] But after observing elements of strength in the administrations of Cleveland, McKinley, and Roosevelt, Wilson began to argue that the presidency could be made the source of leadership. This plan had an important advantage over the original one in that it could be implemented without a Constitutional amendment, which Wilson came to realize would be almost impossible to attain. Yet an amendment of a sort was still necessary. What Wilson called the "living constitution"—the actual regime as fixed not only by Constitutional provisions, but by opinion and practice—would have to be changed by means of a basic transformation of the public's views under which the people would come to regard the executive as the most legitimate source of political authority. Traditional party organizations, with their base in local politics and interest groups, would have to be destroyed at the same time

[3] Wilson, *Leaders of Men*, ed. T. H. V. Motter (Princeton: Princeton University Press, 1952), p. 45. Wilson uses the term "popular leader" as well (p. 42). It is clear for Wilson that modern statesmanship is—or should be—popular statesmanship. For an excellent discussion of Wilson's political thought, see Harry M. Clor, "Woodrow Wilson" in Morton J. Frisch and Richard G. Stevens, eds., *American Political Thought* (New York: Charles Scribner's Sons), pp. 192-218.

[4] Wilson, *Congressional Government* (Boston: Houghton Mifflin, 1885), p. 254. Wilson made the life tenure suggestion on the supposition that the president would not retain his legislative function.

that a new form of parties at the national level would have to be created. The president would stand at the head of his party, recognized by the public and by the members of his Congressional party as its undisputed leader. By such "informal" means, short of an actual Constitutional amendment, Wilson hoped to change the entire system and override the doctrine of checks and balances that the Founders had embodied in the "literary document."

Wilson's plan to transform the Constitution by increasing the power of the executive led him to examine closely the presidential selection process. The selection system, he charged, contributed to leaderless government by producing candidates of limited ability and little stature who were frequently beholden to the "bosses and the machines" that controlled the nomination process. Wilson's initial view was that the quality of nominees would improve on its own accord after the change to a more powerful executive: in response to a greater opportunity to exercise decisive authority, men of ability would enter politics and aspire to the presidency; and with the acceptance of the idea of the public opinion leader, the people would demand from the party conventions nominees who were veritable leaders in their own right. But on further reflection Wilson concluded that such pressures on the selection system were not sufficient, so entrenched were the party power brokers and so great was their hold over the electorate. Wilson's final position was that without a dramatic change in the selection system itself, it would be difficult if not impossible to establish his ideal of executive leadership. Moved by this new understanding, he became an advocate of the presidential primary and formally proposed to the Congress a system of direct national primaries.[5]

[5] Wilson, "First Annual Message to the Congress" in Fred L. Israel, ed., *The State of the Union Messages of the Presidents*, 3 vols. (New York: Chelsea House, 1966), 3:2548. Wilson thought that his proposal might "be handled promptly and without serious controversy of any kind." The proposal is discussed by Louise Overacker, *The Presidential Primary* (New York: Macmillan, 1926), and in "Toward a More Responsible Two-Party System," The Report

Wilson's objective in reforming the selection system, then, was not simply to reduce or remove the influence of the bosses—which was the point at which so many other Progressives stopped—but to increase the authority of the executive and to provide the system as a whole with a greater capacity for change. Under the primary method, the individual aspirant would have the chance to present his own program, and the eventual winner would be in a position to claim a popular mandate for a general direction to public policy. Moreover, aspirants during the campaign would have to address their appeals to the present concerns of the people, for only in this way could the people's imagination be captured and their sentiments moved. Unlike the system of nomination by party organizations, which encouraged inertia and adherence by the candidates to worn-out principles, the new system would emphasize contemporary issues and facilitate changes in public policy. Ultimately Wilson was, in a literal sense, a Progressive; he had a strong preference for change or "growth," alternating between an enlightenment vision that history inevitably brought progress and a more limited Darwinian concept that continuous adaptation was necessary to sustain and nourish society.

Wilson's theory of selection, then, was deliberately calculated to reverse the nineteenth-century relationship between the leader and the party. Instead of limiting the leader, the party would serve him. It would be an instrument at the leader's command helping to further the principles and programs for which he had won approval in his direct appeal to the people. The concept of public opinion leadership is therefore central to Wilson's understanding of how power

of the Committee on Political Parties, American Political Science Association, *American Political Science Review*, supplement vol. 44 (September 1950).

The Democratic Platform of 1912 endorsed the idea of state presidential primaries, while the Progressive Party platform called for a nation-wide presidential primary. See Kirk H. Porter and Donald Bruce Johnson, eds., *National Party Platforms 1840-1964* (Urbana: University of Illinois Press, 1966), pp. 170 and 176.

was to be sought, just as it is central to how he thought power should be exercised. With Wilson's concept of leadership, therefore, one must begin, after which it will be possible to discuss its connection to his theory of parties and selection.

WILSON'S UNDERSTANDING OF POLITICAL LEADERSHIP

Leadership for Wilson was a positive normative concept. He granted that there were always leaders in the ordinary sense of those holding positions of political power: "Leaders of some sort we . . . always have."[6] But in its highest sense leadership was a dynamic kind of rule that achieved its authority by virtue of its intimate contact with and support by public opinion; it was an active force that provided the government with energy. So conceived, it represented a standard against which popular government should be measured. To the extent that popular government provided for leadership and ensured its accountability, it was good government; to the extent that it frustrated leadership and hid its operations from the public view, it was faulty government. Wilson's normative standard was informed by an understanding of necessity. In a direct criticism of the "Newtonian" theory underlying the American Constitution, Wilson argued:

No living thing can have its organs offset against each other as checks and live. . . . There can be no successful government without leadership or the intimate almost instinctive coordination of the organs of life and action.[7]

Although Wilson never discussed his concept of leadership in rigorous, analytic terms, it is possible to focus the discussion around five different elements. Leadership, to Wilson, must be: open, responsible, community-wide in its perspective, democratic, and exercised by persons respected for their excellence and expertise in public affairs.

[6] Wilson, "Leaderless Government," 1:340.
[7] Wilson, *Constitutional Government in the United States* (New York: Columbia University Press, 1908), p. 57.

175

The first element, openness, concerns the obligation of the leader to the public. When planning to implement a policy, the leader must reveal his proposals to the public and directly seek its approval. Power exercised in private and policies enacted behind the scenes are invitations to corruption. Where the leader does not find public support forthcoming, he can and should attempt to persuade the public of the wisdom of his programs, not by tricks or slogans that manipulate public opinion but by rational arguments and earnest advocacy on behalf of the public interest. The opposite of the leader in these respects is "the politician" or "the boss." The politician prefers to deal in private and frequently addresses his appeals to self-interest. "A politician," wrote Wilson, "is a man who manages the organs of the party outside the field of government . . . while the statesman is the leader of public opinion. . . ."[8] Teddy Roosevelt, whose views of leadership often paralleled Wilson's, best elaborated the differences imagined to exist between these two types:

> The leader leads the people; the boss drives the people. The leader gets his hold by open appeal to the reason and conscience of his followers; the boss keeps his hold by manipulation, by intrigue, by secret and furtive appeals to very base forms of self-interest. . . . Leadership is carried on in the open light of day; bossism derives its main strength from what is done under the cover of darkness.[9]

Roosevelt's metaphor of "light" and "dark," which coincides with that of "open" and "closed," was also a favorite of Wilson's. "Let there be light" is the title of one of Wilson's chapters in the *New Freedom*, and elsewhere he remarked that "light is the only thing that can sweeten our political atmosphere."[10] Power exercised "in the dark," often sep-

[8] *Ibid.*, p. 212.

[9] Theodore Roosevelt, *The New Nationalism* (Englewood Cliffs, N.J.: Prentice Hall, 1961), p. 172.

[10] Wilson, *The New Freedom*, Intro. and Notes by W. E. Leuchtenberg (Englewood Cliffs, N.J.: Prentice Hall, 1964), p. 75; and "Committee or Cabinet Government?" 1:115.

arated from official office altogether, was noxious. It could not, like leadership, be judged or held accountable, nor could it elevate or educate the public.

Another way of expressing the contrast between leadership and bossism is to speak of the "public" and the "private." Wilson, along with many others at the time, argued that the public character of political life was being lost in the labyrinth of fragmented governmental authorities and behind the closed doors of party caucuses and conventions. The problem began with the selection of candidates: "Since the choice of candidates for office is a matter of private judgment . . . it follows very naturally that the public business loses its public character and becomes itself a matter of private arrangement."[11] Whether by the phrase "the public character of public business" Wilson meant to exclude the large element of self-interest in politics that the Founders had admitted is never made clear. But what is certain is that he believed that political life in the latter part of the nineteenth century had come too much under the control of private interests and was no longer truly political. The machine led the way: "A machine is the part that has ceased to be political and become an agency of unscrupulous business."[12] Wilson wanted to carve out a domain for public consciousness in American life, and leadership was the means. By continually exhorting people to care about the public good, leaders would promote civic concern and make citizens out of private persons. Leadership thus had a moral and didactic function, and this may help explain why today, in an era dominated by Wilson's understanding of political leadership, one continually hears the call being made for "positive moral leadership" to uplift the people.[13]

[11] Wilson, "Hide and Seek Politics," 2:215.

[12] Wilson, *New Freedom*, p. 134.

[13] The importance of this aspect of leadership for the Progressives is indicated in a study by Otis Graham, *An Encore for Reform* (New York: Oxford University Press, 1967). Graham, who analyzed the views of former Progressive activists at the time of the New Deal, found that most of them quickly became disenchanted with

The second element in Wilson's concept of leadership is the idea of responsibility. In praising the system of cabinet government, which he at first sought to introduce in the United States, Wilson identified responsibility as the regime's "quintessential feature." Responsibility had two basic characteristics. At the level of the governing institutions, it meant the concentration of authority in one place in order to provide the capacity to act directly and energetically. At the level of the electoral process and public opinion, it meant the clear designation of the person charged with the task of governing so that the people would immediately know whom to censure or credit. This, in essence, was accountability:

> Power and strict accountability for its use are essential constituents of good government. A sense of highest responsibility, a dignifying and elevating sense of being trusted, together with a consciousness of being in an official station so that no faithful discharge of duty can go

---

Roosevelt's style of leadership. For the Progressives, Roosevelt was all too comfortable with the machine politicians of the northern cities and all too willing to forget promises of reform for the political process. Nor, in their view, did Roosevelt take seriously enough the idea that power must be based on open appeals to the public interest. For Wilson, "the right methods [of politics] are those of public discussion: the methods of leadership open and above board . . . where honest eyes can look upon them and honest eyes can judge of them" (*New Freedom*, p. 76). Franklin Roosevelt, by contrast, was thought by the Progressives to be secretive, at times manipulative, and not adverse to exercising power through deals made behind the scenes. The Progressives considered a government "of all outside and no inside" (Wilson's words) to be the most important check on political power, since it would assure that support was not based on secret bargains that catered to particular interests. Finally there was the matter of Roosevelt's rhetoric. His excitation of class sentiment stood in marked contrast to the Progressive idea of rational argument which left the individual citizen able to decide policy by himself, uninfluenced by strong passion. Roosevelt employed the technique of division, evidently in the belief that popular support could only be generated by raising the spectre of a threatening force, i.e. an enemy class.

178

unacknowledged and unrewarded, and no breach of trust undiscovered and unpunished—those are the influences, the only influences, which foster practical, energetic, and trustworthy statesmanship.[14]

It has been widely acknowledged that Wilson's model of responsibility came in the first instance from British politics, especially as interpreted by Walter Bagehot. But Wilson also admitted to having been influenced on constitutional theory by Alexander Hamilton, the Founder whose views he respected most. Hamilton, in defending the Constitution in *The Federalist* against those who preferred an executive by a committee or a council, made what is now considered the classic statement on behalf of a unitary executive. Hamilton's two chief arguments for unity—the greater energy possessed when power is given to a single individual and the greater ease with which one person can be watched and held accountable—are both incorporated into Wilson's concept of leadership. But Wilson went much further than Hamilton, proposing in effect to do with political power in its entirety what Hamilton had sought for the executive power alone.[15]

[14] Wilson, *Congressional Government*, pp. 283-84; cited also in Austin Ranney's essay on Woodrow Wilson in his book *The Doctrine of Responsible Party Government* (Urbana: University of Illinois Press, 1962), p. 29.

[15] Wilson even suggested that Hamilton was friendly to the basic goal of his own plan, as Hamilton had never really accepted the "Whig theory" of government that dominated the thinking of the other Founders. It is true, of course, that Hamilton was more favorable than most of his contemporaries to the idea of a strong and vigorous executive. But it would be a mistake to conclude that he was unconcerned about institutional checks and balances. One of the strongest pieces of evidence in *favor* of Wilson's interpretation of Hamilton's views came in a celebrated statement that Hamilton allegedly made about the British Constitution. According to Jefferson, Hamilton in the course of a general discussion of politics claimed that the British Constitution was the best constitution not in spite of, but because of the practice of "corruption." (Corruption was the means by which the British executive power—consisting of the King and his appointed ministers—could control the Parliament, and ac-

The third characteristic of Wilsonian leadership is its community-wide perspective. Political scientists frequently distinguish two ways in which the public interest might be discovered in a popular regime. According to one view, it is found by aggregating parts, each of which should be represented in a bargaining process; according to a second, it is found by consulting the needs of the community conceived as a whole.[16] In practice, the community-wide perspective is emphasized most often by the executive. The executive appeals to the "general public" as distinct from the "special interests." Wilson considered this the only way in which the public interest could truly be ascertained. His sharp criticism of congressional government was often nothing more than an attack on the pluralist concept. To Wilson, congressional government, for which one can read government by aggregation, encouraged in action and partiality to vested interests. Congress was

a collection of men representing each his neighborhood, each his local interest; an alarmingly large proportion of

cording to Bernard Baylin was to colonial thinkers one of the most odious features of British politics.) Jefferson was shocked by this comment and regarded it as certain evidence of Hamilton's monarchic attachments.

But it would surely be incorrect to transfer Hamilton's views on the concentration of executive power in Great Britain to the American case. It is not, I believe, a misstatement of Hamilton's position to say that the executive power was in many respects *more* in need of restraint as it became more popular. In the case of an elective office of a rather short duration, the connection between the occupant's own interest and the public interest was apt to be more tenuous. See *Federalist*, #75, p. 451; Hamilton's convention speech of June 18, Madison's *Notes of Debates in the Federal Convention of 1787*, ed. Adrienne Koch (New York: W. W. Norton, 1969), pp. 135-38.

[16] See Edward C. Banfield and James Q. Wilson, *City Politics* (New York: Vintage Books, 1963), pp. 25-26, 95; Edward C. Banfield, *Political Influence* (New York: Free Press of Glencoe, 1961), pp. 250-60.

its legislation is 'special'; all of it is at best only a limping compromise between the conflicting interests of the innumerable localities represented.[17]

The president, on the other hand, alone had the potential perspective of a national leader:

. . . there is but one national voice in the country, and that is the voice of the President. . . . The nation as a whole has chosen him, and is conscious that it has no other political spokesman. . . . Let him once win the admiration and confidence of the country, and no other single force can withstand him. His position takes the imagination of the country. He is the representative of no constituency, but of the whole people. When he speaks in his true character, he speaks for no special interest.[18]

It is important to point out, however, that this national perspective of the presidency, though encouraged by certain aspects of the office, could easily be negated by the character of the occupant and by the informal pressures that operated upon him. The existing selection process, Wilson often argued, made presidential candidates the captives of political parties which themselves, under the cover of their worn-out principles, were little more than aggregations of various interests. Powerful pluralizing forces were thus at work on the presidency and tended to prevent it from realizing its proper form. Wilson's plan to institute leadership in the executive was designed to ensure that the president would have a view of the whole transcending the level of competing factions and interests. In this respect his views parallel those of the Founders and oppose the brokering concept of the executive that was introduced by Van Buren. But in certain other respects, to be developed later, Wilson's views diverge from the Founders' and raise an entirely different set of problems. His disparagement of the place of interest in poli-

[17] Wilson, *Congressional Government*, p. 73.
[18] Wilson, *Constitutional Government*, pp. 202 and 68.

181

tics, which the Founders admitted into the system in the form of factional bargaining in the Congress, makes one wonder whether his view of power is not too elevated and idealistic, giving rise alternately to moralistic claims (because of attempts to conform to the ideal) and hypocrisy (because of the impossibility of achieving it). And the basis of the executive's "independence," which for the Founders had been in the office's relative freedom from public opinion, lies for Wilson in the leader's mobilization of, or reliance on, public opinion, making one wonder whether the executive is not too powerful (since he claims to speak for the public) or alternatively not powerful enough (since he is limited to following its will).

Fourth, Wilson presents leadership as a fully democratic concept. He called for "popular leaders" and "popular statesmen" who would act with the support and assistance of public opinion. Public opinion in turn becomes the major resource for, and the major constraint on, political leadership. The art of politics is defined wholly in terms of molding public opinion: "Policy—where there is no arbitrary ruler to do the choosing for the whole nation—means massed opinion, and the forming of the masses is the whole art and mastery of politics."[19] Statesmanship, which for the Founders had required a realm of protection from public opinion in which political wisdom could operate with some freedom, now becomes preeminently the art of guiding public sentiment.

Wilson was not the first, of course, to assert the importance of public opinion in a popular regime. Lincoln, referring to opinion on the basic principles of the regime and on basic social attitudes, once declared that "in this and like communities public sentiment is everything";[20] Jefferson saw the revolution of 1800 as a response to a great wave of public opinion; and the Founders acknowledged the crucial role of public opinion, both in its deepest sense of support for the

[19] Wilson, "Leaderless Government," 1:339.
[20] *The Lincoln-Douglas Debates*, ed. Robert Johannsen (New York: Oxford University Press, 1965), pp. 64-65.

regime and in a more immediate sense as a censure and judge of presidential actions. What distinguished Wilson from these others, however, was his insistence that *all* power is based in a very direct sense on public opinion. "I hold," he said in a speech during the 1917 campaign, "that government belongs to the people and that they have a right to that intimate access to it which will determine every turn of its policy."[21]

This publicly expressed view was supported by Wilson's scholarly analysis of the nature of political power. Wilson's effort to strip away the illusions of political science and understand "the life rather than the mere theory" of popular government led him to the conclusion that "the greatest power lies with that part of the government which is in most direct communication with the nation."[22] The "realism" of this last observation would hardly have shocked or enlightened earlier theorists. The Founders were well aware of the tendency of the "part" that claimed to speak for the people to assert its predominance. But it was precisely because the power of this part was potentially so formidable and thus likely to become "imperial" that the Founders sought to place certain impediments in its way. Wilson differed from the Founders in that once having perceived the potential power of popular leadership, he sought to remove all restraints on it—except that of popular approval or disapproval—and make it the central feature of his new political system.

Implicit in Wilson's view, accordingly, is the undermining of what we have called representative government, i.e. government based on the authority of the forms of constitutionally defined powers. Wilson proposed to replace representative government with a form of representative democracy in which public opinion would rule directly through the executive. This understanding of the role of public opinion contrasted with the Founders' understanding, which envi-

[21] Wilson, *New Freedom*, p. 57.
[22] Wilson, *Constitutional Government*, pp. 108-109.

sioned that there would exist at the deepest level a stratum of opinion that supported the forms of the Constitution. For presidential leadership, this meant that opinion could be relied on to uphold the "rights" of the office, thereby allowing a president to gain within the sphere of his authority a degree of freedom from the pressure of opinion at the level of immediate policy preferences. For Wilson, however, there was to be no such deeper stratum of public opinion in support of the Constitution. This followed in part from his deliberate design to undermine reverence for the Constitution and in part from his view that constitutional government meant not an adherence to old forms but development according to the "law of life, not of mechanics." But above all, it followed from his desire to place leadership at the center of the political system. Wilson saw leadership in the final analysis as an informal or extrainstitutional relationship. A solution to the nation's problems, he declared:

> . . . can be accomplished only by some simplification of our methods which will centre the public trust in small groups of men who will lead *not by reason of legal authority, but by reason of their contact with and amenability to public opinion.*[23]

The principal source of the president's power, indeed, was not in the Constitution, either in the sense of being contained in its specific powers or in its originally intended position based upon those powers, but in a new "life" relationship between leader and people.

Wilson's concept of democratic leadership may help explain the curious existence of two very different images of presidential power among contemporary scholars. A recently ascendant view depicts the presidency as an "imperial" institution that has seized over the past quarter century a vast array of powers that were never intended to belong to the

[23] Wilson, *New Freedom*, p. 81, emphasis added. See also pp. 144-45.

president. A second and currently less prevalent view stresses the weaknesses or "colonial" condition of the office. The cause, according to one spokesman of this view, Theodore Lowi, lies not in the president's lack of specific powers but in a general deficiency of authority. When pursuing a policy initiative, the president discovers that he has little to rely on in the way of support for his office and must therefore seek to raise public opinion in his own behalf. In Lowi's words, the president must "turn public because his major resources are public . . . [and] oversell because that is what one must do to sway a large public."[24] These two views of modern presidential power, despite the apparent tension between them, do not rest on conflicting analyses and could both be true.

It is altogether possible for the presidency to absorb a larger and larger share of political power at the same time that presidential authority becomes more reliant on and constrained by public opinion. It seems clear, in fact, that the executive could never have attained its recent status without its first being proclaimed by so many as the nation's only truly representative institution. Yet making popular representation the only, or the primary, basis of presidential power tends to weaken its formal Constitutional claim to authority and to drain the office of its formal prerogatives. Both "imperialism" and "colonialism" as images of presidential power can thus be viewed as complements of one another; and both may be traced to Wilson's efforts to change the way in which Americans understand the presidency, though the results, illustrated by both schools of thought cited above, hardly conform to Wilson's ideal.

Fifth and finally, Wilson held that the qualification for leadership should be political excellence. His conception of leadership, though popular and democratic, was not populist. Far from having his leader appreciated for his commonness,

[24] Theodore Lowi, *The End of Liberalism* (New York: W. W. Norton, 1969), pp. 182-83.

Wilson wanted him to be looked up to and admired for his ability to articulate and promote a political program. Democracy inhered not in the likeness of the leaders to the people but in the people's choice among the views the leaders presented. Wilson looked back admiringly to the nation's first four presidents, each of whom he felt possessed the preparation and skill required for ruling. Not all were popular leaders, but each in his own way was a statesman. It was with Jackson that the standard of popularity became firmly established, though it was with Jackson also, Wilson conceded, that a general decline in the quality of presidents began.[25] Wilson's picture of the ideal executive can be characterized as an attempt to join the features of excellence as found in the distinguished statesmanship of the earliest presidents with democracy as found in the popular executive of Andrew Jackson. That combination he called "popular statesmanship."

The development of a general expectation among the populace that presidents and presidential candidates should serve as active leaders would go a long way, Wilson believed, toward raising the competence of the nominees. No aspirant could become a serious contender unless he was able to articulate a program and move public opinion on its behalf. This would eliminate from presidential competition both the figurehead who possessed no political skill and the broker or "mere representative partisan" who shied away from advocating broad political principles.[26] During the period in which Wilson advocated the cabinet government plan, he envisioned the development of national leaders through Congressional debates which would be attentively followed by the public. Here at last was a means for creating the "conti-

[25] Wilson, "The Making of the Nation," 1:330; "Leaderless Government," 1:343.

[26] Wilson, *Constitutional Government*, p. 66. In his essay "Leaderless Government" Wilson wrote: "It was taken for granted at first that the real leaders of the nation would be put in the presidential chair" (1:343). But after Jackson, Wilson makes clear that this changed.

186

nental characters" sought by Morris and Madison at the Convention and for ensuring that they would be persons of great political ability:

> None but the ablest can become leaders and masters in this keen tournament in which arguments are the weapons and the people the judges. . . . Drill in debate, by giving scope to talents, invites talents; raises up a race of men habituated to the methods of public business, skilled parliamentary chiefs.[27]

Wilson's emphasis on proficiency in formal debate lessened as he gave up the idea of locating leadership in the House. But there was no decrease in the importance he ascribed to being able to communicate a program to the broad public. Any serious candidate for high office must possess this skill, which likewise was the skill that best qualified one to exercise political power. The art of winning power and the art of governing are very much the same. Thus the campaign is seen as a proper, indeed the best, test of a president's qualifications. Wilson, in contrast to the Founders, elevated the art of rhetoric (or communicating with the people) to the highest place among the skills of the executive and proposed that this skill, rather than an established record of service to the state, be made the decisive criterion in presidential selection.

It can be said that Wilson favored rule by a political meritocracy, as long as the meaning of the term in this context is clearly understood. Wilson wanted the "best" to rule, but unlike a true aristocracy the best would be distinguished by how well they served—indeed by how well they spoke for—the people. The price for admission to the high offices of government was a repeated pledge of fidelity to popular democracy, sweetened from time to time by the leaders' flattery of their new master. Whether Wilson's emphasis on democratic leadership and his advocacy of popular primaries

---

[27] Wilson, "Cabinet Government in the United States," 1:30, 37.

would in fact produce merit, however, is another question. The popular devices he suggested to free the regime from the grip of self-interested parties, and which he hoped would produce a "high tone" to politics, could also be the very things which open the door to the kind of populism he abhorred.[28]

WILSON'S VIEW OF DEMOCRATIC OR POPULAR LEADERSHIP

The central element in Wilson's concept of leadership is the idea that the executive should be a "popular leader" or a "popular statesman." This idea immediately raises some important questions. One might wonder, first, whether this kind of leader is not too powerful, able to claim the role of spokesman for the nation after molding its opinions. Wilson, it should be recalled, once referred to leadership as "the art of the forming of the masses"; and the Founders had worried about the kind of rhetorician who, able to communicate with all of the people, might rule "with as complete a sway as if a scepter had been placed in his hand." On the other hand, one might wonder whether this kind of leadership would not be too weak, simply following the currents of public opinion or, more dangerously, seeking to compensate for this weakness by encouraging divisions in the populace in order to generate a following. Wilson's most extended treatment of both these problems appears in an essay entitled "Leaders of Men," which was not published during his lifetime. It is in many respects a remarkable essay, not just for what it reveals about Wilson's political thought but also for the light it sheds on his own presidential leadership, including his un-

[28] One can find a similar attempt by Wilson to establish a meritocracy consistent with democracy in his well-known plans for a professional civil service. See Wilson, "The Study of Administration," *The Papers of Woodrow Wilson*, ed. Arthur S. Link, 18 vols. (Princeton: Princeton University Press, 1966) 5:359-80.

188

compromising crusade for the League of Nations.[29] The analysis below will rely primarily on this essay.

The first problem noted above reminds one of the possibility of a kind of Caesarism or democratic tyranny in which the rhetorical art is so powerful that the proficient leader can implant in the populace the opinions he wants. The leader would then generate his own consensus, and the rule of the public opinion leader would only be a thin disguise for the rule of one man. How seriously did Wilson entertain this prospect? Wilson often contended that the rhetorical skill was one of the best means for attaining power, and in certain private correspondences as a young man he seemed genuinely infatuated with its possibilities.[30] But in his formal public writings, as one might expect, he tended to be more cautious, stressing the limits of political persuasion. Where the public already has in mind a clear idea of what it wants, the leader should carry out that wish: "The nineteenth is a century, we know, which has established the principle that public opinion must be truckled to (if you will use a disagreeable word) in the conduct of government. . . ."[31] But leadership does possess some leeway in those areas in which the public has not yet formed an opinion or fixed on a single

---

[29] Wilson's understanding of leadership may have been a more fundamental cause for his behavior than the psychological traits ascribed to him by Alexander and Julliette George in their biography *Woodrow Wilson and Colonel House* (New York: Dover Publications, 1956). See footnote 35 below.

[30] See Wilson's letter to Ellen Louise Axson, October 30, 1883. In that letter Wilson wrote: "I had then, as I still have, a very earnest political creed and very pronounced political ambitions. I remember forming with Charlie Talcott . . . a solemn covenant that we would school all powers and passions for the work of establishing the principles we held in common; that we would acquire knowledge that we might have power; and that we would drill ourselves in the arts of persuasion, but especially oratory . . . that we might have facility in leading others into our ways of thinking and enlisting them in our purposes" (*Papers*, ed. Link, 2:500).

[31] Wilson, *Leaders of Men*, p. 40.

189

course of action. The potential for leadership here is immense, so immense, in fact, that Wilson again saw the need to limit, or give the appearance of limiting, its discretion. Persuasion, he argued, can not really create new opinions; it can only make manifest those that are already latent:

> [The] general sense of the community may wait to be aroused, and the statesman must arouse it, may be inchoate and vague, and the statesman must formulate and make it explicit. But he cannot, and should not, do more.[32]

He repeated much the same thought, placing even more limitations on the leader, in an oft quoted passage from the *New Freedom*:

> For the business of every leader of government is to hear what the nation is saying and to know what the nation is enduring. It is not his business to judge *for* the nation, but to judge *through* the nation as its spokesman and as its voice.[33]

Wilson called this function of evoking the general sense of the community "interpretation," and this concept, more than that of "forming the masses," seems to have been his public position. As he put it succinctly, "Leadership, for the statesman, is interpretation."[34] The concept of interpretation, however, is not without ambiguities of its own. Though it concedes more weight in determining affairs to the people than does the art of "forming the masses," it also seems to arm the leader with a greater claim to power, for he is not merely asserting his own judgment but expressing the wishes of the people. The leader's self-effacement or humility as a mere spokesman for the people is the basis of his strength. The power of the executive is enhanced, though its discretion

[32] *Ibid.*, p. 44.
[33] Wilson, *New Freedom*, pp. 56-57.
[34] Wilson, *Leaders of Men*, p. 42.

would appear to be more limited, if not in each particular instance then as general institutional tendency.

The concept of interpretation also raises an interesting question with respect to Wilson's views about partisanship. Interpretation carries the dual connotation of variety and singularity: different interpretations are possible but only one is correct. Following this ambiguity, Wilson accepted party competition but continually alluded to a form of leadership that transcended partisanship and could unite the nation on the one "right" interpretation.

Ultimately, Wilson's concept of interpretation seems intended to suggest a kind of middle ground between following or "truckling" to public opinion and commanding or shaping it. While the leader's ear should "ring with the voices of the people," it must listen for their finest pitch. The leader was to be the people's servant, even as he was charged with the task of educating and elevating his master. But whether such a middle ground exists and has genuine substance as an independent position, is not entirely clear. In setting the standards for this middle ground, Wilson continually looks to the two poles that he apparently had rejected. On the one hand, we are told that "uncompromising thought is the luxury of the closeted recluse," and that the leader must learn to make concessions and "twist and turn through the sinuous paths of various circumstances." On the other hand, Wilson allows for a more exceptional kind of leadership that incurs the fullest measure of personal risk and that goes the distance in its effort to persuade. In terms that are very instructive about his subsequent behavior during the League controversy, Wilson wrote:

> Leadership does not always wear the harness of compromise. Once and again one of those great influences which we call a Cause arises in the midst of the nation. Men of strenuous minds and high ideals come forward with a sort of gentle majesty as champions of a political or moral

191

principle. . . . Their souls are pierced with a thousand keen arrows of obloquy. . . . They are doing nothing less than defy public opinion, and shall they convert it by blows? Yes, . . Masses come over to the side of the reform. Resistance is left to the minority and such as will not be converted are crushed.[35]

Of these two views on compromise, it is clear that Wilson regarded the second as the higher or more noble. It sets the standard. Leadership for Wilson tends to be moral leadership, and one of his legacies has been the introduction of a tone of high-mindedness into politics, even where the situation might not call for it. Politics, which usually deals with settling questions of interest, is falsely imbued with a spirit of moralism that inflates the stakes of the issues and trivializes the meaning of morality. Statesmanship is equated with moral leadership, and in this new equation prudence is discounted in favor of gestures that inspire the people.

After deciding on the kind of leadership he wanted, Wilson had to consider how it could be instituted. Given the democratic or popular character of leadership, how as a practical matter could it be distinguished from demagoguery? This question troubled Wilson deeply, as indicated by his own disclaimers of demagogic intent whenever his rhetoric even seemed to "bait" some elements of the population or express overtly populist themes. Thus in one address during the 1912 campaign, Wilson declared that "I should be ashamed of myself if I excited class feeling of any kind," and at another point he hedged, "When I say 'Bring the government back

[35] *Ibid.*, p. 49. It is worthwhile to note that the Georges, who know Wilson's essay on leadership very well, never cite this passage in their book. The omission is significant. One receives the impression from their book that Wilson's actions at the time of the League controversy flowed directly from psychological dispositions. The passage cited here, however, indicates that they might just as well have flowed from a conviction regarding the role of leadership. At the very least, the Georges might have conceded that psychological dispositions worked to produce a set of ideas which, along with the psychological dispositions themselves, became a guide for action.

to the people,' I do not mean anything demagogic."[36] Yet it is not Woodrow Wilson himself, certainly, with whom one need be concerned. His demeanor, training, and even his appearance hardly suited him to being a demagogue, at least of the vulgar sort; hardly any academic plays this role unless for the benefit of his students. The issue with any constitutional doctrine—for such was Wilson's plan for instituting leadership—is not how it applies in any single instance, least of all an instance involving its originator, but how it works over a number of cases as a general "rule of law."

Wilson once again attempted to give a theoretical explanation in his essay "Leaders of Men." "Let us fairly distinguish," he wrote, "the peculiar and delicate duties of the popular leader from the not very peculiar and delicate crimes of the demagogue." A traditional way of differentiating the two which he immediately rejects is the automatic identification of demagoguery with the kind of leadership that claims authority by virtue of representing public opinion. This conception, he argues, cuts too deeply, separating not legitimate leadership from demagoguery, but popular from nonpopular leadership. It was therefore a definition that was used to support aristocracy. Wilson declared himself prepared to engage in the "ancient and honorable pastime of abusing demagogues," but insisted that, "you must allow me to make my condemnation tally with my theory [of popular government.]"[37] Lest one think that Wilson viewed the problem lightly, it should be noted that in another context he wrote that "the most despotic of governments under the control of wise statesmen is preferable to the freest ruled by demagogues."[38]

If not by this traditional aristocratic definition, how then did Wilson propose to distinguish legitimate popular leadership from its perversion? Wilson mentioned two criteria, each of which has certain difficulties. First he cited the durability

[36] Wilson, *The New Freedom*, pp. 50-51, 57.
[37] Wilson, *Leaders of Men*, pp. 42-43.
[38] Wilson, "Cabinet Government in the United States," 1:33.

of the issue evoked. The leader appeals to the "firm and progressive thought" of the community while the demagogue plays on "the momentary and whimsical popular mood, the transitory or mistaken popular passion."[39] As a practical matter, however, it would seem difficult to know beforehand which opinions are "firm" and which "transitory." And unless Wilson was prepared to advance the extraordinary thesis that all opinions which are durable are necessarily progressive—a view which he at times comes very close to embracing, but never asserts unequivocally—this basis for distinction is insufficient. But Wilson also was reluctant to take the alternate path and distinguish "progressive thought" from "mistaken popular passion" by means of some objective criterion, for this would be to admit the existence of a standard beyond public opinion. The closest he comes to making any such substantive identification is in *The New Freedom*, when he indicates a direct connection between demagoguery and the fomentation of the poor against the rich. He goes on to suggest a rough identification of demagoguery with any act of dividing permanent economic or sociological groups within society.[40] Only those issues that divide the public on the basis of "political" beliefs resting on general conceptions of the public good would seem to be legitimate issues for a leader to evoke. (Later on, many of the old Progressives would reject Franklin Roosevelt on the grounds that his class appeals were demagogic.) Because political differences are not rooted in the social structure of the community and are thus matters on which people can be persuaded, Wilson holds out the prospect that a true leader can win a consensus, as in the case of the battle between the forces of reform or corruption or—as he later hoped—in the battle over the League.

The second criterion that Wilson suggests to distinguish

[39] Wilson, *Leaders of Men*, p. 42.

[40] Wilson, *New Freedom*, pp. 50-51, 57. See also Theodore Roosevelt's speech "The Menace of the Demagogue" in Theodore Roosevelt, *Campaigns and Controversies* (New York: Charles Scribner's Sons, 1926), pp. 258-74.

194

leadership from demagoguery turns on the question of personal intent. The demagogue is interested solely in maintaining or augmenting his personal power, while the leader, though not oblivious to such concerns, has in mind the permanent interests of the community:

> This function of interpretation, this careful exclusion of individual origination it is that makes it difficult for the impatient original mind to distinguish the popular statesman from the demagogue. The demagogue sees and seeks self-interest in an acquiescent reading of that part of the public thought upon which he depends for votes; the statesman, also reading the common inclination, also, when he reads aright, obtains the votes that keep him in power. But if you will justly observe the two, you will find the one trimming to the inclinations of the moment, the other obedient to the permanent purposes of the public mind. . . . The one ministers to himself, the other to the race. . . .[41]

But this distinction is likewise inadequate, for it does not provide a practical basis by which to identify or prevent demagoguery. Often there is no correspondence between intent and result: an issue raised with no more than the usual calculation of maintaining power may yet, because of its nature, result in the most bitter sort of division involving the deepest and basest passions. Sincerity is no guarantee of rectitude, though in politics it frequently portrays itself in that light. A second and more serious difficulty is that intent is not "visible" and therefore cannot serve as a basis for an unmistakable identification. Although people always make judgments about the character attributes of a candidate, such judgments are hardly "objective" and are strongly influenced by the candidate's stand on the issues. The champion of a cause is seldom considered by its adherents as a demagogue.

Because of these considerations, earlier theorists of the selection system thought it was necessary to go beyond intent in their search for a method to discourage dangerous

[41] Wilson, *Leaders of Men*, pp. 45-46.

leadership styles. Their approach was first to distinguish demagogic leadership by means of some concrete and "visible" standard, and second, by relying on this standard, to implement an institutional arrangement that would limit or exclude demagoguery from the process of selection. Some degree of approximation was inevitably involved in such attempts, since what could be identified and excluded necessarily encompassed both more and less than demagogic leadership. But this was understood as the price of any kind of institutional solution. For the Founders, the net was cast very broadly. Dangerous leadership was identified with popular leadership, which is to say with the attempt to raise a popular following by direct issue appeals. It is not certain whether the Founders felt that popular leadership was generally undesirable and detrimental or whether they merely believed that it could not be admitted without also admitting outright demagoguery. Whatever their exact opinion, however, the limitations they had in mind on leadership appeals were very restrictive, and perhaps too much so for a republican regime. The chief institutional check they initiated to prevent demagoguery—the electoral college system and nonpartisan competition—lost its original function, in large part because of Jefferson's successful experiment with popular leadership. The effort to prevent demagoguery then moved outside the formal Constitutional sphere. For Jefferson and Van Buren, popular leadership was admitted as long as it was tied to one of the two "natural" parties. Under the control of these parties—or perhaps, by extension, any established party— leadership was relatively safe; outside of parties, leadership was apt to be dangerous, for no check existed on the ambitions of the candidates. For Jefferson and Van Buren, accordingly, nonpartisan leadership became the visible approximation of demagoguery, and party competition became the institutional device to prevent it. Under this solution the public would accept party competition as the norm in political affairs, and parties would obtain *de facto* control over access to presidential consideration.

196

Though expressing concern for the problem of demagoguery, Wilson failed to identify it by any concrete standard. He thus broke with a long tradition that saw demagoguery as an evil that required certain institutional arrangements for its prevention. Wilson placed his reliance, as we do today, on the people, trusting all to their insight and self-restraint.

WILSON'S VIEW OF POLITICAL PARTIES:
THE RELATIONSHIP BETWEEN PARTIES AND LEADERSHIP

Advocates of the party government or responsible political party school might take exception to the view expressed here that leadership, and not party, constituted the central element of Wilson's program for political reform. Members of this school, which a short time ago included many of the leading political scientists in the field of American government, claimed Wilson as one of their own. In one sense, this is true. Wilson was the first major American figure to introduce and popularize the British model of party democracy. But it does not follow that establishing strong parties was his principal goal. On the contrary, Wilson molded his view of parties to fit his view of political leadership; the party system was the means and leadership the end. Party government advocates, by contrast, often obscure the question of whether party government is an end or a means. This follows from their frequent unwillingness to confront the central problem of who is to control the party and consequently who is to rule in the regime as a whole.[42]

[42] The most well-known proposal for establishing party government in America is found in the report of the Committee on Political Parties of the American Political Science Association, entitled "Toward a More Responsible Two Party System," *American Political Science Review*, supplement vol. 44 (September 1950). Wilson's ideas on parties are cited throughout the report. Party also is made the central facet of Wilson's thought in Austin Ranney's essay on Wilson in *The Doctrine of Responsible Party Government*.

The importance of leadership, however, has certainly not gone unnoticed. Herbert Croly emphasized this aspect of Wilson's thought

It would hardly be worth emphasizing the distinction between party and leadership if the two always reenforced each other, such that every step taken to strengthen leadership also strengthened party. But this is not the case. At certain crucial points the institutional requirements for the two concepts diverge; and when this occurs, Wilson supports what sustains leadership, though without acknowledging the damage that this does to party. Wilson favored a strong party at the governing level where it could help to carry out the president's program; at the electoral level he also claimed he wanted a strong party, though it is here that his claim was more rhetorical than real. He called candidly for the destruction of the old local party organizations based on self-interest and for the formation of a new kind of electoral organization that would form around national leaders. Yet it is difficult to see in what sense such an organization can be called a party, if by a party one has in mind Weber's minimal definition of a "group of individuals who assume the active direction of party affairs, including the formulation of programmes and the selection of candidates."[43] Wilson's "party" seems, on the

---

and the tension it created with his views on political parties. See *Progressive Democracy* (New York: Macmillan, 1914), pp. 337-46. See also Arthur S. Link's essay "Woodrow Wilson: The Philosophy, Methods and Impact of Leadership" in Arthur P. Dudden, ed., *Woodrow Wilson and the World of Today* (Philadelphia: University of Pennsylvania Press, 1957), pp. 1-22.

The question of who rules under the party government model has long been disputed in the debates on this proposal. Some critics have argued—and some proponents have conceded—that party government is only a means for establishing a plebiscitary presidential system. See Edward C. Banfield's essay "In Defense of the American Party System" in Robert A. Goldwin, ed., *Political Parties, U.S.A.* (Chicago: Rand McNally, 1961), pp. 21-29; and E. E. Schattschneider, *Party Government* (New York: Holt, Rinehart and Winston, 1942), p. 53.

[43] Max Weber, *The Theory of Social and Economic Organization*, ed. Talcott Parsons (New York: Oxford University Press, 1947), pp. 410-11.

contrary, to be a temporary organization—perhaps under a traditional party label—that is "owned" by a particular leader and that exists to promote that leader's interest. Moreover, the real basis of the leader's claim on the party rests not with his acceptance by members of the ongoing organization and not even perhaps with its traditional adherents, but with the mass of voters who take part in the primaries.

Wilson's analysis of the relationship between the existing parties and the crisis of leadership was much more complicated than that of many of his contemporaries. Unlike most late nineteenth-century reformers, Wilson refused to blame the absence of leaders entirely on the parties. Although the parties had many defects and could be considered the proximate cause of many current problems within the regime, Wilson continually stressed that the parties were a natural and even a desirable addition to the original Constitution. Parties had not, of course, been planned on by the Founders, but they were "absolutely necessary to hold things thus disconnected and dispersed [by the Constitution] together and give some coherence to the action of political forces." Wilson frequently criticized the parties for their excesses, but on reflection usually excused them from most or all of the responsibility for the regime's failings:

> The part that party has played in this country has been both necessary and beneficial, and if bosses and secret managers are often undesirable persons, playing their parts for their own benefit or glorification rather than for the public good, they are at least the natural fruits of the tree. It has borne fruit good and bad, sweet and bitter, wholesome and corrupt, but it is native to our air and practice and can be uprooted only by an entire change of system.[44]

[44] Wilson, *Constitutional Government*, pp. 206, 210. Wilson blames leaderless government on the Constitution in spite of the fact that the problem became less acute the closer one went to the Founding: "The singular leaderless structure of our government never stood fully revealed until the present generation . . ." ("Leaderless Government," 1:330). Wilson thus believed that the success of the first

Wilson was also disposed to forgive the performance of the parties during the nineteenth century on the grounds that the nation had not yet become a full national community and consequently did not require sustained national leadership. The nation, of course, had been partly and sporadically a community and therefore required an assertion of a vigorous national viewpoint on certain occasions. But it was a fragile community plagued by sectional divisions, and it was best held together throughout most of the century not by pressing too much of a "rational" perspective on the people, but rather by relying on organizations that worked on subrational and self-interested motives: "The very compulsion of selfishness has made them [i.e. parties] serviceable; the very play of self-interest has made them effective." Parties had played so important and pervasive a role that Wilson believed that there was "a sense in which our parties have been our real body politic. Not the authority of Congress, not the leadership of the 'President, but the discipline and zest of parties has held us together, has made it possible for us to form and carry out national programs."[45]

But a change was taking place in the nature of the American community. Localism, Wilson argued, was giving way to a new national focus, primarily as a result of the completion of the westward expansion and the growth of a national economy. Sensing an end to what Robert Wiebe has called "island communities," and the advent at last of a national community, Wilson called for a new political order to meet

---

generation came in some measure despite the Constitution and not because of it.

Wilson's view that the Constitutional system was at fault for causing the crisis in American government should be contrasted on the one hand with the explanation of reformers like Carl Schurz, who put the blame on parties, and on the other hand with the ideas of Herbert Croly, who contended that the problem derived from the dominance of the laissez faire ideology of Thomas Jefferson.

[45] Wilson, *Constitutional Government*, pp. 217-25; p. 220; p. 218.

the needs of modern times.[46] The reign of old-style parties now could, and should, be ended: "Party organization is no longer needed for the mere rudimentary task of holding the machinery together or giving it the sustenance of some common object. . . ."[47] It was time for power to be transferred from the parties to the formal institutions, and for party to be put in the service of political leadership. The "price" the nation had paid for its unity in the mediocrity of its presidents was now one that no longer could be afforded.

The new order that Wilson envisioned would still have need of parties, but they would perform different functions. The first objective of the new party system was to overcome the dispersal of power that existed under the Constitution. For this, party government—meaning an extrainstitutional agent binding the party in Congress to the president—was required. That a reform of parties could become a major element in the reform of the entire system of which the parties were said to be a product would seem to present a logical difficulty. But Wilson thought it resolvable on the grounds that party reform would be preceded by a wholesale change in the public's attitude about the regime. The second objective of the new party system would be the establishment of a new vehicle through which the majority could express its opinions. According to Wilson, "representative government is, indeed, only another name for government by partisan majority, and government by majorities is party government." But not any kind of majority would do. To be a genuine majority the people had to be freed from the grip and drill of the nineteenth-century parties and permitted to express themselves on current issues of concern:

> Such parties as we have, parties with worn-out principles and without definite policies, are unmitigated nuisances. They are savory with decay and rank with rottenness. . . .

[46] Robert Wiebe, *The Search for Order* (New York: Hill and Wang, 1967), p. xiii.
[47] Wilson, *Constitutional Government*, p. 220.

201

These parties must be roughly shaken out of their inso-
lence, and made to realize that they are only servants. . . .[48]

It is evident, then, that the new parties would be formed
on the basis of a division on issues or principles. The interesting fact, however, is that as a scholar Wilson made no effort
to supply the content of a new partisan division. He spoke
time and again of the need for clear choice, but never indicated what that choice should be.[49] His vigorous defense of
reform and of new political arrangements is no exception,
for Wilson never envisioned that either of these issues would
form the basis of a party division. These were matters that he
believed should be accepted by all as the basis of a new
political order, after which the partisan divisions on issues

[48] Wilson, "Committee or Cabinet Government?" 1:109-10. Wilson's assessment of the condition of parties at the time corresponds
with a recent analysis of the period by Robert Marcus in his book,
Grand Old Party (New York: Oxford University Press, 1971).
Marcus adds the point that the parties' continued adherence to worn-
out principles began to be felt by the general public in the 1880s
and led to a steady weakening of partisan attachment. The decline
in the parties' electoral strength contributed to a decline in their
moral fibre. Faced with an electorate comprised of a diminishing
number of intense partisans, the parties sought to buy with money
what they could no longer win with principle. Other party strategists,
however, saw the best response to this new situation was to field
a candidate with great personal appeal who could pull votes which
the party no longer controlled. For Marcus, this new style of personal politics was realized, at least in one possible form, in the first
truly modern campaign, run by Mark Hanna on behalf of William
McKinley in 1896. Hanna's campaign emphasized efficient, central-
ized organizational management and fund-raising, and developed a
successful "advertising" campaign which carefully cultivated an image
of solid responsibility for McKinley. Wilson, also sensing a vacuum
in the politics of the time, called for a somewhat different solution.
Parties, he claimed, could be reinvigorated by providing them with
genuine leaders and with genuine programs relevant to the immediate state of affairs.

[49] This point, which is evident from a reading of Wilson's articles,
is also made on psychological grounds by the Georges in *Woodrow
Wilson*, p. 29.

and principles might take place. Paradoxically, Wilson's true "party"—in the eighteenth-century sense of the term as a movement to change the form of government—was never acknowledged as a party, but was "hidden" behind a non-partisan movement for political reform.

Why was it that Wilson made no attempt to establish a partisan division, even on the level of policies and programs on which he proposed that partisanship should exist? Was it because he did not, until very late, hold partisan views? Or was it because he did not fully appreciate the need for a party to have an enduring principle to serve as an incentive to attract and motivate members? In each of these possible explanations there may lie some part of the truth. But there is a third explanation that Wilson himself offered and that is fully consistent with his general political thought. When Wilson analyzed the source of the absence of genuine principle in the political parties, he attributed the problem ultimately to an institutional failure and not to an intellectual failure to provide the substance of a political program. Supply leadership, Wilson argued, and principled political parties would directly follow:

> The two great parties . . . are dying for want of unifying and vitalizing principles. Without leaders they are also without policies, without aims. With leaders there must be parties. . . . Eight words contain the sum of the present degradation of our political parties: *No leaders, no principles; no principles, no parties.*

To establish the principles before the parties, Wilson implied, would be to reverse the way in which matters should work; party exists for the sake of leadership and not for the sake of party. "Among a free people there can be no other method of government than such as permits an undictated choice of leaders and a strong, unhampered making up of bodies of active men to give them effective support."[50]

[50] Wilson, "Cabinet Government in the United States," 1:36-37; "Leaderless Government," 1:399.

It is evident that Wilson's perspective on party and leadership differed completely from the traditional nineteenth-century view. According to Van Buren, party principle exists "prior" to political leadership and is designed to circumscribe leadership appeals within safe limits. Political leadership is restricted in its function to reiterating partisan principles and applying them to changing circumstances. The task of formulating party principles is a quasi-constitutional act, undertaken only occasionally and with the object of setting the boundaries of political conflict for the ensuing era.

Wilson no doubt could have proceeded by supplying new partisan principles to fill the void of the irrelevant old ones, thus changing the substance of the partisan division but maintaining the traditional role of political leadership. But his objective was different. He sought to institute a constitutional change under which political leadership would have the prerogative of formulating new principles and reshaping the broad outlines of electoral division at each election. The nation needed continual renewal or rejuvenation, and the selection system for Wilson was the institution that would help initiate it. Like Jefferson, Wilson asked for change in the system to keep pace with improvement (or growth). But while Jefferson remained wary of national elections and popular leadership, Wilson had great confidence in them.

The fact that Wilson's major objective was to strengthen leadership and not parties makes one wonder about his final attitude toward partisanship. Leadership needs party in the sense of a "body of active men to give support," but it does not require traditional partisan divisions. Indeed, in the last analysis, leadership for Wilson is not a partisan concept at all, but transcends party and exists for the nation as a whole. The full identification with a political party thus becomes a hindrance, because the party label is still laden with past meanings. The problem with the nomination of any "mere partisan representative," Wilson felt, is that such a person is regarded immediately as a spokesman for a part and not the whole, and thus cannot unify the nation. The nation, however, "craves" such unity, which again may help explain why Wilson never set forth the basis for a permanent partisan division. A new program expressed by a party through its leader could become the basis of a national consensus:

> Its [the nation's] instinct is for unified action, and it craves a single leader. It is for this reason that it will often prefer to choose a man rather than a party . . . He [the presidential candidate] may stand, if he will, a little outside party and insist as if it were upon the general opinion. It is with the instinctive feeling that it is upon occasion such a man that the country wants that the nominating conventions will often nominate men who are not their acknowledged leaders, but only such men as the country would like to see lead both its parties.[51]

Wilson at first thought that this "nonpartisan" dimension to the selection of leaders could be accomplished within the forms of the traditional partisan institutions of selection: the delegates to the convention, aware of the nation's needs, would on their own look beyond the "mere partisan leader" and choose the individual best suited for national leadership. But in 1912 Wilson gave up on this idea and proposed abandoning the convention system as the mode of nomination in favor of the national primary. This shift, it seems clear, was designated to wrest control of nominations not only from the selfish bosses but from traditional partisans as well. Under a national primary system the individual leaders could appeal over the heads of party intermediaries directly to the people, whose instinct was understood to be unitary or nonpartisan. Whether Wilson, in adopting this proposal, realized what its full implications would be for the party as an electoral organization is not clear. But his suggestions of nonpartisanship certainly make one think that, at the electoral level at least, he was willing to go the limit to attain "freedom" for the individual leader. It is at this point that Wilson seems to part company with members of the party-government school that

[51] Wilson, *Constitutional Government*, pp. 68-69.

205

he helped to found, for while many of these persons favor strong executive leadership, they have always felt obliged by their original premises to proclaim the continual need for permanent partisan divisions.

For all his attacks on the Founders, Wilson had apparently imbibed much of the form, if not the substance, of their position. Wilson wanted to put the president above partisanship, and relied first on the convention delegates and later on the national primary to accomplish this goal. One or the other of these was to provide the executive with a kind of independence or elevation analogous to that which the Founders had sought through their own proposed nonpartisan electoral system. It is highly doubtful, however, that the Founders would have approved of Wilson's ideas or even thought them likely to accomplish his own objectives. To the Founders, whose nonpartisan system was based on excluding popular leadership, opening the system to this kind of leadership would risk the creation of bitter divisions within the electorate, not to mention a gradual loss of the discretion needed for the exercise of statesmanship. It may well be that by elevating leadership at the expense of traditional parties, as Wilson wanted, partisanship as we have known it can be destroyed. Indeed, according to certain "end of party" theorists, such as Walter Dean Burnham and Gerald Pomper, the evidence for this conclusion is already nearly at hand.[52] But these scholars give no indication that the result is likely to be the kind of unitary nonpartisanship that Wilson favored. The results of a modern system of candidate oriented parties may not be known for some time, but if past experience can serve as a guide, there is reason to believe that a popular nonpartisan system will risk the dangers of "image" appeals and increased divisions among different political groups,

---

[52] See Walter Dean Burnham's essay "American Politics in the 1970's" in *The American Party System*, 2nd ed., ed. William Nisbet Chambers and Walter Dean Burnham (New York: Oxford University Press, 1975), pp. 308-40; and Gerald Pomper, *Voters' Choice* (New York: Dodd Mead, 1975), pp. 38-40.

exacerbated if not created by leaders operating under no restraints; and if parties do ultimately collapse, the old problem of how to keep the presidential election from the hazards of a House selection would again be reopened.

THE PROBLEM OF AMBITION AND THE RELATIONSHIP OF THE SELECTION SYSTEM TO THE CHARACTER OF THE EXECUTIVE

Like Hamilton, Wilson conceived of the selection problem in very broad terms and held that the quality of the person chosen was determined not solely by the machinery of the selection process but by the arrangement of public offices as well. To attract the best men into politics, Wilson argued that it was necessary to have offices of great power and visible authority:

> Government forms will call to the work of administration able minds and strong hearts constantly or infrequently, according as they do or do not afford them at all times an opportunity of gaining and retaining a commanding authority and an undisputed leadership in the nation's councils.[53]

In his early writing Wilson stressed this aspect of the selection question to the exclusion of all others. The low state of the presidential office, rather than any defect in the mechanism of choosing its occupant, accounted for the poor quality of our candidates. "I am disposed to think," he wrote in *Congressional Government*, "that the decline in the character of the Presidents is not the cause, but only the accompanying manifestation of the declining prestige of the Presidential office."[54]

While the necessity of having a powerful office to attract the ablest men suggested certain problems to Hamilton, to Wilson it seemed to present no special difficulties. Hamilton

[53] Wilson, "Cabinet Government in the United States," 1:35.
[54] Wilson, *Congressional Government*, p. 43.

207

reasoned that if politicians sought recognition and honors, one could assume that they were dominated by a powerful ambition that needed both channeling and checking. For Wilson, on the other hand, the assumption is implicitly made that those with the "strong hearts" also have good character. Ambition is not so vigorous or dangerous a force as it had appeared to the Founders. It was not that Wilson was entirely unconcerned with the possibility of dangerous men winning power. When he was pushing his cabinet government idea, he outlined the following means by which dangerous men might be discovered:

> Thorough debate can unmask the most plausible pretender. The leaders of a great legislative assembly must daily show of what mettle they are. . . . Rhetorical adroitness, dialectical dexterity, even passionate declamation, cannot shield them from the scrutiny to which their movements will be subjected at every turn of the daily proceedings. The air is too open for either stupidity or indirection to thrive. Charlatans cannot long play statesmen successfully when the whole country is sitting as critic.[55]

He may have felt that this same process would work under a national primary, as some proponents of the present plebiscitary system now argue. Yet what is characteristic of Wilson's approach in the final analysis is the abandonment of all institutional devices and a reliance on both the self-restraint of the leaders and the wisdom of the people. Not perceiving the same passions or dangers in politics as the Founders, Wilson was much more trusting of political authority, so long as it was democratic. This, of course, helps explain the ease with which Wilson and his followers in the party-government

---

[55] Wilson, "Cabinet Government in the United States," 1:37; "Committee on Cabinet Government." For a similar view, adopted to the process of presidential primaries, see Stephen Hess, *The Presidential Campaign* (Washington, D.C.: Brookings Institution, 1975), pp. 37-42 and 114.

school could dismiss separation of powers and checks and balances.[56]

As Wilson turned from the problem of how to implement cabinet government in America to the problem of how to strengthen the executive, his initial position, which attributed the low quality of candidates entirely to the character of the office, gave way to a more comprehensive view. The lack of power in the office was at fault, but so, too, was the selection process. Candidates were chosen "by the management of obscure men and through the uncertain chances of an ephemeral convention which has no other part in politics." Where convention selection was not the product of manipulation, it was the result of confusion—of the "unpremeditated compromises or the sudden impulses of huge conventions."[57] Because of their search for "available" candidates—candidates who had done nothing offensive (or spectacular) and who happened to practice politics in a large, highly contested state—the conventions often chose men who were little known to the country and who lacked the support and respect of the members of Congress. That a candidate of this sort might find it difficult to lead was a matter of little concern to the party conventions; the power brokers who dominated the conventions were interested in selecting a successful candidate, not in choosing a good president.

[56] One finds the best statement of this view by a modern student in James MacGregor Burns' *The Deadlock of Democracy* (Englewood Cliffs, N.J.: Prentice-Hall, 1963). Burns writes (p. 6):

We have become too much entranced by the Madisonian model of government. . . . this is also the system of checks and balances and interlocked gears of government that requires the consensus of many groups and leaders before the nation can act. . . . In glorifying the Madisonian model we . . . have underestimated the powerful balances and safeguards that are built into a system of majority rule and responsible parties. We have thwarted and fragmentized leadership instead of allowing it free play within the boundaries of the democracies process.

[57] Wilson, "Mr. Cleveland's Cabinet," 1:218; "Leaderless Government," 1:346.

Nor did the independence of presidential candidates from Congress under this system enhance the power of the president. As evanescent and unpopular bodies, the conventions could add no weight to a candidate's claim to being a national leader; in fact, the unpopular overtones of the conventions tended to cancel out whatever gains came from the final election. In terms of promoting leadership in the presidency, Wilson even thought that the old caucus system was superior to the existing system, in that it at least guaranteed the president a measure of confidence in the legislature.[58] Although one might wish to dispute Wilson's interpretation of the effects of the caucus, his general point about the relationship between selection and presidential power bears consideration. The weakness of the presidency—at least as measured by Wilson's standards—was not solved by freeing presidential nominations from the grip of the congressional caucus or by introducing democratic choice into the final election. Even after these two conditions were met, the presidency following the Civil War showed many of the same weaknesses as the presidency of the one-party caucus era (1812-28). According to Wilson, the only solution was to provide the candidates with a source of independence and strength in the nomination process to go along with the power and independence generated by the final election. Having the nomina-

---

[58] Wilson, "Leaderless Government," 1:343-46. Wilson also wrote ". . . in rejecting that system [congressional selection] to pass to the use of nominating conventions we certainly render it impossible— or, at any rate, in the highest degree unlikely—that our presidents should ever be leaders again" (1:344).

Note that Wilson sought to reinstitute part of the idea of the caucus system in his direct primary proposal: after the nominee was selected, a convention to write the party platform would be held consisting "not of delegates chosen for this single purpose, but of the nominees for Congress, the nominees for vacant seats in the Senate . . . and the candidates for the presidency themselves, in order that platforms may be framed by those responsible to the people for carrying them into effect." State of the Union Message, December 2, 1913 in Fred Israel, ed., *The State of the Union Messages of the President*, 3 vols. (New York: Chelsea House, 1967), 1:2548.

tions decided by the people would assure that the candidates would be in a position to proclaim that they were "in most direct communication with the nation" and that the winner, as the nation's acclaimed spokesman, could not be denied the leadership of either his party or the Congress.[59]

WILSON'S INFLUENCE ON PRESIDENTIAL SELECTION

Wilson influenced the development of presidential selection by promoting the view that popular leadership is the only legitimate basis on which to solicit power, and that all restrictions and constraints upon it should be removed. This view has been gaining ground since the beginning of the century. It supplied a large part of the impetus for the Progressive movement and for the recent reform movement that followed the 1968 presidential election. Before analyzing the development of selection in this century, it may be helpful to recall the basic assumptions underlying this view. First is the idea that a "closed" system of nomination controlled by a party organization is an evil—certainly a political evil and perhaps a moral evil as well. Second is the belief that the people on their own can fully be trusted to choose leaders without the guidance of restrictive electoral institutions. And finally there is the view that no serious side effects flow from an open pursuit of the nomination, that self-interest and ambition, if they exist, do not lead aspirants to divide and inflame the populace.

In these last two assumptions one finds a new optimism toward national elections. Earlier "legislators" of the selection process looked upon elections as problematic. When considering the two basic issues of institution-building—how to prevent evils and how to promote benefits—they placed their emphasis at least as much on the first as on the second. For both the Founding Fathers and the founders of permanent political parties, there was a deliberate concern for the pernicious effects of unchecked ambition, particularly as

[59] Wilson, *Constitutional Government*, pp. 108-9.

it might be expressed in dangerous popular appeals. To Wilson such concerns seemed unwarranted. National elections could be looked on as "positive" events. For the burden he asked them to bear, his optimism was perhaps necessary. Elections were entrusted not simply with the responsibility of determining national policy, but also with the task of choosing a president who would possess the full scope of political power. Under Wilson's conception of constitutional government a statesman must always be at the helm, or the system would fail.

CHAPTER V

The Development of
the Presidential Selection System
in the Twentieth Century

THE history of presidential selection in this century can best be viewed as a struggle between two different models of the national electoral process, one having its origin in the views of Martin Van Buren and the other in the thought of Woodrow Wilson and the Progressives. Each model consists of a particular nominating arrangement, a theory of the role of political parties, and a general shape or pattern of electoral behavior. These three elements are related as parts of a whole "system," such that a change in any one element is likely to produce a change in the other two. As an "output," each system promotes a certain kind of presidential candidacy, which in turn reacts on the political regime as a whole, influencing the nature of the authority of the executive and the character of presidential leadership.

Van Buren's conception of the electoral process, which will be referred to as the party-dominance model, has the following characteristics: nomination by "regulars" of the party organizations, a favorable attitude within the populace toward political parties, and a strong partisan identification among the voters rooted in a combination of affective attachment to their party and a commitment to its general principles.[1] Under this model candidates pursue the nomi-

---

[1] The best account of voter attitudes toward parties may be found in the sample of statements by the voters given in Campbell, Converse, Miller, and Stokes, *The American Voter* (New York: John Wiley and Sons, 1964), pp. 129-55. It is the concern of the authors here to show the level of ideological awareness within the electorate. But what comes through most clearly from a reading of the statements themselves is that most of the voters have an affective attach-

nation by an inside strategy of negotiation with party leaders; open popular appeals are discouraged until after the nominations and are then largely contained by traditional party principles. The type of candidate that is favored is either a "politician" possessing the skill of brokering among elements of a diverse coalition, or a politically neutral but personally illustrious figure under whose auspices the process of accommodation can take place.

The Progressive idea, to be referred to alternatively as the candidate-supremacy or plebiscitary model, is characterized by: nomination by interested amateurs or by the rank-and-file through primaries, an ambivalent attitude in the electorate toward parties (with a special concern about party organizations), and a "responsive" electorate concerned with current issues and open to continual political change.[2] Aspirants solicit the nomination under this model by an outside strategy of direct popular appeal. In the final election campaign the party forms itself around the nominee, adopting his vision as the party's program. Under this model candidates may aspire to achieve a consensus victory in which the triumphant candidate's personal constituency transcends traditional party lines and includes strong backing from all segments of the population. In the Wilsonian version of this model the type of candidacy favored is one which emphasizes popular statesmanship—high-minded appeals by a per-

---

ment to one or another of the parties based on their acceptance of a certain principle of justice, e.g. the Democrats are the party "concerned with all the people," while the Republicans "stand for big business, at the expense of the farmer and the working man" (pp. 133-34). If one begins with the view that the vote is an expression of a certain principle of justice, connected with particular issues when they are salient, then there is no reason to be disappointed with the level of opinions found in this survey. It is only when one judges voting by the standard of ideological sophistication that the voter fails to live up to some mythical ideal of the perfect citizen.

[2] The picture of the "responsive" voter is drawn most clearly by Gerald Pomper in the *Voters' Choice* (New York: Dodd Mead, 1975), pp. 31-35.

son of great reknown and accomplishment. In the modern party reform version, to the extent a distinct theory exists, the Wilsonian ideal is scaled down and transformed into the idea of a candidacy based on "issue advocacy"—a willingness to take stands on the "hard" issues of the day and to make issue positions the focus of the campaign. These conceptions of leadership represent, of course, the theoretical ideals of their respective proponents, and it remains to be seen if their institutional arrangements actually promote these results.

The struggle between these two models has passed through three identifiable phases in this century. In the first phase, dating from the election of 1912 through the election of 1920, the idea of candidate supremacy was introduced into an electoral system that had been based since Van Buren's time on the party dominance model. The new theory won wide public support and gained ground in the form of state primary laws for the selection of national convention delegates. For a time it appeared as if the candidate-supremacy model might fully replace the older system. But the primary movement lost momentum and by 1920 a resurgence of the power of party organizations began to take place. In the second phase, lasting from the 1920s until the 1960s, the selection system included elements of both models and has therefore been referred to as a mixed system. In certain respects, as will be seen, the "mix" became a "blend" and won support for its own distinctive properties; in most respects, however, it remained a combination of two competing and conflicting systems, each maintaining its own identifiable characteristics. During this period there were marginal shifts in the influence of these two systems, but neither had the strength or support to displace the other. The third phase can be dated from the mid 1960s when the balance that existed between these two systems began to break down. By the election of 1972 the selection process had been transformed into what is essentially a plebiscitary system. This transformation was a result first of a shift in the dominant

215

motivation for organizational participation from a professional to an amateur orientation and second of a large increase in the number of presidential primaries. Both of these
changes were related, though in a complex way, to the reform movement that began within the Democratic Party.

This chapter will survey the three phases outlined above
with a view to showing how the prevailing system in each
phase structures the ambition of presidential aspirants. This
approach abstracts to some extent from the empirical data,
as the attempt is to isolate the influence of the institutional
arrangements. It is understood, of course, that any particular outcome is the result not only of institutional factors, but
of political factors as well, i.e. of the particular personalities
and issues involved in each race. But since these political
factors may be considered largely "accidental" or uncontrollable, they will not be treated in a systematic fashion.
The attempt, then, is not to develop a comprehensive theory
that explains all nomination outcomes, but only to indicate
the tendency of the selection system.[3] Finally, it needs to be

[3] Whether it is possible to integrate all the factors that influence
nomination politics into a general theory of presidential selection
remains an open question. The most recent attempt at such a theory
—or at least of a full typology—is contained in William Keech and
Donald Matthews' book, *The Party's Choice* (Washington, D.C.:
Brookings Institution, 1975). These authors attempt to "explain"
nomination outcomes largely in terms of the different situations that
exist among the aspirants at the commencement of each campaign,
e.g. the circumstances in which an incumbent is running or in which
a clear early front-runner exists, etc. Many interesting observations
are generated from this approach. But it suffers from a failure to
acknowledge, at least in its theoretical argument, the importance
of the effect the institutional arrangements have on the outcome in
each situation. The authors speak, for example, of the "modesty of
the impact of presidential primaries on the competitive situation"
(p. 114), a conclusion which obviously cannot do justice to the events
of the past two elections. The authors' conclusion is probably a valid
assessment of the role of primaries under the mixed system; but
with a change in the system itself, different influences come into play
and what tended to occur in a given situation under one system may
no longer tend to occur under another.

pointed out that the material in this chapter overlaps in part with the subject of the next chapter, which treats the objectives of the recent reform movement. This organizational scheme has been adopted for the sake of continuity in presenting the effects of each selection system, though it reverses the usual order we have followed of discussing theory before practice.

THE RISE OF CANDIDATE SUPREMACY (1912-1920)

The introduction of presidential primaries in 1912 provides a good "test" for one of the central theses of this study, namely that the development of the selection process has been strongly influenced by deliberate attempts to "legislate" its character with a view to long-range institutional effects. The influence of deliberate legislation, we have said, has been greater at some periods than others. But overall it has been argued that beginning with rational theories of the selection process provides the best starting point for understanding political development. Even where practice deviates from theory, an approach that begins from theory can be useful. One can point out the areas in which legislators were unclear about their own objectives, which may then help explain why the institution developed in ways they did not foresee; or, one can indicate the areas in which legislators may have known what they wanted but failed to understand or implement the institutional arrangements that would promote their own objectives. In both of these cases, the assumption is not that theory directly governs practice, but that an approach that begins from theory may be most helpful in understanding practice.

The alternative to this thesis is that the development of the selection system is explained by certain nonrational forces, such as changes in communications technology, basic swings in the attitudes of the mass electorate unrelated to theories of selection, or calculations of politicians regarding some immediate political advantage. (The last two, of course, may

217

be rational actions in one sense, but not with respect to long-term institutional development.) There is no question that these factors have often played an important and in some instances a decisive role. But the general thesis here is that they are usually of secondary importance and can be used to explain aspects of the development of each system but not the origination of the system itself.

The introduction of the candidate-supremacy model during the Progressive era seems on first glance to confirm the general thesis that theory was the decisive factor in shaping practice. The Progressives pressed for a new institutional arrangement on the basis of their commitment to a set of principles, and they succeeded, at least in part, in transforming the selection system along the lines they desired.[4] To be sure, they fell far short of obtaining all the institutional changes they sought, and even where they were successful their institutions did not always produce the consequences they wanted. But neither of these points contradicts the validity of the approach that begins from a treatment of theoretical ideas.

Against this apparent control of practice by theory, proponents of the "nonrational" school of political development might offer two objections. The first would hold that the decisive factor that led to the Progressive changes was the attempt of certain politicians to gain political advantage, specifically, the search by Progressives within the Republican Party in 1912 to find some method that would give the

---

[4] Speaking of the Progressives as if they had a single set of objectives is obviously an oversimplification. In fact, as many have shown, people with very different persuasions and goals adopted the label of Progressivism and espoused various progressive reforms. See for example Walter Dean Burnham's account of the undemocratic objectives of certain elements of the Progressive movement, *Critical Elections and the Mainsprings of American Politics* (New York: W. W. Norton, 1970), pp. 77-81. What is being referred to in the text is the dominant tendency of the National Progressive Movement, especially as expressed by its leading spokesmen such as La-Follette, Roosevelt, and Wilson.

nomination to LaFollette or Roosevelt. Certainly, it cannot be denied that without the "energy" provided by this attempt to secure a political advantage, no transformation of the selection process would have taken place. But it is equally certain that without the general Progressive theories already in existence, this attempt would never have met with any success. The order of causality, then, is best described as follows: ideas were responsible for the overall strategy and for giving it a justification of legitimacy; the search for political advantage then provided the immediate force for its enactment.

The second objection is more significant. It holds that the transformation of the Progressives was in a sense prepared for by a basic change in the attitude of the people toward parties that began in the 1880s. This objection has never been directly stated in these terms, but it is implicitly the thesis of two important books on late nineteenth-century politics: Robert Marcus's *Grand Old Party* and Richard Jensen's *The Winning of the Midwest*.[5] According to both these authors, the strength of partisan commitment began to diminish in the Guilded Age as a result first of a growing belief within the electorate that the principles of the major parties, which derived from the Civil War, were no longer relevant, and second of a change in the communications network from one characterized primarily by partisan newspapers to one based on nonpartisan newspapers and magazines. In response to these changes, which loosened the ties of many voters to the old parties and left a large "floating" element within the electorate, party leaders were forced to give greater weight in their nomination decisions to the popularity of individual candidates and to current issue constituencies. The archetype of the new campaign was the McKinley candidacy of 1896, which relied extensively on image techniques and mass persuasion. It follows from this analysis

[5] Robert Marcus, *Grand Old Party* (New York: Oxford University Press, 1971), p. 3; Richard Jensen, *The Winning of the Midwest* (Chicago: University of Chicago Press, 1971), pp. 269-308.

that even if the Progressive reforms had never taken place, there would have been some important changes in the character of the nominating process, if not in its formal institutional arrangement then at least in the norms that guided the participants. But even if one grants that a new equilibrium in the selection process would have evolved in which candidate personality and current issues played a greater role, it would still have been very different from the model of candidate supremacy and electoral responsiveness favored by many of the Progressives. While the evolution spoken of by Marcus and Jensen may have helped to facilitate the acceptance of the Progressives' reforms, the fact remains that in 1912 the Progressives were still reacting against what they considered to be the overwhelming strength of political parties. It was in their deliberate attempt to overthrow the "tyranny" of parties and create a new electoral system that the theoretical and institutional foundations of the candidate-supremacy model were established.

The use of presidential primaries on a significant scale began with the election of 1912. Fourteen states held primaries in that election and nine more added primary laws by 1916. After some additions and deletions, the number of primaries in 1920 stood at twenty-one. States adopted primaries for different reasons, with local considerations playing a prominent role. But national Progressive ideas provided the proponents of primaries with their basic arguments and claim to legitimacy. Indeed, the reform that best illustrates the theoretical design of the Progressives was the national primary, which was endorsed in the Progressive Party platform of 1912 and by President Wilson in an address to the Congress in 1913. This plan made little headway, and the Progressive forces had to turn their attention exclusively to the individual states. Yet the objective of the state primary movement remained national in scope. The plan was to transform the delegate selection process into what in effect would be a national party plebiscite in which the people would choose the nominee. Convention delegates would become agents of the voters' will at the nominating stage, much as the electors had once been transformed into agents of the people's choice at the final election stage. If enough of the delegates were chosen by the primary method, the convention would be changed from its earlier role as a deliberative body to a body that merely tallied the popular votes. Only in the event that none of the candidates won enough delegates in the primaries to secure the nomination would the convention recapture its deliberative role, and even then some proposed that its choice be restricted to the top two or three vote getters.

In order for the new system to produce the kind of candidacy sought by many of the Progressive theorists, namely an outside campaign in which the candidates would take their case directly to the people, a large percentage of delegates, probably well over the number needed for the nomination, would have to be chosen in the primaries. Unless this number was obtained, the party organizations would continue to maintain control and candidates would have to tailor their outside strategies to fit the requirements of their inside strategies. Since a major advantage of the pure outside strategy was supposed to be its effect in freeing the candidates from the deals and compromises of an inside strategy, a mix between the two systems in which the party organizations were dominant offered only a partial prospect for improvement. Moreover, anything less than a full reliance on outside strategies by the candidates would tend to lessen the demand for primaries. Without the candidates "going to the people," the voters would lose interest in the primaries, and state legislators could legitimately question whether they should be maintained. Accordingly, it was necessary to reach a certain "critical mass" of delegates selected through primaries, or else the movement would lose impetus. As Louise Overacker wrote in 1926: "The effectiveness of the presidential primary as at present in operation is limited . . . most of all by the fact that it is in use in less than half of the states."[6]

The "critical mass" in the Democratic Party at this time was very high because of the party rule requiring a two-thirds majority to choose a nominee. The percentage of delegates selected in primaries—around forty percent in 1912, sixty-five percent in 1916, and fifty-five percent in 1920—fell far short of what a candidate needed for nomination in the Democratic Party. This was an important reason that discouraged full-scale outside campaigns in the Democratic races of 1912 and 1920. The only outside campaign in these two hotly contested races was Attorney General Mitchell Palmer's brief attempt to build a popular constituency on the "Red Scare" issue in 1920. As long as the two-thirds rule remained in effect, there was little point in making a full-scale assault on the nomination by an outside strategy, and especially one that might upset the established party leaders. It was not until the abolition of this rule in 1936 that a predominantly outside strategy could have much chance of success, and the first such actual attempt awaited until 1952 when a Democratic incumbent was finally vulnerable.

On the Republican side, the situation was very different. With a simple majority required for nomination, the importance of the primary component was much greater. In 1912, the primaries could not yet supply enough delegates for a majority, but they could provide a very substantial bloc. It was the strategy first of Robert LaFollette and later of Teddy Roosevelt to win all or nearly all the primaries, thereby capturing most of the delegates needed for the nomination and impressing enough of the regulars to carry the day. The strategy failed. LaFollette, bitter at being replaced by Roosevelt, refused to throw his support to his fellow Progressive, thus dividing the primary contingent; and Taft's support in the nonprimary states remained firm. But

[6] Louise Overacker, *The Presidential Primary* (New York: Macmillan, 1926), p. 126.

222

what is significant from the point of view of the impact of the institutional arrangements on candidate behavior is that both LaFollette and Roosevelt pursued pure outside strategies and even forced the incumbent to take to the campaign trail. In 1916, the delegates selected in primary states numbered more than a majority. But in this election none of the active candidates was strong enough to run an extensive national campaign. Senator Cummins pursued a half-hearted outside strategy in which he avoided most of the states where a strong favorite son was on the ballot. The nomination went to Justice Hughes, who never campaigned or formally entered any of the primaries, although he was aided by a victory on a write-in campaign in Oregon. In 1920, two Republican contenders again paid close attention to the primaries. Hiram Johnson took to the stump in a vigorous outside campaign, while General Wood, though not campaigning in person, entered most of the primaries and spent lavishly to promote his candidacy. Already in this campaign, however, the selection of the delegates in primary states was often divorced from the race among the national candidates. This change from a national candidate orientation in primaries to the *de facto* dominance of the party organizations signaled a decline in the importance of the primary component and began the shift to the mixed system.

Although none of the candidates following an outside strategy won the nomination in the period of 1912 to 1920, the experience with the outside campaigns is worth considering. The demagogic appeal of the Palmer campaign, although it never caught fire, indicated the manner in which some candidates might make use of their new freedom, while the Republican campaign of 1912 showed the potential threat to party unity that the new system could create. (Some struggle within the Republican Party was undoubtedly inevitable in 1912, though it is significant that the party was only able to be put back together in 1916 by a nomination that was "brokered" by party leaders.) The introduction of

223

the primaries was also marked, surprisingly enough, by widespread complaints about the system's inequities. More surprising still is that one of the leading critics was Robert LaFollette, widely known as the father of the primary movement. And while one should be wary of accepting at face value the comments of a disappointed loser, it is fitting in this instance to hear out the complaints of the father on the topic of his first offspring, the Republican nomination campaign of 1912.

LaFollette's first criticism focused on the organizational advantage Roosevelt possessed, an advantage he attributed to the greater amount of money that Roosevelt had at his disposal. LaFollette charged that Roosevelt obtained this money by "selling out" to special interests:

> Contributions from men with these connections [e.g. Perkins of United States Steel] would account, in part, for the character of campaign which Roosevelt carried on for months, the lavish expenditures of which were proof of unlimited sources of supply. Headquarters were established east and west, north and south, and an army of men employed and put in the field.

Next LaFollette pointed out the advantages of Roosevelt's name and the ease with which he established a personal appeal that co-opted but was not entirely true to Progressive ideals:

> Progressive principles were lost sight of in his campaign. For definitive issues and purpose there was substituted a standard of personal loyalty to him. . . . Into this [the Progressive] movement, when it gave promise of national success, Roosevelt projected his ambition to be President a third time.

Finally, LaFollette struck out at the unprincipled character of Roosevelt's campaign, its lack of concern with consistency, and especially its low-level appeals: "It had . . . the out-

224

ward seeming of success—the sort of success that intoxicates the crowd."[7]

What is striking about LaFollette's complaints is the extent to which they echo Van Buren's criticisms of a nonpartisan electoral process. Nor should this come as a surprise. The primary system is, in effect, a nonpartisan election at the nomination stage. As such it is bound to present many of the same characteristics identified by Van Buren for nonpartisan elections: personal factions, undesirable forms of popular leadership, and alleged inequities deriving from differentials in the potential to organize, including an unequal access to money. Van Buren's solution to these problems in the case of the final election was permanent organizations. But this solution, apart from the fact that it does not seem applicable to the nomination stage, would directly contradict the antiorganization purpose for which the primary system had been instituted. Not being able to solve these difficulties by any kind of organizational plan, LaFollette focused his attention (as modern reformers do) on the one problem that can be remedied by legislation: inequities in campaign financing. Aside from the question of whether legislation in this area might not create more difficulties than it solves, the larger point remains that control over financing does not affect all, or even the most serious, problems of the plebiscitary system.

By the end of this period, one can perhaps speak of certain lessons that the candidates and the organizational regulars had learned from the new institutional arrangements. The candidates, seeing that the number of delegates selected in primaries fell well short of the "critical mass" intended by the Progressives, would now have to think twice before undertaking a pure outside strategy. Serious contenders would have to concern themselves with how an outside campaign, in the event one was used, would affect the attitudes of the

[7] Robert LaFollette, *Autobiography* (Madison: Robert M. La-Follette Company, 1913), pp. 636, 640, 644.

organizational regulars. On the other hand, there is probably something to the account of the Hughes Commission that the regulars now felt something of a check on their discretion:

> . . . [popular] preferences could be disregarded by the party at the party's peril. [After 1912] Conventions were ill-disposed to disregard the mandate expressed by primary contests, at least where the primaries produced a mandate that could be interpreted with clarity. Party managers indeed welcomed the primaries as a proving ground which provided them with a much more adequate guide than their own hunches as to who would make an appealing candidate in the November election.[8]

Although it is doubtful that the regulars actually welcomed the primaries, they may well have learned to appreciate the hazards involved in passing over a demonstrated popular figure. But even in the case the Hughes Commission mentions—the Republican selection process of 1912—one wonders whether the regulars were not taught their lesson more by Roosevelt's third-party candidacy than by his string of primary victories. The "closed" parties of the old system, after all, had always operated under the check imposed by a threatened or actual bolt of one of its factions. Far from showing the inflexibility of the old system, it could be argued that the selection process in 1912 and 1916 demonstrated the kind of responsiveness of which this system was capable. Closed parties in conjunction with an open electoral system, i.e. open to third parties, constituted the traditional solution to the need for periodic political change. The advantage in practice enjoyed by the major parties introduced a bias against change, but the possibility of a challenge by a third party could pressure them to make changes when the demand was great enough. It was the operation of this traditional system more than the new primary system that led to the

[8] *Report of the Commission on the Democratic Selection of Nominees* reprinted in the *Congressional Record*, vol. 114, 90th Congress, 2nd Session.

compromise candidacy of Justice Hughes in 1916, which represented just about the degree of change to which the Republicans were committed in that year.[9]

THE MIXED SYSTEM (1920s-1960s)

With the decline of Progressive idealism following the War and the settling of the great schism within the Republican Party, the impetus for more primaries began to subside. Perhaps, too, the failure of any candidate following an outside strategy to win the nomination dampened support for the new system. The return to normalcy, at any rate, brought a return to power of the party organizations. The retrenchment in the primary movement assumed three different forms: the outright repeal of primary laws as occurred in Iowa (1917), Minnesota (1917), Vermont (1921), Montana (1923), North Carolina (1927), Indiana (1929), Michigan (1931), and North Dakota (1935); the insulation of primaries from a national focus, sometimes by tradition and sometimes with the assistance of legal provisions that barred delegates from specifying on the ballot which presidential candidate they preferred, as occurred in Pennsylvania, West Virginia, New York, and Illinois; and finally, the development of a tradition of favorite son candidacies, which took place in California and Ohio. As compared with the period of 1912-20, the era of the mixed system had fewer primaries; and of those which existed, more were isolated in practice from the influence of national candidates.

The complex laws and traditions in the various states need not concern us here. It is enough to say that while somewhere between forty and fifty percent of the delegates in each party were chosen in primaries, the actual percentage that any national candidate could hope to win was considerably less. The primary system had to a very substantial degree become "denationalized" and taken over by local party leaders. This

---

[9] See James Sundquist, *Dynamics of the Party System* (Washington, D.C.: Brookings Institution, 1973), pp. 165-66.

result is illustrated best by the Kefauver campaign of 1952. In the twelve primary states that Kefauver won, he managed to obtain only fifty percent of their delegate support on the second ballot.[10] (The sum total of his votes from these states was 203, less than one-third of the number required for the nomination.) While in certain instances Kefauver was himself to blame for a lack of careful planning, the chief obstacle to his winning delegate support lay in the various state laws and traditions that made it difficult and sometimes impossible for a candidate to convert a primary victory into delegate votes.

The legal situation throughout the period from 1924 to 1964 remained relatively stable. Yet because this legal situation itself reflected two competing theories of selection, no single method of soliciting the nomination emerged. The mixed system was in reality less a distinctive system in its own right than a compromise between two different systems. Some aspirants, such as Stassen in 1948 and Kefauver in 1952 and 1956, relied chiefly on an aggressive outside strategy, hoping that they could win every crucial race and force themselves on the hostile regulars. Others, such as Stevenson in 1952, Johnson in 1960, and Humphrey as late as 1968, pursued a completely inside strategy, avoiding the primaries and working through the party leaders. In some measure, however, the system with its two conflicting elements pointed to a "mixed" campaign in which the candidate would pursue simultaneously an outside strategy to demonstrate popular support (and win some delegates) and an inside strategy to capture the bulk of the delegates needed for victory. This general type of candidacy, called by Hugh Heclo an "entrepreneurial" style, required a candidate who ideally could both project a strong public image and bargain with local organization leaders.[11] The campaigns that adopted

[10] Keech and Matthews, *The Party's Choice*, pp. 185-89.

[11] The term entrepreneurial is Hugh Heclo's, from his article "Presidential and Prime Ministerial Selection" in Donald R. Matthews, ed., *Perspectives on Presidential Selection* (Washington, D.C.: Brookings Institution, 1973).

228

this approach varied from the type in which the candidate himself would refrain from directly campaigning but "allow" a vigorous organizational effort on his behalf to those in which the candidate would actively solicit votes. The former type is illustrated by the campaigns of Hoover and Smith in 1928 and Roosevelt in 1932, the latter by the campaigns of Dewey in 1940, Taft in 1952, and Kennedy in 1960. Though the candidacies in this second category resemble a pure outside strategy—and perfect lines are difficult to draw—they can be distinguished by the close attention they gave to winning nonprimary votes. In no sense did these candidates ever burn their bridges with the party leaders. Even in Kennedy's campaign, which was clearly the most active of those mentioned, it is significant that Kennedy stayed out of a number of primaries—California included—as part of a "deal" with organizational leaders. The outside element in his strategy was carefully adopted with a view to its effect on the inside element.[12]

It is impossible to say which general strategy—outside, inside, or mixed—was the "correct" one, for this depended on the situation and on the strengths and weaknesses of the particular candidate. Of the three strategies, however, it seems clear that the "pure" outside campaign was the least likely to succeed and was usually adopted more from necessity than choice. The power relationship within the system favored the organizational interest over that of the rank-and-file, meaning that where the candidate had at least a chance of winning the organization's backing, it did not pay to run as an "insurgent" attacking the party establishment. With the possible exception of Eisenhower's candidacy in 1952, a campaign that is very difficult to classify, no candidate following a predominantly outside strategy won the nomination. An inside strategy was better suited to the system and yielded a number of successes, but it, too, had certain drawbacks. It was risky simply to concede the delegates that could be captured in the primaries; and opponents could point to the fail-

[12] Theodore White, *The Making of a President, 1960* (New York: Atheneum, 1961), pp. 96-97.

ure to contest the primaries as an admission of weakness. James Davis, a leading authority on the subject of presidential primaries, argued in 1967 that after the Kefauver campaign of 1952 a norm evolved to the effect that a viable candidate would have to prove himself in the primaries. Davis contends that Stevenson was more or less compelled to take on Kefauver in 1956 and that Johnson's 1960 candidacy was never really credible in light of his failure to enter any primaries.[13] This view of the importance of a norm as distinct from the character of the institutional arrangements was partly disproved by Humphrey's success with an inside campaign in 1968; on the other hand, it was partly vindicated by the great opposition which met Humphrey's selection, an opposition based not only on his policy positions but on the alleged illegitimacy of a campaign that did not submit its case to the people. In retrospect, and most likely from the perspective of candidates as well, it was the "mixed" strategy, if one had the strengths to follow it, that offered the best chance of success. It had none of the drawbacks of the inside strategy and offered the opportunity for a candidate to build popular support and enthusiasm that could carry over into the final election campaign. On the question of the effect of the mixed system it may thus be said that it tended to channel presidential ambitions away from extreme campaigns and toward either a "traditional" appeal to party regulars or a moderate outside campaign that won some public support for the candidate but not in such a way as would alienate the regulars.

Defenders of the mixed system have usually spoken of the "check" that its two conflicting elements placed on one another. The candidate-supremacy element, it was said, prevented stagnation by opening up the process to candidates who could appeal beyond the interests of the party regulars, while the party dominance element discouraged extreme appeals and directed serious contenders to seek a position that

[13] James Davis, *Presidential Primaries* (New York: Thomas Y. Crowell, 1967), pp. 61-65.

would maintain the delicate balance of coalitional parties. But it was symptomatic of the difficulty of winning a theoretical consensus for this system that its defenders usually split among themselves and emphasized the virtues of one component of the system over the other. There were "partisans" of the plebiscitary element whose views are best illustrated by the argument of the Hughes Commission report in 1968. While conceding the legitimacy of both aspects of the system, at least for the era prior to 1964, the commission reserved all of its praise for the "open," democratic side:

> . . . the basic importance of the primaries lay in their role as symbols. They reflected a national commitment to the principle that the nomination of presidential candidates was not a matter to be decided simply by convention delegates or by power brokers working behind closed doors. The fact that many states declined to provide for delegate selection entirely by primary was acceptable to the nation —but only because the system did not override or *frustrate the national commitment to direct democracy in the naming of presidential nominees.*[14]

According to this version, the "closed" side had no virtues worthy of mention and was tolerable only because it never seriously frustrated the expressed will of the people.

By contrast, a number of leading political scientists, among them V. O. Key, Gerald Pomper, Aaron Wildavsky, and Nelson Polsby, stressed the importance of the party dominance element of the mixed system.[15] Their case for the "closed" aspects of the system was usually stated in opposition to the idea of a direct national primary, but it was meant to apply equally to a system dominated by state primaries in

[14] *Commission on Democratic Selection of Nominees,* p. 31546 (emphasis added).

[15] V. O. Key, *Politics, Parties, and Pressure Groups,* 5th ed. (New York: Thomas Y. Crowell, 1964), p. 392; Gerald Pomper, *Nominating the President* (New York: W. W. Norton, 1966), pp. 210-35; Nelson W. Polsby and Aaron B. Wildavsky, *Presidential Elections,* 3rd ed. (New York: Charles Scribner's Sons, 1971), pp. 234-53.

which the delegates were selected with a national candidate orientation. Their first concern was over the type of leaders that "direct democracy" might promote. Wildavsky and Polsby contended that direct democracy

> might lead to the appearance of extremist candidates and demagogues, who unrestrained by allegiance to any permanent party organization, would have little to lose by stirring up mass hatreds or making absurd promises.[16]

The party organization, in this view, provides restraint because its members have an interest that extends beyond any particular candidate to the long-term well-being of the party. In the words of Allan Sindler, the party has "a past and a future as well as a present."[17] The party will accordingly tend to shun aspirants such as a Huey Long, a Joe McCarthy, or a George Wallace, each the type who might succeed in deluding the public in the short-run but who would bring discredit to the party over the long-run. To find a practical example of this kind of reasoning, one can do no better than to go all the way back to Alexander Hamilton's partisan plea in the election of 1800, when the choice of the president lay before the House and when many Federalist representatives were attempting to strike a deal with Aaron Burr. In a letter to one Congressman, Hamilton argued that "if the Federalists substitute Burr, they adopt him and become answerable for him . . . if he acts ill, we must share blame and disgrace."[18]

In addition to citing the beneficial effects of parties on the immediate compaign, their defenders point to their constructive influence on potential aspirants far in advance of an actual attempt for the presidency. The selection system

---

[16] Polsby and Wildavsky, *Presidential Elections*, p. 230.

[17] Allan P. Sindler, *Political Parties in the United States* (New York: St. Martin's Press, 1966), p. 33.

[18] Alexander Hamilton, letter to James Bayard, January 16, 1801, *Works of Alexander Hamilton* ed. H. C. Lodge, 12 vols. (New York: G. P. Putnam's Sons, 1904), 10:435.

establishes the kinds of leadership appeals that are more likely to bring success and in so doing influences the behavior of prospective candidates. If the party-dominance and mixed systems suggested moderate appeals, the open system, according to its critics, encourages posturing and extremism. This point has even been conceded by a well-known defender of the open-party system, James Sundquist:

> The reforms of the twentieth century have gone a long way toward ensuring that whenever the country polarizes on an issue, the polarization will be quickly and faithfully reflected by the parties. . . . This prospect will encourage more politicians to take their chances with extremism, giving it even greater potential. This is the hazard of an open party system.[19]

A further point cited by supporters of the party-dominance element is its positive role in maintaining political parties. Delegates controlled by the regulars or party power brokers are said to be more likely than those committed to the individual candidates to look for accommodation among the various elements in the party. Groups of regulars, perhaps attempting to maximize their local organization's interest or to play the decisive role of king maker, frequently refrain from committing themselves to any one candidate and therefore remain in a position to break a deadlock. Even those who commit usually maintain a degree of independence and can therefore at some point withdraw their commitment and negotiate. Party power brokers are thus in a certain sense in the position of "judges" rather than "plaintiffs"; they retain the independence to survey the situation and to "weigh" the different claims—for example, the claim of popularity. According to Nelson Polsby and Aaron Wildavsky, "sharply increasing the number of pledged delegates would introduce great rigidity into the convention [in the event of a deadlock] because of the increased likelihood of stalemates which could

[19] James L. Sundquist, *Dynamics*, p. 307.

233

not be overcome because no one would be in a position to switch his support."[20] By contrast, the immediate goal of the individual aspirant and his supporters is to win the nomination. If possible, this will be accomplished in a way that does not damage the party or detract from its chance of success in the final election. (Dignified statements in support of party unity are often issued by a centrist front-runner who can afford the luxury of such magnanimity and who may be seeking to discredit the more strident appeals of his challengers.) But if the nomination cannot be won by promoting consensus, the aspirant will not hesitate to adopt the strategy that is most likely to bring him victory, regardless of its effect on the long-term well-being of the party. Here again is where the party's interest may conflict with that of the candidate's. The thesis of the defenders of a dominant role for the party organization in the nomination process is that the sum total of the regulars' interest comes closer to representing the long-term interest of the party than does the interest of any particular candidate.

American parties have often been praised by consensual theorists for their moderating influence. According to Seymour Lipset, "elections become occasions for seeking the broadest support by convincing divergent groups of their common interest." To some extent, as Lipset argues, this tendency is encouraged by the nature of our electoral system, under which, because there is only one winner and no reward for runner-ups, factions have a strong incentive to coalesce in order to form a potential majority. But such accommodation does not follow automatically from the winner-take-all system. It depends also on a nominating system dominated by parties constituted in such a way that they can usually maintain harmony among their diverse factions. The primary, as Lipset contends, can "give minority interests an opportunity to openly express themselves in opposition to those in office in their own party and thus helps to keep them within the

[20] Polsby and Wildavsky, *Presidential Elections*, p. 237.

234

party."[21] But this expressive function works only as long as the primaries do not become the final arbiter of the selection process; the primary component can be a plaintiff, but not the judge and jury.

During the period of the mixed system, the electorate evidenced an ambivalent attitude toward partisanship. It was less attached to parties than it had been during most of the nineteenth century, but it was not nearly as independent minded as many of the Progressive theorists had hoped. This ambivalence, it may be suggested, was linked to the two alternative roles prescribed for parties under the mixed system. A large portion of the electorate was influenced by traditional party allegiances, but a significant number of voters—enough, according to V. O. Key, to constitute the decisive swing vote—responded to current issues and to an assessment of the incumbent's performance. In Key's view, the existence of these independent-minded voters was a necessary condition for electoral "responsibility," i.e. for the capacity of the electorate to move from party to party and thereby to keep the parties and the government responsive to the voters.[22] But Key should not be classified among the Progressive theorists. His model of a responsible electorate is incompatible with both the open selection system envisioned by one strand of the Progressive tradition and the "responsible party" system advocated by another. To work effectively his model requires a system in which parties provide choice within a range that most citizens would find acceptable. An appeal by the out-party regarded as too extreme by voters dissatisfied with the performance of the in-party would preclude them from registering their protest. Yet this is what would most likely occur under a "responsible party" system or a system of open, candidate-dominated parties. Key's model of responsibility is thus most compatible

---

[21] Seymour Martin Lipset, "The Paradox of American Politics," *The Public Interest* 41 (Fall 1975): 156.

[22] V. O. Key, *Politics, Parties, and Pressure Groups*, pp. 225-27.

with parties that are mindful of the feelings of their traditional partisans but able at the same time to judge and respond to the concerns of the swing portion of the electorate. The mixed system, it would seem, is best suited to this task.

THE TRIUMPH OF CANDIDATE SUPREMACY

During the 1960s the party-dominance component of the mixed system came under attack from a growing number of amateur participants and especially from reformers in the Democratic Party. The reforms were deliberately intended to reduce the influence of the party regulars, and they also precipitated—some would say inadvertently—a resurgence of the primary movement. The theory that guided reformers will be treated in the next chapter; the discussion here will focus on the general characteristics of the plebiscitary system which they established.

The most significant change in the selection process since 1920 has been the dramatic increase in the percentage of delegates chosen by primaries, shown below in Table V-1. All of the new primary laws allow or require the delegates to identify their national candidate preference on the ballot. Some of the states which formerly had primaries that barred candidate identification changed their laws to follow the new trend, among them the crucial state of New York. Republicans, who had nothing to do with initiating these developments, have nevertheless been swept along in the process of change and have found their selection process transformed by Democratic legislatures and governors, much as the Democrats were often the "victims" of the Progressive Republicans between 1912 and 1920. The new laws, as one might expect, have sharply increased the national candidate orientation among the delegates, as shown by the estimate in column 2 of Table V-1. By 1976, the selection system had evolved to the point where the state primaries were functioning in most instances as contests among delegates committed to different national candidates. The "critical mass" spoken

TABLE V-1: Extent of Primary Component in
Delegate Selection, 1960-1976

	Democrats			Republicans		
Year	Number of Primaries	% of Total Delegates	Est. % of Total Delegates Elected with National Candidate Orientation*	Number of Primaries	% of Total Delegates	Est. % of Total Delegates Elected with National Candidate Orientation*
1960	18	43	17	17	41	
1964	18	48		18**	47	16
1968	17	42	24	16	45	
1972	23	65	57	23	65	
1976	31	74	62	29	72	56

* Estimates derived from reading case-by-case surveys of the primaries; made only for years in which primaries were extensively contested.
** Includes advisory primary in Texas.

of earlier, which would virtually compel aspirants to adopt a vigorous outside strategy, had been reached.

The Democratic Party reforms of 1974 also mandated the use of proportional representation in delegate selection for all nonprimary states and for primaries under certain circumstances. The Republican caucus states remained unaffected by this change, since the rules that govern delegate selection in these states are made by each party. In the primary states, however, the legislation was usually written to apply to both parties. The extent of the use of proportional schemes is indicated below in Table V-2. What the long-term effects of this change will be is still unclear, especially as the laws on this point are still in a state of flux.[23] Gerald Pomper has argued that the system has made it even more difficult

[23] The Democratic convention in 1976 called for the use of proportional representation in all primaries by 1980.

237

TABLE V-2: Numbers of Delegates Elected under each System of Representation in 1976

Party	Plurality Primary	Non-Primary*	Quasi-Propor-tional**	Proportional Primary	Caucus	Total
Democratic						
Number of Delegates	989	2	226	1100	691	3008
Percent of total	32.9	0.1	7.5	36.6	23.0	—
Republican						
Number of Delegates	1151	711	5	392	—	2259
Percent of total	51.0	31.5	0.2	17.4	—	—

* Includes delegates selected in caucus states or appointed and those in primary states mandated at discretion of state conventions or committees.

** Includes statewide delegates that reflect proportionally the candidate preferences of delegates elected at district levels under plurality primary systems. (Statewide delegates reflecting candidate preferences of district delegates elected under proportional methods are counted under proportional.)

for party power brokers to control large blocs of delegates and that it will therefore encourage national candidates to contest directly for delegates; and since some delegates can usually be gained even where a candidate is not a plurality winner, the incentive for a candidate to compete in most races will be all the greater.[24] If this view is correct, proportional representation will reinforce the tendency to transform the selection process into a direct struggle among national candidates for committed delegates.

The final institutional change of recent years has been the regulation of campaign financing by the federal government.

[24] Gerald Pomper, *The Election of 1976* (New York: David McKay, 1977), pp. 6-7.

238

Prior to the 1970s, financing was largely a "market" affair, restricted only by certain limitations on contributions from banks, corporations, labor unions, and government employees.[25] With the campaign finance legislation of the 1970s, however, this area has been brought under extensive government regulation, as the Progressives had wanted. The complex legislation in this field, as modified by the Supreme Court decision of *Buckley v. Valeo*, provides for disclosure of contributions, limitations on campaign contributions, and public funding in both the primary and final election campaigns (with different rules applying in each case). Acceptance of public funding also brings with it a limitation on the total amount that a candidate can spend. The full effects of this legislation cannot yet be determined. But if the experience of 1976 serves as a guide, it suggests that more candidates may be encouraged to enter the race and that they will be forced to declare much earlier to meet the various requirements, both trends that were already encouraged by the plebiscitary system. The tendency toward early declarations does not exclude an incumbent, as Gerald Ford's campaign illustrates. According to Richard Neustadt, this remarkable extension of the official campaign into the process of governing constitutes a significant loss of flexibility for the president.[26] One might add, going beyond Neustadt's characteristic concern with the president's power alone, that this change also tends to drain constituted authority of a claim to confidence and impartiality. The campaign finance legislation also provides for the distribution of funds directly to the candidates during the nomination stage, which Gerald Pomper thinks will further "weaken established party organizations and their ability to control the selection of con-

[25] For a review of this legislation and a discussion of its enforcement (or lack thereof), see William Crotty, *Political Reform and the American Experiment* (New York: Thomas Y. Crowell, 1977), pp. 169-77.

[26] Neustadt, *Presidential Power* (New York: John Wiley's Sons, 1976), pp. 19-21.

vention delegates."[27] Indeed, the form in which the funds are distributed amounts very nearly to a legal endorsement of the plebiscitary system and the candidate-dominated party. The law also implicitly endorses, as will later be explained, the current reform view that favors substituting "open" parties for an open electoral system. It is quite possible, then, that the most important effects of this legislation will not be on the financing of campaigns but on the character of the party system and the way in which candidates seek the nomination.

The evolution of the modern selection system can be traced to the Goldwater candidacy of 1964, though 1964 was not the decisive year. Goldwater's nomination campaign, unlike the pure outside strategies that would follow, relied only secondarily on the primaries. Goldwater's greatest strength was in the nonprimary states where he captured more than half of his delegates.[28] But what made his emphasis on the nonprimary states different from the usual approach of the past and redolent of the outside strategies that would follow was his extensive use of a personal "grass roots" organization to capture delegates. Rather than negotiating with delegates already chosen, the Goldwater organization sought and succeeded in winning delegates already committed to his candidacy. A candidate-oriented strategy was pursued in the domain that had usually been controlled by the regulars. Efforts of this kind had played a role in the candidacies of Wilkie, Stevenson, and Eisenhower, but Goldwater's planning was much more elaborate and constituted, according to Keech and Matthews, "the most effective and elaborate candidate organization seen in presidential politics up to that time."[29]

[27] Pomper, *The Election of 1976*, p. 4.

[28] Goldwater had 492 votes from the nonprimary states (out of a possible 655) and 392 votes from the primary states (out of a possible 653). Source: *Congressional Quarterly Weekly Report* 33, December 20, 1975, p. 2808.

[29] Keech and Matthews, *The Party's Choice*, p. 194.

The successful nomination campaign of George McGovern in 1972 employed a strategy similar to Goldwater's in the nonprimary states, but unlike the Goldwater candidacy it relied greatly on the primaries. The truly critical change from 1964 was not in the practices of the candidates but rather in the new institutional arrangements. As a result of the reforms in the Democratic Party, the exceptional strategy that Goldwater employed in the nonprimary states became, so to speak, the institutionally preferred strategy, at least in the Democratic Party; and the increased number of primaries meant that primaries had to be given more attention than in 1964 or 1968. The primaries gave McGovern over 800 committed delegates, more than half of the total needed for victory. The principal focus of every active campaign, Republican and Democratic, now had to be on an outside strategy in the primaries.

The two distinguishing features of the campaign under the modern plebiscitary system are strong personal campaign organizations and direct popular appeals by the candidates. Both of these features were evident in the elections of 1972 and 1976, and it will be helpful to explore the range of possibilities in each case. This can best be done by focusing on the campaigns of George McGovern and Jimmy Carter.

1972

The large personal campaign organization is at the center of the modern nomination campaign. Its distinguishing characteristics are loyalty to the individual candidate and an *ad hoc* organizational structure. As the organizations exist only for the one campaign in which the candidate participates, power relationships are seldom fully institutionalized. The struggle for offices within a stable party organization is replaced, according to James Q. Wilson, by "a struggle for access to the candidate's ear and favor."[30] To the extent the

[30] James Q. Wilson, *Political Organizations* (New York: Basic Books, 1973), p. 115.

241

organization as a whole is formalized, power extends from the top down, with the candidate being the ultimate source of power.

The organization is needed to do the "work" of the campaign. In primary states this means helping to mobilize and get out the vote, a critical factor in primaries because of the relatively low turnout. Xandra Kayden, one of the first students of electoral politics to study a campaign from a purely organizational perspective, described the strength of the McGovern campaign as being based on "its ability to turn out its supporters at the polls on election day, [a factor] that is particularly important where there is a 'field' of candidates."[31] The role of the organization in the nonprimary states can be even more important, for here the organization can almost "substitute" for the people, providing the manpower to contest in caucus meetings. A concerted effort was made by the McGovern campaign organization to recruit volunteers in the nonprimary states. Because McGovern himself had chaired the Democratic Party's reform commission and drew some of his campaign aides from its staff, he was more aware than the other candidates of the potential effects of the new rules, and in particular of the increased vulnerability of the caucus processes to amateur participation. Moreover, in what some might describe as an inequity potentially as serious as that deriving from a differential in monetary resources, McGovern drew his support from a constituency of the educated upper-middle class that is much more likely to participate in political activities than the average American.[32] With no apparent

[31] Xandra Kayden, "The Political Campaign as an Organization," *Public Policy*, 31 (Spring 1973): 277.

[32] See Keech and Matthews, *The Party's Choice*, pp. 207-10. These authors comment that "Governor Wallace was also campaigning on an emotional issue in 1972—anti-busing. But his predominantly working-class following was less easily organized than McGovern's. . . ." For a general discussion of the relationship between class and organizational participation, see Wilson, *Political Organizations*, pp. 56-90 and Sidney Verba and Norman H. Nie, *Participation in America* (New York: Harper and Row, 1972), pp. 99-101.

attempt to belittle his own candidate, Gary Hart summed up the importance of organization by noting that "we always felt that the best organization was going to win [the nomination]."[33] This was hardly a democratic defense for a supposedly democratic system, but then Hart made this comment at a Harvard University Institute of Politics seminar in which the managers and consultants from the 1972 campaign were asked to discuss the real, as distinct from the publicly avowed, determinants of presidential selection.

The incentives for participating in a personal campaign organization can be classified according to the usual categories for participation in voluntary associations. The motive may be solidary (to be where the action is), material (to derive a specific tangible benefit), or purposive (to promote certain policies or to serve a person in whom one believes).[34] Mention of the first two might seem out of place in an age of supposed amateurism. But to be identified by the media magnates as a "tough, young organizational genius" and to have this mild form of Machiavellianism universally admired is no small inducement for many campaign workers. More important is the prospect of obtaining an interesting job if the candidate is victorious. Although patronage in the regular bureaucracy is a thing of the past, staff jobs in the White House serve as a partial replacement, at least for those near the top of the campaign organization. The White House staffs of Kennedy, Nixon, and Carter all illustrate the possibilities for the young campaign workers, and in light of this "function" for the White House staff it seems unlikely that its size will ever be dramatically reduced.[35] Because Mc-

[33] *Campaign '72, The Managers Speak*, eds. Ernest R. May and Janet Fraser (Cambridge: Harvard University Press, 1973), p. 40.

[34] This classification is taken from Wilson, *Political Organizations*, pp. 30-51.

[35] See Stephen Hess, *Organizing the Presidency* (Washington: Brookings Institution, 1976), p. 80. Although one shouldn't push the point too far, the "institutionalization" of the campaign staff in the White House staff represents a continuation of the influence of the "campaign mentality" into the process of governing. As cam-

243

Govern was not elected, his own plans for rewarding his campaign staff are not known. But the commitment of his principal aides was such as to lead one to suspect that the normal reward would be forthcoming. The campaign organization, according to Xandra Kayden, was controlled "by politicians whose primary loyalty was to the candidate and not to some abstract ideology, and whose main objective was to win by whatever means possible—not to keep pure some ideology or implement some new decision-making procedure."[36]

Since only a relatively small number may actually be seeking (or can be given) jobs, the greater part of the candidate's campaign organization must be recruited on the basis of some other motivation. In the case of the McGovern organization, it was a purposive commitment to certain issues. The effects of recruiting volunteers by this means was a topic of a good deal of commentary during the 1972 campaign. The dynamics of an organization in such cases can impose unwanted constraints on a candidate. The candidate's objective is to obtain the needed volunteers as "cheaply" as possible, which is to say with the fewest commitments beyond what the candidate himself, for reasons of policy or strategy, wishes to make. The volunteers, however, may only be willing to give their support in exchange for firm policy stands. As Xandra Kayden explains:

> . . . when the initial strength of the campaign comes from the participation of purposive members (as was true for McGovern and by every indication is likely to be true for those who follow), there is an expectation that their interests will not be entirely neglected.[37]

---

paign workers, especially in insurgent campaigns, tend to be drawn from young outsiders, the function of counseling the president at the highest levels is likely to be affected in a significant way. The highest advisors may come from the campaign staff rather than being drawn from the group of Washington professionals.

[36] Kayden, "The Political Campaign as an Organization," p. 265.
[37] *Ibid.*, p. 289.

The candidate may then find himself in a dilemma at the point at which he wants to seal his nomination and become the party's standard bearer, a situation that McGovern confronted on a few key occasions at the 1972 convention. Having made commitments during the preconvention period to secure an organization cadre, the candidate must either honor them, thus confirming himself as an uncompromising representative of a faction, or else shift positions in an effort to broaden his base, thus leaving himself open to the charge of hypocrisy. Such a dilemma may be almost unavoidable for any candidate who seeks to build his initial base of volunteers through issue appeals. This aspect of the modern campaign led Benjamin Page to declare that "perhaps a two-stage campaign is an impossible dream. Perhaps voters refused to forget earlier positions and the character of original supporters."[38]

The second characteristic of the modern campaign is the extensive use of popular leadership, i.e. direct appeals by individual candidates seeking to rouse and capture a mass following. Candidates now conduct their campaigns in the "exposed" situation in which support must be sought on grounds other than party identification. In the fully open campaign, candidates are even denied the one source of identification that was associated in the past with many outside strategies—running against the party organization. James Barber has noted that under present conditions of presidential selection, candidates display much less "coyness" than in previous times.[39] If the analogy to courtship is apt, one might say that the current selection process is distinguished by an openness bordering on permissiveness. Candidates announce earlier than ever and press their suits with an almost shameless persistance. But the situation is not so unfavorable to the

---

[38] Denis G. Sullivan, Jeffrey L. Pressman, Benjamin I. Page, and John J. Lions, *The Politics of Representation* (New York: St. Martin's Press, 1974), p. 114.

[39] "Introduction" in James David Barber, ed., *Choosing the President* (Englewood Cliffs, N.J.: Prentice Hall), p. 3.

uninitiated as one might think. In the frankness allowable in discourse among the experienced, Charles Guggenheim, Senator McGovern's media advisor for the 1972 campaign, told an Institute of Politics seminar that "what happened [in 1972] was that McGovern came on as sort of the political virgin, and that's always attractive to a group who wants to make a change."[40] McGovern's virginity was not, of course, the only image in the 1972 Democratic campaign, nor the only one to be soiled. Much was done in an effort to promote the steady trustworthiness of Ed Muskie and the youthful "charisma" of John Lindsay.

But in the final analysis it was not images but issues that were decisive in 1972.[41] This is best illustrated by the turn-about of Senator Muskie during the campaign. Muskie, the initial front-runner, sought at first to downplay the significance of specific "position-taking," arguing that the choice of a president should revolve around an assessment of the person:

> When we choose a president we are choosing more than a set of speeches or a series of programs and promises. Indeed, the great issues which end up on a president's desk are often far removed from the heat and tumult of an election year.

This elevated posture failed to generate a firm constituency, and Muskie's initial support disintegrated under attacks from both the Right and Left within the party. After a poor showing in the Florida primary, Muskie sought to transform himself from an "old" to a "new" Ed Muskie. The new Ed Muskie, born on March 16, 1972, admitted to having spread himself too thin on the issues. Leadership for him henceforth

[40] May and Fraser, *Campaign '72*, p. 126.

[41] Arthur H. Miller, Warren E. Miller, Alden S. Raine, and Thad A. Brown, "A Majority Party in Disarray." Paper delivered at the annual meeting of the American Political Science Association, 1973, pp. 12-15; see also Orren and Schneider, "Democrats versus Democrats."

246

would mean "offering solutions." Note the new Senator Muskie in action during the primary campaign in Pennsylvania:

> Our people are fed up with the great institutions—public and private—that ran their lives without responding to their issues. . . .

> The important question is not what a candidate is against but what is he for—and how would his election as President make a difference to you. I have proposed a freeze on food price increases. No other candidate has. I say freeze food prices now. You can say the same thing by voting for me on Tuesday.[42]

Given an election year of high issue salience, was there something inevitable in Muskie's fall from a "statesman" to a butcher?

Muskie's initial lack of understanding of the necessities of the modern primary campaign was perhaps best illustrated in his denunciation of George Wallace after the Florida campaign:

> What disturbs me about this campaign or about this election result in Florida is that it reveals that to a greater extent than I had imagined, some of the worst instincts of which human beings are capable have too strong an influence in our elections. . . . George Wallace is a demagogue of the worst possible kind.[43]

By contrast, Senator McGovern avoided a direct denunciation of Wallace and sought instead to capitalize on the dissatisfaction of the Wallace voters by putting them together with his own dissatisfied followers in a coalition of the alienated, Left and Right. McGovern seemed to understand much better than Muskie the nature of the modern campaign.

[42] Speech, January 7, 1972, in Tallahassee, Florida; speech, April 10, 1972, in Pittsburgh, Pa.; speech, April 24, 1972, Pennsylvania Television Address. From the records of Senator Muskie.
[43] Speech, March 12, 1972. From the records of Senator Muskie.

In addition his boldness, in contrast to Muskie's hesitancy or moderation, was better suited to the times. Whatever the explanation, McGovern was not ashamed to pick up on a number of Wallace themes, including the appeals to anger on which Wallace's campaign fed. In opening his final drive for votes in Wisconsin, McGovern described the Wallace victory in Florida as:

> . . . an angry cry from the guts of ordinary Americans against a system which doesn't seem to give a damn about what's really bothering people in this country today. It was a vote to stop the whole damn Democratic Party and make it listen to the people for a change—instead of just to political strategists.[44]

This strategy, which represented part of McGovern's master plan for the general election victory, did not succeed beyond the Wisconsin primary. McGovern was already, or would soon become, too strongly typed within the electorate as a liberal. The alienated voter, according to the SRC analysis of the election, turned out to be more "Left" or "Right" than alienated.[45] But McGovern's attempt was most instructive. It suggested the idea of an appeal that "transcended" images and issues, one based on being the spokesman for a deep-seated feeling or mood within the electorate. This idea, which relies on the pollster to keep his punchcards on the electorate's pulse, seems almost to parody Wilson's notion of interpretation and is known in the campaign consulting business as "articulation." It was this new strategy of popular leadership that would help win the day for Jimmy Carter in 1976, a year in which specific issues were much less salient than in 1972.

[44] Speech, March 23, 1972. Milwaukee, Wisconsin, from the records of Senator McGovern.

[45] Miller, *et al.*, "A Majority Party in Disarray"; Richard W. Boyd, "Electoral Trends in Postwar Politics," in Barber, ed., *Choosing the President*, pp. 200-1.

248

1976

If the nearly successful campaign of Ronald Reagan illustrated many of the same themes as the McGovern candidacy of 1972, that of Jimmy Carter was something quite different. Carter avoided an emphasis on "hard" issues, choosing instead to emphasize a number of well-chosen "valence" themes. These were reinforced by a focus on certain character attributes which often conveyed the same message as the content of his political appeal. Carter succeeded in holding together the diverse elements of the Democratic Party's coalition in a feat that would have been the envy of the party power brokers of the Van Buren tradition. Carter pursued a vigorous outside strategy and in so doing managed to build his own constituency without alienating any major group within a party. This result defied some of the dire predictions of the opponents of a fully open campaign and served to silence much of the criticism of the selection process from within the party. But to the student of institutional arrangements certain questions remain: was there a disturbing undertone to the kind of appeal that brought Carter his success? Was the consensus he achieved the result of certain unique personal skills and certain fortuitous political factors, rather than an outcome encouraged by the system? And finally, since institutional arrangements meet their test in troubled rather than calm times, does the success of 1976 really disprove the major complaint against the plebiscitary system?

At the outset of the 1976 campaign, most electoral analysts assumed that to win the Democratic nomination it would be necessary for a candidate to build a constituency by emphasizing a "hard" issue appeal.[46] What had been de-

---

[46] Pomper, *The Election of 1976*, p. 1. Keech and Matthews, *The Party's Choice*, p. 156. This point was confirmed by the discussion of many experts who participated at a Harvard University Institute of Politics seminar in 1975. The ground rules of this seminar, however, required confidentiality, so no names or quotations can be provided.

cisive in 1972 must be decisive in 1976. This conclusion, we now know, misread the possibilities inherent in a plebiscitary system. Although the experience of 1972 may represent the most likely outcome in a year of intense political conflict, it is now clear that in quieter times the campaign can assume a different character. The result should not come entirely as a surprise: Van Buren's analysis of popular leadership suggested that, depending on the times, a personal constituency might be generated either by issue appeals (as in 1824) or by a general personal appeal (as in 1828); and much the same conclusion has been drawn by V. O. Key and Allan Sindler from their studies of political leadership in the candidate-dominated system in southern states during the one-party era.[47]

It was not the case, of course, that issues were entirely without significance in 1976. If Carter did not emphasize an issue appeal in his campaign, others did, and by a combination of strategy and good fortune this redounded to Carter's benefit. The *New York Times*/CBS poll data, analyzed by political scientist Gary Orren, shows clearly that in Carter's two crucial early victories in New Hampshire and Florida, he picked up alternatively the conservative vote against a field of liberals and the liberal vote against George Wallace.[48] In contrast to the situation in 1972, when the centerist Muskie was squeezed from both sides, Carter found himself in these two campaigns in the enviable position of running against only one wing of the party at a time.

The poll data also shows, however, that voters were responding largely to the personalities of the candidates and to more general valence issues that transcended the traditional liberal-conservative cleavage.[49] The two most successful can-

[47] V. O. Key, *Southern Politics* (New York: Alfred A. Knopf, 1949); Sindler, *Political Parties*, p. 33.

[48] *New York Times*, February 26, 1976. The analysts note (p. 18) that "more than 3 to 1 the New Hampshire voters sampled said they considered the issues more important than the personal qualities of the candidates."

[49] *New York Times*, June 9, 1976.

didates in the 1976 campaign, Carter and Brown, both es-
chewed—and defied—traditional categorization; and both
stressed aspects of their characters designed at least in part
to differentiate themselves from the usual Washington politician—integrity in the first case and downright unconven-
tionality in the second. The Carter campaign, according to
Hamilton Jordan, was premised on the assumption that
issues often are too complex for most voters (at least in
1976) and that "the average fellow out there is looking beyond them to what sort of person the candidate is."[50] Carter's
very effective stump speeches early in the campaign often
began with what amounted to a boy scout pledge: "I'm
Jimmy Carter and if I'm elected President, I'll never tell a
lie." Carter's campaign organization which at the top had its
usual share of those harboring career ambitions (though
without having the usual gloss of issue commitment), was
built at the bottom with those committed to the candidate
himself, many of whom were won over by Carter by personal
contacts in a long campaign. The time and energy Carter
put into his campaign before the calendar year of 1976 made
it the closest thing yet seen to a national friends and neigh-
bors campaign and thereby gave him a good deal of discretion about the issue positions he could adopt.

The personal characteristics Carter stressed fit perfectly
with the mood in the electorate to which he appealed. Carter
seized on the "issues" of dishonesty in Washington and the
irresponsiveness of our major institutions to run a general
campaign against the entrenched powers—against Washington, against the bureaucracy, and even, where he could make
it stick, against the power brokers of the regular party. The
campaign was run in the name of the people in the form of
a mild form of populism that promised to make the government become as "decent and competent as our people."[51]
Carter's attacks as an outsider were directed against symbols
that were the scourge of the Left: "those who play golf at

[50] *New York Times*, June 10, 1976, p. 42.
[51] Cited in Pomper, *The Election of 1976*, p. 11.

251

the same country clubs," and the Right: "the inefficiency, waste, and bureaucratic mess in Washington." In the latter appeal one can see undertones of Wallace's campaign themes, and it was a key element of Carter's strategy not to attack Wallace but to replace him.[52] Carter's ability to appeal to dissatisfaction on the Right without alienating the Left was a crucial factor in his success, allowing him to pursue a viable campaign against Wallace in the south without sacrificing his position as a plausible candidate among moderates, blacks, and some northern liberals. Carter had managed to tap a mood of dissatisfaction that went beneath or above ideological divisions. He thus managed to achieve what McGovern had sought but failed to accomplish during the latter part of his 1972 primary campaign, although it must be added that Carter faced a much less divisive climate of opinion. Carter defined his own dragon—Washington—and slew it, following the general tactic of popular leadership of raising oneself by attacking something else. Yet the object of his attack was such that he managed to pit virtually the entire population against no one. In one of the most astute analyses of the 1976 primary campaign, William Schneider observed that Carter had succeeded in doing what few other candidates in America had done: he became a genuine insurgent of the middle.[53]

The basis of Carter's new "New Politics" left many of the originators of the New Politics with an uneasy feeling. Contrary to their intent, Carter did not make use of the new system to solicit his following by appealing to "hard" issues. Udall expressed the typical New Politics sense of frustration with Carter's avoidance of the issues in the following complaint: "The *New York Times* told liberals he was liberal,

[52] Interview with Hamilton Jordan, *New York Times*, June 10, 1976.

[53] *Los Angeles Times*, May 23, 1976. Schneider writes: "What Jimmy Carter has done is to separate protest from ideology. . . . His protest against Washington—the symbol of the party regulars, the establishment, and the system—is a rare phenomenon in American politics: a protest movement of the center."

the conservatives thought he was conservative, and the moderates thought he was moderate. In Iowa he had both the abortion and the anti-abortion vote, he had labor and anti-labor, he had opposites on all sides."[54] In the view of many on the Left, Carter's campaign was little more than a shrewd image appeal. What is of interest to the student of electoral behavior, however, is not this partisan evaluation of Carter's campaign, but the "shallowness" of his electoral support. This was illustrated in the primary races against Governor Brown, who at the last moment enjoyed considerable success running as an outsider to the by then "establishment" candidacy of Carter. If the outcome of the nomination is determined by such appeals as these, there is reason to fear not only a debasement of electoral politics but also the possibility of success of a truly fraudulent campaign. Perhaps the most accurate picture of the New Politics, then, is not the one that its originators had in mind but instead the "Replacement Party" candidacy depicted in Robert Altman's insightful movie on American politics, *Nashville 1975*.

Carter's success in uniting the Democratic Party silenced some critics of the new system who had argued that it would inevitably produce divisive issue candidacies which would destroy party consensus. But this criticism might still prove accurate for election years in which the importance of issues is greater than it was in the Democratic race of 1976. Indeed, on the Republican side in 1976, an issue campaign that finally focused on the Panama Canal treaty very nearly divided the party. Moreover, if the test of institutions is how they work under circumstances of stress, the substance of the charge that the new system tends to destroy party consensus has yet to be refuted. Even in the calm race on the Democratic side in 1976, the happy consensual result can perhaps be said to have occurred in spite of the selection system and not because of it. In addition to Carter's own considerable skill, one cannot fail to notice the contingent

[54] Cited in Kandy Stroud, *How Jimmy Won* (New York: William Morrow, 1977), p. 258.

factors that worked in his favor. With the divisiveness of the 1972 campaign still in the minds of many Democrats, there was probably a greater than normal disposition for voters to resist the choice of their issue favorite and look for a winner. And as a southerner, Carter was able to appeal to a large constituency that otherwise would have found him less attractive. Even his success here, the polls indicate, was partly attributable to Wallace's paralysis, which many voters felt disqualified him from serious consideration.[55] Finally, Carter's strong support among blacks could also be related to his being a southern candidate: as a governor in Georgia with a Progressive record, especially with respect to black political appointments, Carter was able to win the confidence of many blacks without a stand in terms of the issues that would have earned him this degree of support.

The effects of the plebiscitary system on the political system as a whole will not be fully known for some time. But some of its influences and tendencies are already discernible. First, it was posited earlier that a systematic connection exists between the form of the selection system and the general pattern of voting behavior. Since the emergence of the candidate-supremacy system, there has been a sharp increase both in the percentage of those who identify themselves as independents and in the rate of defection among self-proclaimed partisans. Two presidential landslides for candidates of different parties have occurred since 1964, in both cases without any permanent long-term alignment in favor of either party. All this has prompted a number of experts on voter behavior, led by Walter Dean Burnham, to speak of a period of electoral dealignment, a period in which voter attachment to parties declines and voters choose among candidates without regard to party label.[56] It is not necessary

[55] See the *New York Times*/CBS National Poll, reported on March 29, 1976.

[56] Walter Dean Burnham, "American Politics in the 1970s: Beyond Party" in Chambers and Burnham, eds., *The American Party Systems*, 2nd ed. (New York: Oxford University Press, 1975), pp. 308-57.

to deny the influence of two factors usually cited as causing dealignment—an increasing educational level within the electorate and the disruptive effect of certain recent issues—to suggest that the ascendancy of the candidate-supremacy model has also contributed to this change. By focusing the voters' attention on individual candidates, the plebiscitary system can be said to "teach" the lesson that current issues and particular candidate qualities are more important than parties. The institutional influences that tend to weaken party organizations at the nomination stage inevitably spill over to the final campaign. As the authors of *The Changing American Voter* argue:

> Party organizations have grown weaker; they are less relevant as electioneering institutions than they once were, especially on the presidential level. Presidential campaign organizations are created anew for each election. They represent the personal entourage of the candidate rather than a continuing partisan institution. . . . The individual candidates are more independent of party; they run on the basis of their own characteristics and programs, not as representatives of continuing party institutions.[57]

This empirical description of the current electoral system could just as well serve as a theoretical statement for what many of the Progressives sought for the electoral process. It sets forth the basic components of the candidate-supremacy system, a system that was supported institutionally by nomination by plebiscite and low levels of partisan attachment. Finally, it is likely that the current nominating system has contributed to voter independence in a more direct and concrete way. There are grounds for supposing that a decline in partisanship since 1964 has been accelerated by a nomination process that leads parties to divide their coalitions and desert part of their constituencies, thus forcing some of

[57] Norman Nie, Sidney Verba and John Petrocik, *The Changing American Voter* (Cambridge: Harvard University Press, 1976), pp. 346-47.

their traditional voters out of the partisan fold. The problem might be just as much one of runaway parties as one of a runaway electorate. It is possible, certainly, that at some future point a realignment might occur and partisan sentiment increase. But current institutional features, if continued, would work shortly in the direction of a disintegration of steady partisanship and toward the reemergence of a politics based on the supremacy of the individual candidate.

How does this decline in partisanship relate to the functions of the selection system that have been identified in this study? At the extreme, it could lead to a collapse of the usual monopoly over nominations held by the two major parties. This in turn could result in the problems of formal legitimacy associated with elections decided by the House. Short of this dramatic effect, the decline in partisanship raises questions about the role parties play in ensuring a candidate with a valid national following. If parties manage to restrict the primaries to their actual identifiers, the number of participants will hardly be characteristic of a national cross section. If on the other hand most primaries remain open in practice to all voters, there are apt to be disputes within each party about whether the candidate is truly the party's nominee. Finally, the decline in partisanship reduces the number of people whom the president can rely on to support his initiatives on the grounds of traditional partisan attachment. Presidents may thereby be forced to rely more on techniques of popular leadership in an effort to win public opinion.

Second, the candidate-centered campaign erodes the ability of elections to affix responsibility, which is one desirable aspect of the selection system's function of promoting choice. According to Hamilton's suggestion in *The Federalist*, it is important for the psychological well-being of the nation for the voters to believe that they can affix responsibility on their officials by rejecting them in an election. This serves the purpose of maintaining a sense of optimism among the people, as if in venting their frustrations there is new hope for solving

256

difficult problems.[58] (The benefits of this doctrine were clear in the election of 1932, where the rejection of Hoover provided a temporary sense of relief.) Under the system the Founders envisioned, the function of affixing responsibility would usually be served by the electoral judgment passed on the incumbent, who could continue to run without any limitations. But with the emergence of the two-term norm—and now the Twenty-Second Amendment—this solution works only part of the time. A partial substitute for the same function, however, was found in the doctrine of holding a party accountable for the failures of its incumbent. No doubt, as Edward Banfield has argued, there is something that is fictitious in holding a new nominee accountable for the past mistakes of an incumbent of his own party.[59] But the importance of the people's feeling that there is accountability—and the relief that this feeling can provide—makes the fiction of party responsibility well worth preserving. Under the current system, as Nie *et al.* argue, "Voters are less able to vote on the basis of past performance (as V. O. Key and others argued they did), since the candidate cannot be held responsible for what others in his party have done while in office—unless, of course, the incumbent is the candidate."[60] This belief follows from the awareness of the voters that the party is no longer a collective institution with a past and a future but merely a label temporarily owned by a particular candidate.

Third, an electoral system based on candidate supremacy will in turn have certain influences on the character of the executive, a matter to be discussed in more detail in the following chapters. Here it is sufficient to point out that the influence works in the direction of a Wilsonian executive—one

[58] This point is also suggested by James Barber when he speaks of the affective role of politics and the presidency in *The Presidential Character* (Englewood Cliffs, N.J.: Prentice Hall, 1972), pp. 448-50.

[59] Edward Banfield, "In Defense of the American Party System," in Goldwin, ed., *Political Parties U.S.A.*, pp. 32-33.

[60] Nie, Verba, and Petrocik, *The Changing American Voter*, p. 347.

who is "free" of party (but who cannot thereby call on it to aid him in winning public support), one who may raise great expectations about what a president as an individual can accomplish, and one who is led to emphasize authority based on an informal relationship with the people rather than the authority of the office itself.

Finally, the modern campaign, based as it is on the individuals' own characteristics and programs, has put the art of popular leadership at the center not only of presidential selection but of the American constitutional system as a whole. The Progressives who proposed this kind of leadership anticipated that it would result in an elevated popular statesmanship; but there are grounds for at least suspecting that the institutional arrangements intended to foster such leadership may instead result in a politics that favors demagoguery, image candidacies, and a sophisticated pandering known as "articulation." This type of leadership, should it result, will apply not only to presidential campaigns but will radiate throughout the entire system, by the force both of example and the pull of presidential ambition on prospective candidates. This influence would already appear to have been exerted on the Senate, the new incubator of presidential candidates. Given their advantages of strategic location, access to the media, control over their own legislative area, and, perhaps most importantly, their freedom from the responsibility of making executive decisions, senators are ideally suited in the present context to becoming presidential candidates. Their activities are likely to push the Senate further in the direction of being an institution committed to arousing public opinion rather than to serious lawmaking.[61] Indeed this trend, which began in the 1950s, may have been inaugurated by the presidential ambitions of such men as Estes Kefauver. In his retirement address to the Senate in 1975, Senator Aiken went so far as to suggest a Constitutional amendment barring active senators from running for

[61] Nelson W. Polsby, *Congress and the Presidency*, 2nd ed. (Englewood Cliffs, N.J.: Prentice Hall, 1971), pp. 67-69.

258

the presidency.[62] It would no doubt be unseemly for the Constitution to lump senators with those under thirty-five years of age as one of the few groups legally ineligible for the presidency, but the general reasons that led Senator Aiken to propose such a drastic step are worth considering. Perhaps the best way to realize his goal would be through a reform of the electoral process, reinstituting in some measure the power of the political party.

[62] Congressional Record, vol. 120, no. 172, 93rd Congress, 2nd Session, 1975, p. 21027.

CHAPTER VI

Modern Party Reform

THE theory that has guided the current changes in the selection system is generally referred to by journalists and political scientists by the name of "reform." This label admittedly poses certain difficulties for analysis. It is the name of a diverse movement (or tendency) in recent times that has touched many aspects of American politics besides the presidential selection system. Moreover, different groups having differing and sometimes conflicting objectives have pressed their claims under its banner. Yet the name reform remains, for better or worse, the only one with which to begin a discussion of contemporary developments in presidential selection. It is the label of the political marketplace, chosen alike by the proponents and opponents of the recent changes.

There is another and more serious difficulty in treating the theory of reform. Unlike the other theories of selection discussed in this book, there is no single body of thought for reform that sets forth a complete description of its premises and objectives. This may be merely an accident of history (the failure of any one theorist to articulate its goals), or it may reflect the fact, as Everett Ladd has suggested, that reform is not a genuinely new theory but merely an elaboration of Progressive views.[1] Whatever the cause, however, it will be necessary in discussing reform to look for a statement of its premises in sources other than those relied on thus far —in the general ideas of certain groups of party activists as described by political scientists and in public documents

[1] Everett Ladd in *Transformations of the American Party System* (New York: W. W. Norton, 1975) writes, "The Democratic Party changes of the 1970's are largely in the spirit of the earlier Progressive reforms" (p. 317).

260

such as the reports of the various Democratic Party reform commissions.

In spite of these problems, however, it can still be said that reform is an identifiable movement which has certain distinct ideas on presidential selection. Three values or concerns stand out as most characteristic of the reform view: (1) opposition to any role for interest groups and self-interest in the selection process, and thus a strong antipathy to traditional party organizations, reflexive partisanship, and private contributions to presidential campaigns; (2) support, in the name of republican legitimacy, of more openness, participation, and democracy in the selection process, both during the nomination and the final election stages; (3) a belief that presidential selection is preeminently the occasion for the people to make policy choices on "hard" issues.[2]

There is no question that these ideas are very general and, especially in the case of the desire for more democracy and openness, vague as well. Because of this lack of precision, the reform theory has been able to serve only as partial guide for practical prescriptions. Theory was frequently followed as far as it would lead; but it was often too broad or confused to make a direct link to practice. Three consequences, characteristic of the recent reforms, have followed. First, the results of changes that reformers made often deviated from their intent, in part because their intent was never clearly specified or worked out in advance. Second, there was a great deal of room under general reform principles for groups to fashion proposals that were designed to advance certain short-term political interests; and finally, the broader objectives of reform, to the extent they existed, were often lost sight of in the name of certain procedural formulae that were derived initially from the general goals but which then became reified as ends in themselves.

[2] This list is not exclusive nor does it apply to all reformers. It represents a distillation of the reformers' dominant objectives as revealed in the reform documents and the many surveys of reformers conducted by political scientists.

261

The plan of this chapter will be to begin by asking what kind of institutional arrangements the reformers favored, a question that immediately raises the problem of distinguishing intent from consequences. Next we shall search for a more comprehensive description of the theory of reform by tracing the reform movement to its origins in the amateur club movement of the 1950s and following its development through the reform commissions of the national Democratic Party and certain recent federal legislation. Some effects of reform on party structure that could not be treated in the previous chapter will then be explored, after which we shall ask how successful the reformers were as judged by their own standards. A broader evaluation of reform, making use of the criteria developed by earlier thinkers, will be saved for the concluding chapter.

THE INSTITUTIONAL OBJECTIVES OF THE REFORM MOVEMENT

The reform movement brought about the establishment of a plebiscitary selection system very much along the lines proposed by the Progressives. Although two other movements of the late 1960s, the New Left and the New Politics, helped prepare the way for the plebiscitary system by calling for a more democratic selection process, the actual revisions that took place were carried out not under the black flags of these leftist movements but under the sanitized white banner of reform. Wherever rules and laws were rewritten, people spoke of "reforming" the system.

But if the reform movement was responsible for establishing a plebiscitary system, it does not necessarily follow that reformers actually intended this result. Indeed, many of those who sat on the reform commissions of the Democratic Party claim they had something very different in mind. According to Austin Ranney, a member of the McGovern-Fraser Commission and a former president of the American Political Science Association, the reformers never envisioned a large increase in the number of primaries:

I well remember that the first thing we members of the Democratic party's McGovern-Fraser commission (1969-72) agreed on . . . was that we did *not* want a national presidential primary or any great increase in the number of state primaries. Indeed, we hoped to prevent any such development by reforming the delegate-selection rules so that the party's nonprimary process would be open and fair, participation in them would greatly increase, and consequently the demand for more primaries would fade away . . . But we got a rude shock . . . We accomplished the opposite of what we intended.[3]

Much more, then, was done in the name of reform than its architects intended. Though reformers did succeed in achieving two very important goals—a curb on the power of the regular organizations and an end to a number of practices

[3] Austin Ranney, "Changing the Rules of the Nominating Game," in Barber, ed., *Choosing the President* (Englewood Cliffs, N.J.: Prentice Hall, 1972), p. 73.

Exactly why the states adopted the primaries has never been researched in detail. Ranney has little doubt that it was the reform rules that were the principal cause of the change. The chief reason, he suggests, was the desire of the state parties in existing caucus states to avoid the great complexity that the new rules imposed in the case of caucus proceedings. The following reasons can also be added: (1) Some may have felt that the spirit of reform was best met through primaries, for whatever the reformers may have intended, much of what they said suggested the desirability of maximizing popular participation. (2) Moderates and regulars, realizing the advantage that the New Politics activists might have under the new open caucus procedures, in some instances actually came to favor the primaries on the grounds that the people were more supportive of their views than those of their opponents. (3) Certain presidential candidates believed that they would do well in particular states and so lent their support to primary legislation. While it was not, therefore, always the reform-minded elements within the party who pushed for primaries, almost every group when seeking to make the party more democratic used the name of reform to justify its position. This paradox has its source in the fact, to be explored below, that party reform was defended publicly on democratic grounds, and it was this public defense that became the deepest cause for the change to primaries.

deemed unfair or undemocratic—it was the unanticipated effects of their actions that have been most significant in shaping the development of the selection process since 1968.

Thus as far as the explicit intention of the reformers is concerned, a distinction can be drawn between the reformers and the Progressives. Many reformers, in fact, resent the inference that they have served as the foot soldiers of the Progressives. Their goal, they claim, was to strengthen parties, not to create the empty shells favored by the Progressives. In the one full-length academic defense of the reform movement, *Parties*, John Saloma and Frederick Sontag assert that the purpose of reform was to build "effective citizen parties."[4] If anything, these authors look to the party-government school for their inspiration, and the book is even blessed with an introduction by one of the spiritual fathers of that school, James MacGregor Burns.

Yet such expressions, or confessions, of a "pro-party" intent on the part of reformers do not alter the plain facts of the current situation. The results of reform speak a Progressive language, and the best that reformers can therefore claim is that they were the innocent victims of an accidental series of events. But how innocent were they? The blame for unintended results may be considered less as it involves consequences that could not be reasonably foreseen and greater as it involves consequences that flow logically from the position that is defended. By this criterion, reformers cannot escape a measure of guilt, at least in the second degree. Whatever they may have intended, their doctrines never discouraged, and in fact paved the way for, weaker parties and a plebiscitary system. Their justification of change in the name of greater democracy and participation, which borrowed heavily at times from certain themes of the New Politics, undermined any role for a party organization in the selection process and did nothing to prevent a movement to primaries. And the emphasis reformers placed on designing

---

[4] John S. Saloma, III, and Frederick H. Sontag, *Parties* (New York: Vintage Books, 1973), p. 8.

a selection process that provided for each person's candidate preference, to the exclusion of any considerations of the needs of a party organization, resulted in a system in which the role of the party, however conceived, would be overshadowed by that of the individual candidates and their organizations. Given the rhetoric and principles of reform as they were publicly revealed, it is no surprise that many have identified the reform movement with the current system rather than the one the reformers apparently favored.

THE ORIGINS OF THE REFORM MOVEMENT

The difficulties reformers experienced in obtaining their goals was in part the result of the vagueness of their doctrines. Never before their moment of triumph in the Democratic Party in 1968 had they been compelled to articulate a positive statement of their position. Until that time they had been a small minority within the party, and as long as they functioned in the role of the "opposition," they could define their movement largely in terms of what it was against. Reformers found that it was sufficient to attack boss-dominated parties and to suggest, without the need to be very specific, that there was an alternative form of party organization at once stronger and more democratic than the existing one. But once the reform movement pushed aside the bosses, it lost the luxury of free criticism and was forced to assume responsibility for its own doctrines. And as this has occurred, it has become more and more apparent, not only to unbiased observers but to many reformers as well, that the ideas of the reform movement for restructuring the electoral process were in many instances vague and contradictory. In a certain sense, then, the reform movement is now paying the price of its own success.

We can best attempt to identify and sort out the various objectives of the reform movement by tracing its origins to the amateur club movement in the 1950s. The amateur movement was first studied in depth by James Q. Wilson in

The Amateur Democrat.[5] Wilson applied the term "amateur" to the participant who wants to promote certain policy goals and for whom these goals provide the motivation or incentive to take part in partisan activities. The amateur is also committed to a certain view about how politics should be conducted. Parties should be controlled by fellow amateurs, by those who share and care for a particular set of policies. Indeed, the amateur's animus against those serving in politics for less elevated reasons is itself a factor that stimulates his desire to participate. Politics for the amateur must be saved from the confusion and lack of clear principles that come from a party system dominated by those unconcerned with policy objectives.

The object of the amateur's contempt is the "professional." The professional style of politics reflects a long tradition in American party organization that dates back to the founding of permanent parties in the 1820s. The professional, according to Wilson, is motivated to participate in politics by incentives other than policy preferences—by material interest (a job, and sustaining an organization that relies heavily on jobs), by traditional allegiance, and by the friendships and excitement that come from belonging to a political organization. While professionals have generally adhered to certain policy positions—the New Deal liberalism of many of the big city organizations' Democrats being a case in point—they do not, so to speak, wear their ideological positions on their sleeves.[6] The professional is dedicated to maintaining the party as an ongoing organization and not simply as an instrument for accomplishing certain policy objectives. And since the professional is concerned less about policy or "ideology," he is more apt than the amateur to look for consensus and strike bargains with those with whom he might

---

[5] James Q. Wilson, *The Amateur Democrat* (Chicago: University of Chicago Press, 1962).

[6] Wilson, *The Amateur Democrat* (Chicago: University of Chicago Press, 1962), p. 22. Wilson states that "no one relied more heavily on big-city machines than Franklin D. Roosevelt."

266

have some disagreements. The usual characterization of the two political types is that the professional prefers victory to purity, the amateur purity to victory.

There is, however, one exception which Wilson noted to the professional's usual accommodating stance. When it comes to deciding who should run the party, as distinct from what policies it should pursue, the professional can be as uncompromising in his opposition to the amateur as the amateur is to the professional. There is, accordingly, nothing surprising in the well-documented findings of Denis Sullivan *et al.* on the Democratic Party convention of 1972. These researches found that delegates who began the 1972 convention as "professionals" (as defined by an attitude of concern for the party) in the end adopted a viewpoint about the fate of the party that was characteristic of the amateur. These professionals were reacting not to the usual kind of defeat but to a takeover of the party by a new political type. Their animosity was similar to that observed by Wilson in their struggles with reformers at the local levels in the 1950s and 1960s.[7]

Wilson's study of party organization and political motivation became the starting point for much of the subsequent scholarship on parties and the nomination process.[8] His identification of the conflict between those motivated by these two different political incentives on the local scene provided the general framework within which scholars analyzed the struggles in the Republican Party in 1964 and the Democratic Party in 1968 and 1972; and his discussion of the connection between amateurism and reform has shed a good

[7] Denis Sullivan, *et al., The Politics of Representation* (New York: St. Martin's Press, 1974), pp. 124-27.

[8] One can follow Wilson's concepts through the following studies: John Soule and James Clark, "Amateurs and Professionals: A Study of Delegates to the 1968 Democratic National Convention," *APSR*, 64 (September 1970): 888-99; Aaron Wildavsky, *The Revolt Against the Masses* (New York: Free Press, 1971), chaps. 12-14; Denis Sullivan, *et al., The Politics of Representation*, pp. 116-34; and Everett Ladd, *Transformations*, pp. 304-31.

267

deal of light on the difficulties and failures that the reform movement has met with on the national scene. While it would be incorrect to say that Wilson's views have been misinterpreted by those who have made use of his categories, a few points of clarification or elaboration are nevertheless worthwhile.

First, some have tended to identify the party too closely with the professional, implying that the party member is by definition a professional and the amateur always an outsider.[9] Although this positioning of the two groups reflected the actual state of affairs throughout most of the period up to 1964, Wilson never meant to suggest that it represented a "natural" or permanent condition.[10] The behavior of parties, in his view, is strongly influenced by the particular incentive that is dominant among the party's membership. This incentive is subject to change in response to shifts in political norms, the class structure of society, and the kinds of inducements available to the party organization. While Wilson expressed serious reservations about amateur parties, doubting in particular their capacity to promote the kind of coalitions American politics requires, he nevertheless presented a good deal of evidence to suggest that amateurs were becoming a stronger force within the party organizations. Parties had fewer of the inducements that supported professional participation—principally, less patronage—and there was a large increase within society in the educated, upper middle-class stratum from whose ranks amateurs generally come.[11]

[9] This view it seems, is adopted by Ladd in *Transformations,* p. 308.

[10] Wilson, *The Amateur Democrat*, p. 340, and *Political Organizations* (New York: Basic Books, 1973), p. 115. One should recall in this context that amateur "intrusions" have taken place before 1960, especially in the Republican Party. The GOP nomination campaigns of 1940 and 1952 were both greatly influenced by amateurs. Unlike the others, however, the amateur movement of 1964 appeared to signal a permanent and decisive shift in the direction of a greater role for amateurs.

[11] Ladd, *Transformations,* p. 317; Wilson, *The Amateur Democrat,* p. 268.

If the party member is not by nature a professional, there might nevertheless be something to the related hypothesis that amateurs will begin to behave somewhat more like professionals if ever they come to dominate a national party. The case for this hypothesis is based first on an unavoidable problem in the studies Wilson and others made of political motivation in the 1960s, namely that there were always two distinct influences acting on the amateur, each of which could explain his tendency to behave as a purist. One was his purposive motivation and the other was his temporary position as an outsider fighting to win control of the party from the regular, if not at the local then at the national level. Since both of these influences were operative at the time, it was impossible to know the extent to which each might have accounted for the amateur's behavior. By way of building an alternative model of predicted amateur behavior, it could be argued that the amateur might act more cautiously once faced with the responsibility of exercising power and maintaining the party against the opposition or against the possibility of displacement by a third party. This issue of behavior of the amateur is obviously of great importance to anyone making recommendations about the future character of the selection system. Any proposal that would restore the influence of the party organizations within the selection process would have to take into account the fact that what today we call amateurs will almost certainly occupy a more prominent position within the party organizations of the future than they did in the past.

A second point of clarification relates to Wilson's understanding of the connection between amateurism and reform. The two in his view are related but not, as some have supposed, identical. The amateur is one who participates in politics because of a commitment to furthering certain policy goals; the reformer, above and beyond this, is one who wants to make electoral procedures more open and democratic. Indeed, if it is possible to imagine a "pure" reformer, he would be one concerned primarily with these procedural objectives and hold them more dear than any policy goals.

Few persons, of course, are capable of such olympic detachment, and it suffices for practical purposes to define the reformer as one who, whatever his policy goals, is also committed to some notion of electoral democracy—not simply for the purpose of winning control of the party, but as an end in itself.

During the 1950s and early 1960s, when the party organizations were dominated largely by professionals, there was always some temptation for amateurs to adopt the rhetoric of reform. A call for more democracy offered a readily available, "principled" appeal that could be used to support the legitimacy of a challenge to the regulars. But the degree to which amateurs were actually committed to this principle varied with their ideological orientation. Among amateur liberal Democrats—and it was the clubs comprised of these persons that Wilson studied directly—amateurism was always found in conjunction with a belief in reform. Democratic procedures were an important part of their ideological beliefs. Among conservative amateurs, on the other hand, Wilson reports no great enthusiasm for procedural democracy. It was a minor concern, invoked perhaps on occasion, but having no intrinsic appeal either to the conservative amateur himself or to the constituency which he cultivated. The important point to stress, then, is that the reform movement was not a product of the amateur movement *per se*, but primarily of liberal amateurism. It was a force emanating from the Left, tied to the value of further democratization.

But while liberal amateurs believed in more democracy, they never agreed exactly on what it meant in the context of party affairs, especially at the level of the presidential selection process. Specifically, they never decided whether the best arrangement was one in which democratic procedures predominated within a party of amateurs but wherein the party organization maintained certain of its "undemocratic" prerogatives, or one in which the power of decision-making, to the extent possible, was extended to the rank-and-file.

270

The reformers could avoid this choice because they were largely on the outside. Moreover, they could think of it as a secondary problem because of their belief that the reform movement itself was somehow representative of the people's wishes. The people, it was felt, backed reform—or would, if only the unfair advantages that enabled the professionals to maintain an unnatural grip upon them were removed.[12]

At the national level, the modern amateur movement first achieved success in the Republican selection process in 1964. (Liberal amateurs, stung at being beaten to the punch, could nevertheless derive solace from the humiliating defeat suffered by their ideological opponents.) The amateur conservative movement of 1964 that took control of the Republican Party was described by one observer as a "vast grass-roots army of dedicated volunteers who regarded their effort as a crusade to save the country."[13] In the sense that this movement was a crusade, involving as it did many persons who had never participated before in party politics, it could be described as a "popular" movement. But in no sense was it a movement for reform. Despite occasional attacks on the party hierarchy in the name of more openness, the conservative amateurs did not wed their struggle to the cause of procedural democracy. Nor did they undermine the prerogatives of the state organizations. Thus in those places where they managed to take control of the party, conservative amateurs found the privileges of the organization intact and were able to enjoy them to their own advantage. And in many cases they subsequently became party "regulars."[14]

The emergence of the reform movement as a force on the national level occurred four years later in the Democratic Party. The immediate impetus for change came from "radical" reform elements, from those favoring the most demo-

[12] Ladd, *Transformations*, p. 7.

[13] Lee W. Huebner, "The Republican Party, 1952-1972" in Arthur Schlesinger, Jr., ed., *History of U.S. Political Parties*, 4 vols. (New York: Chelsea House, 1973), 4:3012.

[14] John Bartlow Martin, "Election of 1964," in Schlesinger, ed., *History of American Presidential Elections*, 4:3580-81.

cratic conception of the electoral process. The forces supporting Eugene McCarthy, Robert Kennedy, and George McGovern, adopted for themselves the label of advocates of the "New Politics." By this they meant, in procedural terms, a selection process in which the candidates took their case to the people, circumventing the party organizational hierarchy and traditional interest-group leaders. The New Politics was direct, popular, and—what does not necessarily follow logically from the other properties—oriented toward serious issue appeals. Under the Manichean distinction that the New Politics advocates adopted and which was accepted widely in the journalistic writing of the day, the opponents of direct democracy were said to favor the "old politics," a politics based on negotiation with organizational and interest group leaders that resulted in political payoffs and confused issue stances. To the supporters of the New Politics there was no question, at least in their moments of greatest enthusiasm, that a majority of the rank and file ("the people") supported a New Politics candidate. The call for a change in procedures in 1968 was thus made in the name of the people, against not only the existing party organization but party organizations of any sort; and many of the New Politics advocates could be found in the forefront of a revived effort to abolish the national party conventions and establish national primaries.[15]

Those who actually wrote the reform rules for the Democratic Party, however, rejected the national primary proposal. Indeed, they justified their reforms largely on the grounds that it was necessary to save parties from the misguided attacks of the New Politics advocates. Change, they argued, had to be made within the party in order to stave off the movement to a national primary. No doubt some reformers saw an advantage in playing up the seriousness of this threat as a way of satisfying the public of their modera-

[15] See Alexander Bickel, *The New Age of Political Reform* (New York: Harper Books, 1968), p. 2, and *Mandate for Reform*, published by the Democratic National Convention, April 1970, p. 11.

tion. In much the same way they used the threat of violence (from others) to win support for their proposals. "Unless changes are made," Senator McGovern warned in 1970, "the next convention will make the last look like a Sunday school picnic by comparison."[16] Much of this was probably rhetorical excess, but it nevertheless reveals the reformers' sincere desire to save at least some notion of a party from what was perceived to be at least a possible threat.

Reformers differed, however, on just what kind of party they wanted to save. One can distinguish two major groups within the reform commission, each with a different view about the proper character of the reformed party. The first group, to be referred to as the "establishment reformers," was concerned primarily with patching up the breach that had opened within the party in 1968. The new rules were desirable because of their fairness, but also because they would satisfy the New Politics dissidents and bring them back into the party. The establishment reformers' aim was not to alter radically the notion of a party, but to make those changes which, under new circumstances, would maintain the coalitional character of the party.

The second group, the "ideological reformers," was comprised of those who were committed to the substantive political programs of the New Politics advocates and those who had been connected with one or another of the New Politics candidates. They could be said to have represented the dissidents' claims within the party circles, and as such they were in a position to say what was needed, in terms of new rules and procedures, to mollify their followers. Like the New Politics advocates, their conception of a party was of a body that offered to the people a clear principled program. A party was obliged to address the issues, appealing to the citizens as individuals concerned with the issues, not as members of traditional intermediary groups. The new rules should be designed to help build this kind of party.

[16] Quoted in Richard C. Wade, "The Democratic Party, 1960-1972" in Schlesinger, ed., *Parties*, 4:2843.

The ideological reformers also had an immediate political goal, consistent as they saw it with their understanding of a party: they wanted to wrest control of the party from its existing leaders and take it over to promote a political program that sponsored the policies of the New Politics. One naturally is led to ask if this practical goal could be accomplished through democratic means. The general response of these reformers was simply to say that they favored an "open" party. Openness meant destroying the undemocratic privileges enjoyed by the existing organizations and allowing free and easy access for those wanting to participate in the delegate selection process. To this extent democratizing the party was consistent with the ideological reformers' objectives. But openness also implied—or many construed it to imply—a process that resulted in the selection of the candidate most favored by the rank and file. This understanding of democracy presented the ideological reformers with a problem. While many of them believed that the people backed a New Politics program, the practical strategy dictated that as little as possible should be left to chance. The ideological reformers thus favored the "open caucus" rather than primaries, for under this system the strong motivation of the New Politics amateurs could be relied on to provide them with an advantage. Even though many realized that this kind of open system might not be democratic in the sense of producing a representative result, they were nevertheless content to allow and even foster the confusion that associated openness with democracy. The aura of democracy would lend legitimacy to their plans and allow them to take control of the party in the name of the people.[17]

[17] The distinction developed here between the ideological and the establishment reformers is one that I derived from interviewing a number of persons involved in the reform movement. I was helped especially by an interview with Samuel Beer of Harvard University, who had been a member of the McGovern-Fraser commission and who has observed closely the subsequent development of events. In no way, however, do the views developed here represent those of Professor Beer.

Thus two groups combined to push for reform, one with a view to preserving the coalitional character of the Democratic Party and the other with a view to transforming it into an agent for principled action. Neither group favored an increase in the number of primaries. The establishment reformers opposed it because they believed that a predominantly primary system would make it impossible for the various interests within the party to settle their differences, something which could only be accomplished through the negotiation and bargaining of group leaders. The ideological reformers opposed it because primaries were less likely than open caucuses to promote their immediate goal of taking over the party. Yet both groups in the end found it impossible to stop the rush to primaries. Their own publicly stated principles, as will shortly be seen, contradicted their desires. Instead of cautioning against a totally popular system and justifying some role for the party organization, we find the McGovern-Fraser Commission citing approvingly the populist adage that "the cure for the ills of democracy is more democracy."[18]

In looking back over the development of the selection system since 1960, it is clear that two major forces have been responsible for initiating the changes that brought down the mixed nomination system. One was amateurism and the other reform. Amateurism strictly speaking was a broad movement whose defining characteristic was the effort to replace the prevailing material and solidary incentives dominant among the members of the party organizations with a purposive incentive, thereby making parties more self-consciously oriented to achieving policy objectives. Reform, a movement whose initial sponsors were largely liberal amateurs, sought not only to make parties more issue-oriented but also to make parties somehow more open and democratic. These two forces, which one might have thought would complement each other, turned out in the end to work at cross purposes. Although the reform movement helped to weaken the influ-

[18] *Mandate for Reform*, p. 14.

275

ence of the professional, it also espoused principles that helped undercut the basis of all organizational prerogatives, amateur no less than professional. What form the selection process might have assumed in the absence of reform cannot be known, but it seems likely that the amateurs would have more influence than they possess under the present system.

THE OFFICIAL CASE FOR PARTY REFORM

The description of the reformers' underlying objectives offered above was based on interviews and secondary accounts. It was necessary to begin in this fashion, going so to speak "behind the scenes," because the official reports of the reform commissions do not provide a satisfactory account of the reformers' overall intentions. The reports tell us what the reformers could collectively agree on, but that agreement did not extend as far as a positive statement of the kind of parties or selection system that should exist. This deficiency in the documents is no reason, however, to treat them less seriously than the revelations of the reformers' "real" intentions. It is in large measure through public documents that public officials communicate with the nation, and these documents are therefore often more influential in their impact on subsequent events than privately held views. They accordingly merit our close attention.

The Hughes Commission (1968) and the McGovern-Fraser Commission (1969-72)[19]

The reports of these two commissions offer the best account in the reform literature of the need for a change in our

[19] The Hughes commission was set up initially on private initiative, though its report was presented to the 1968 rules committee of the Democratic convention. Its arguments laid the groundwork for national reform, and the McGovern-Fraser commission, an official party body established pursuant to a resolution passed at the 1968 convention, followed its reasoning and suggestions on most points. The guidelines or rules established by the McGovern-Fraser commission, which will not be discussed in any detail, included the fol-

electoral institutions. Change, the commissions argue, is a matter of necessity: the Democratic Party must be reformed in order to save the party, the two-party system, and even the regime. The existing mixed system has lost the confidence and support of the American people, a loss all the more crucial because it coincides with Americans' growing disillusionment with other major institutions of the regime. The crisis in the selection system derives specifically from a crisis in representation originating in the breakdown of the New Deal coalition:

> The crisis of the Democratic Party is a genuine crisis for democracy in America and especially for the two-party system. Racial minorities, the poor, the young, members of the upper middle class, and much of the lower middle and working classes as well—all are seriously considering transferring their allegiance away from either of the two major parties.[20]

This argument assumes, of course, the validity of the conventional position that the well-being of the regime depends on a healthy two-party system. The McGovern-Fraser Commission proceeds to make this point in a bold and even threatening way:

---

lowing: quotas for delegate representation for minority groups, youth, and women; timely selection of delegates, i.e. within the calendar year of the convention; a uniform date in each state for the selection of delegates; a ban on the selection of any more than ten percent of the delegation by a state committee; a ban on the use of the unit rule. Beyond these requirements, the commission "urged," among other items, a complete termination of selection of delegates by state committees and a guarantee of "fair representation" of minority views on presidential candidates. The latter, of course, referred to winner-take-all primaries and was the basis for Humphrey's challenge of the California delegate selection process.

[20] *Report of the Commission on the Democratic Selection of Presidential Nominees*, reprinted in *The Congressional Record*, vol. 114, 90th Congress, 2nd Session, 1968, pp. 31544-31555; current reference is to p. 31545.

If we do not represent the demands of change, then the danger is not that people will go to the Republican Party, it is that there will no longer be a way for people committed to orderly change to fulfill their needs and desires within our traditional political system. It is that they will turn to third and fourth party politics or the anti-politics of the street.[21]

The reformers' basic argument for changing the selection process, then, is based on the need to maintain the legitimacy of a system in which parties play a central role; and this argument is based in turn on the proposition that legitimacy for the parties can be achieved only if the major parties represent the "demands of change." The function of legitimacy is defined in terms of the function of promoting change. There is clearly some point at which this argument holds merit. But it is worthwhile pondering for a moment some of the possible implications of the commission's position as stated above. If the commission is intending to argue merely that a major party should make an effort to include those forces that "demand change," few would take exception with its sentiments—although one might question the assumption that such forces are seeking, and would be willing to make accommodations with, the more traditional groups within society. But if representing the demands for change means simply acceding to them, regardless of the number of their adherents, there are certainly sound reasons to question whether this is the obligation of a major party or whether it would promote the legitimacy of the party system.

There is an even more disturbing overtone to the commission's argument on behalf of the two-party system. The commission implies that the major parties are the only vehicles for valid partisan participation, a position that casts doubt on the legitimacy of all third-party activity. This position would seem to encourage those who cannot find a place within either of the two major parties to think that the electoral

[21] *Mandate for Reform*, p. 49.

system as a whole is illegitimate. The "traditional political system" is identified entirely with a monopoly of the two-party system. This view contradicts the usual defense of our two-party system which holds that third and fourth parties on occasion play a positive role as instruments for representing new forces, testing their support, and, by virtue of these last two functions, pressuring the two major parties into maintaining responsiveness. The two major parties, in this view, may await cautiously to see if the "forces of change" are viable; if so, one or both of the parties will find it necessary, for its own preservation, to attempt to make some accommodation. The third party, then, is one source of "renewal" for the two-party system.[22]

The alleged crisis in representation to which the commissions refer is admitted to be of recent origin. The Hughes Commission conceded that the mixed system, though not fully open or democratic, had been able to serve the nation quite adequately from its inception in the 1920s until the 1960s. It had allowed for an adequate expression of the interests of the major groups within American society and established a framework within which these groups could settle their differences. But two developments in the 1960s undermined its effectiveness. The first was a growing dissatisfaction among black Americans with being represented in northern states, especially in the big cities, by white party leaders. Blacks felt that their views were no longer being adequately taken into account by the existing organizations and began to demand a new basis of representation. The second development was the increase in the number of "issue-oriented individuals" within the electorate. These persons related to the political world through their views on vital questions of public policy, not through a stable set of interests that could be represented by a traditional interest group. The Democratic Party, which

[22] V. O. Key, *Politics, Parties and Pressure Groups*, 5th ed. (New York: Thomas Y. Crowell, 1964), p. 281; Daniel L. Mazmanian, *Third Parties in Presidential Elections* (Washington, D.C.: Brookings Institution, 1974), pp. 27-66.

was built largely around the representation of major groups, thus could not in its present form express the will of the electorate. The only way the views of these individuals could be accurately accounted for was through a process in which they could each register their issue preferences by voting for the candidate whose position accorded most closely with their own.[23]

These two elements of the crisis of representation are clearly different. Blacks are said to be more group conscious while the electorate as a whole is said to be less group conscious. This "tension" is resolved, as one might have expected, by the implicit acknowledgement that the tendency toward individual issue-consciousness is taking place primarily within the (white) upper-middle class:

> . . . the increasing education and affluence of the electorate generally have combined to erode substantially the role of well-defined interest groups in presidential politics. . . . Whereas bargaining among representatives of party organizations once could be said to represent the interest and views of the mass constituency of the party, the decline of the interest groups behind the bosses has undercut that rationale.[24]

Assuming that this presentation of the problem is accurate, toward what end should the selection process have been changed—to accommodate blacks or the white upper-middle class? Accommodating the former, it is clear, could have been accomplished by reforming the *party*, whereas accommodating the latter required a change in the character of the delegate selection system as a whole. By reforming the party, we mean that steps could have been taken to encourage or ensure greater access for blacks within the party. Indeed, though both reform commissions leave the impression that it was an absence of democracy that was the cause of black underrepresentation, it was frequently in the caucus states

[23] *Report of Commission on Democratic Selection*, p. 31547.
[24] *Ibid.*, p. 31547.

and party-controlled primaries that black representation was highest relative to the population; and in many northern cities blacks were on the verge by 1968 of controlling the party organizations.[25] It would have been possible to draw a distinction between practices that harmed the long-term interests of the party organization, e.g. the unit rule, and those deemed unfair only from the point of view of those rejecting organizational prerogatives of any kind. Reform could have been directed solely at the former.

Instead of changing the party, however, reformers adopted the strategy of revamping the entire delegate selection process, opening it to the expression of the participants' candidate preferences. Replication of candidate preference in the delegate totals was the central theme of the McGovern-Fraser Commission reforms. This representational theory, which previously had been one theory among many, was now extended to embrace the entire selection process, replacing such alternative theories as representation of state and local parties. Meanwhile, the problem of underrepresentation of blacks, which was expanded to include underrepresentation of women and young people, was handled through the imposition of quotas for these groups, but quotas within a system intended to reflect candidate preferences. Those designated under the minority categories were not, accordingly, representatives of their groups in any real sense, but were

[25] *Mandate for Reform*, p. 26. In 1964 two percent of the convention delegates were black; in 1968, the number had increased to over five percent. More important, the commission made no attempt to show that the states using the closed system were actually the ones that had underrepresentation of blacks. A study done subsequently by John Jackson proves, in fact, that there was no relationship in 1964 or 1968 between the type of selection system (caucus or primary) and the degree of minority representation. See "Some Correlates of Minority Representation in the National Conventions, 1964-1972," *American Politics Quarterly* 3 (April 1975), pp. 171-88. When one considers that all but two of the southern states used caucus or committee systems in 1968, it becomes clear that outside of the south the caucus system actually did a better job of securing black representation than the primary system.

281

instead agents selected in the first instance to vote for a particular candidate. Group representation—though it is doubtful that young people in any way constituted a meaningful group—was subsumed under candidate representation.

This new approach to selection was plainly intended to satisfy the desires of the "issue-oriented individuals" of the upper-middle class, an observation made not necessarily to discredit the reformers but only to indicate their particular bias. The new process met the contention that such individuals could not be represented on an ongoing basis within a party organization because they only discovered their political views in response to their assessment of current issues. A party in this view has no long-term identity that is determined by the concerns of an activist cadre; rather, it assumes its identity at the last moment in the voters' choice of a particular candidate.

The actual form that this expression of candidate choice should take—the open caucus or the primary—was never stipulated in the commission reports, nor was a preference directly indicated. The closest the McGovern-Fraser Commission came to revealing its partiality to the open caucus was in its statement that "we are concerned with the opportunity to participate rather than the actual level of participation. . . ." But this statement, which contains only a glimmering of the notion of an amateur party, was balanced by a good deal of thoroughly democratic rhetoric. The McGovern-Fraser Commission went out of its way to commend the states that had passed new primary laws and singled out for special recognition those that had adopted the most explicitly democratic system of proportional representation.[26] The Hughes Commission was even more clear in its praise of "direct democracy":

> The fact that many states declined to provide for delegate selection entirely by primary was acceptable to the nation —but only because the system did not override or frustrate

26 *Mandate for Reform*, pp. 49-50.

the national commitment to direct democracy in the naming of presidential nominees. . . . [By 1968] a confluence of forces has made the Democratic National Convention an occasion of great moment in the inexorable movement of Presidential politics in America toward direct democracy.[27]

The term "plebiscitary system," which thus far has referred to the choice of the nominee by the people, has an additional connotation. It is often used in contradistinction to a pluralist system and implies the rule of mass opinion in contrast to the rule of settled groups which compromise their interests in a bargaining process. The mixed system contained both a pluralistic and plebiscitary element. The system created by the reformers was designed expressly to diminish the influence of groups and to expand that of opinion. There is admittedly some ambiguity in the reformers' view about just how responsive the system should be to *mass* opinion, but the emphasis on the rule of opinion is unmistakable. Coupled with the democratic character of the rhetoric, it leads directly to the notion of rule by public opinion. Just how public opinion is formed is never carefully explored by the reformers. Their idea seems to be that opinion "grows up" from the bottom, from the autonomous decisions of discrete individuals reacting to the issues of the day. Their system is designed to produce a nominee who is a public opinion "leader" in the sense of one who expresses the strongest current of opinion within the electorate. But one finds no notion of leadership similar to that of Woodrow Wilson in which the leader possesses a formative influence over public opinion. There is, in fact, no attention given to the question of the type of leadership or the type of executive that is desired. The reformers' views on groups and leadership were no doubt influenced by the general ideas current in the late 1960s that group politics was obsolete and that politics was now directed by mass movements. Yet one might well wonder whether in

---

[27] *Report of Commission on Democratic Selection*, p. 31546.

abandoning themselves to this view, reformers did not help to perpetuate and institutionalize it, even before one could be certain that it represented the wave of the future.

The Commission on Delegate Selection and Party Structure (the Mikulski Commission)

The 1972 Democratic Party convention established another commission on delegate selection which was asked to look into the operation of the 1972 rules, suggest revisions, and outline new procedures consistent with the call for the 1976 convention "that delegates . . . be chosen in a manner which fairly reflects the division of preference by those who participate in the presidential nominating process . . ."[28] At the time, the reform-minded convention probably had in mind a new set of rules that would implement some of the guidelines that the McGovern Commission had suggested but not required for 1972. But when the commission was actually appointed in the following year, the situation within the party had changed greatly. A "reform" candidate had suffered a humiliating defeat, brought on in large measure by the intraparty split that many felt had been encouraged and fueled by the reform rules. It became impossible now to ignore the claims of the regulars, and a shake-up within the party took place.

The new commission, headed by Baltimore City Councilwoman Barbara Mikulski, faced pressure from the national party to proceed cautiously. From Democrats around the nation, meanwhile, the commission received conflicting demands for still further reforms and for a return to traditional procedures. By its rhetoric the commission sought to placate both groups, laying stress on the importance of openness—"We have spent this past year searching for the best way to insure the opportunity for every delegate to participate in the

[28] *Democrats All, Report of the Commission on Delegate Selection and Party Structure,* Democratic National Committee, December 6, 1973, p. 5.

delegate selection process"—but also emphasizing the coalitional character of the party:

> The purpose [of the convention] is to wield a diversity of state organizations, special interest groups and rank and file Democrats. . . . The commission faced a difficult task in developing rules that would be oriented to party unity and coalition building among its pluralistic constituencies.[29]

What is most striking in reading the report, however, is the absence of any serious argument on behalf either of further reform or retrenchment. The commission apparently sought to avoid the controversy that might be generated by taking a firm stance of any kind. The proposed rules are justified on the grounds simply of procedural values: "fairness," "participation," and "openness" are all invoked as givens, needing no further defense in terms of the benefits they bestow.[30]

But the tameness of the commission's rhetoric provides no indication of the importance of the changes it proposed. Like the rhetoric, the new rules strike a balance between the demands of traditionalists and reformers, though it is reform goals, reified as procedural formulae, that come out on top. As concessions to traditionalists, quotas were formally renounced, the slate-making process was closed, and a provision was adopted to allow for greater participation by party regulars. Yet this last provision, supposedly the greatest concession to the regulars, indicates just how far the formal goals of reformers had come in winning acceptance within the party. The way in which the commission posed the problem is itself revealing:

> The central question that this Commission faced was not whether to include Party leaders and elected officials in the decision-making process, but rather how best to do so without jeopardizing the ability of the rank and file to influence the outcome of the Convention.[31]

[29] *Ibid.*, p. 1.   [30] *Ibid.*, pp. 3-4.   [31] *Ibid.*, p. 11.

285

A rule was adopted that allowed for up to twenty-five percent of the delegates from primary states (not caucus states) to be selected by state committees; it stipulated, however, that these delegates must reflect the same division of candidate preference as the delegates who are directly elected. The party organization was thus obliged to follow the decision of the people.[32]

Most of the other changes explicitly promoted the formal reform principles. The most important principle advanced is that of "fairness." Translated into its meaning for presidential selection, this principle requires that the selection process replicate as precisely as possible the candidate preferences of those participating. (Candidate preference could include a designation of uncommitted or no preference.) In caucus states, where delegates had traditionally been elected without having to make a formal declaration of the candidate they supported, the emphasis on candidate preference was met by a rule requiring that all delegates designate their candidate preference at the time of their selection. This rule applied at all levels of the process, meaning that delegates selected to the district conventions from the mass meetings had to identify their candidate choice. In effect, the mass meetings in caucus states resembled primaries, with "ballots" on which participants indicated their preferred candidate and an official tally of the results. (Indeed, at all levels, the persons actually selected as delegates were not chosen until after it was determined how many delegates a candidate was entitled to; the delegate, except where elected as an uncommitted, was thus no longer viewed as a trustee but as an instructed agent.) In primary states in which the state law did not allow the delegates to identify their preference on the ballot, the state party was required "to publicize to all eligible voters the candidates for delegate approved by each presidential candidate."[33] Finally, another rule gave to the candidates the right of approval over the delegates who ran com-

---

[32] *Report of the Commission on Delegate Selection and Party Structure*, as amended and adopted, March 1, 1974, rule #12.
[33] *Ibid.*, rule #10.

mitted to them, thus providing the candidates with more leverage over their delegations than had been the case in the past. What one finds in the new rules, then, is an implicit acknowledgment of the candidate-supremacy model: the selection process revolves around the expression of the candidate choice of the participants, and there is no direct provision for the representation of the organizational interest of the party.

The search for precision in the replication of candidate preferences led the Commission to adopt the novel principle of proportional representation in delegate selection. This decision is yet another indication of the degree to which the theory of candidate representation had supplanted the theory of representation of party organizations. Under the provision for proportional representation, electoral districts had to award their delegates in proportion to the percentage of voters supporting each candidate within the district. National rules allowed states to cut off representation for a candidate who received below fifteen percent of the vote, a figure that proved high enough to prevent the fractionalization that was widely feared before the 1976 selection process began. Also exempted from the requirement were delegates running as individuals—i.e. not on slates—from units the size of a Congressional district or smaller. But no longer was this exception explicitly recognized as "fair," as it had been by the McGovern-Fraser Commission; and a provision that all elections be conducted under proportional representation was passed at the 1976 convention, though whether the states will pass legislation needed to achieve compliance remains to be seen.[34]

[34] The party commission now drafting the rules for 1980 has adopted a regulation requiring proportional representation in all primary elections except those in single member districts. State democratic parties must take "provable positive steps" to enact legislation that conforms with the rules. See *Openness, Participation and Party Building: Reforms for a Stronger Democratic Party*. Report of the Commission on Presidential Nomination and Party Structure (Washington, D.C.: Democratic National Committee, 1978), p. 54, 57.

SOME FURTHER CONSEQUENCES OF PARTY REFORM

Now that the case for reform has been discussed, it remains to treat the effects of the reform movement on the character of political parties and on the national conventions. A point that has been emphasized throughout this analysis is that the reform movement, notwithstanding the reformers' intentions, served to weaken the role of the party within the selection process. By "party" here we mean some sort of formal organization, or for that matter an informal cadre of activists, committed on an ongoing basis to promoting the interests of the party's label. By 1976, with primaries dominating the selection process, the party, in this sense, played a minimal role. It was "the people" that had become the decisive force, and observers and candidates found themselves consulting pollsters in an effort to discover the whims and inclinations of the new sovereign. It was no accident that the major media sources allocated large sums of money in 1976 to pay for polls. This merely acknowledged the fact that the major "story" in nominating politics was no longer to be found in what party leaders were thinking, but in what the people wanted and in how they were responding to the blandishments of the candidates. The Old Politics for all intents and purposes was a thing of the past.

Yet there is one sense in which it could be said that the reform movement strengthened the Democratic Party. For those who measure strength in terms of the degree of dominance of the national party over its state counterparts, progress certainly could be claimed: national standards for delegate selection were implemented, and the state parties—and even in some measure the state governments—recognized the primacy of the national party in determining the character of the selection process. The national party's assertion of control over the delegate selection process actually began before 1968 in response to the problem of discrimination in delegate selection and party affairs in some of the southern states. The 1964 convention, in the compromise over the Mississippi

288

delegate challenge, laid down national criteria for participation in party affairs that barred racial discrimination. But the action taken by the reform commission was of a different order altogether: it was directed not only, or even primarily, at discrimination but at the character of the selection process as a whole.

Never was the abstract "right" of the national party to enforce such procedures against its state party counterparts in doubt. Yet, because the national party itself tended to be an amalgam of the state parties and to reflect their interests, and in particular their desire for autonomy, there was little chance that this right would actually be exercised. The reform movement, however, changed this. Born of a national impulse for change, the reform movement seized the initiative at the 1968 convention and established a mandate for instituting national standards; and by using the McGovern-Fraser Commission to the fullest extent of its authority—and perhaps beyond—reformers boldly challenged the traditional autonomy of the state organizations. The acquiescence of the state parties established the precedent of national control, and this precedent was used without challenge by the Mikulski Commission.

Only in one area was the potential "sovereignty" of the national party over the states a matter of some legal doubt. This was where a national party might establish regulations for the selection of delegates that conflicted with or went beyond what state *law* required. In such instances, the issue was whether the national party, if it chose, could refuse to seat delegates selected in accordance with valid state laws. Again, this issue had not been raised for some time because of the national parties' acceptance of state autonomy; and again the reform rules forced the issue. In the Illinois delegate selection challenge of 1972, the national party chose not to seat delegates elected validly according to state law (Mayor Daley's slate) because the election procedures did not fulfill all the requirements for delegation selection under the party's new rules. Although the status of a party as a

289

"private" or quasi-private association might have suggested that the convention was fully within its rights, some believed otherwise and could cite on behalf of their position a whole line of court decisions dating back to the 1940s which called into question the private character of the American political party. It was, moreover, not only those "wronged" by reform rules who sought redress in the courts, but other groups who contended that the selection system was not sufficiently reformed. In both parties, the formulae apportioning delegates to the states were challenged, and the Americans for Democratic Action even threatened legal action in 1975 against the exemption of certain primary states from the provision for proportional representation.[35] In the Illinois delegate case and in some of the apportionment challenges, a number of the lower courts decided that these issues were proper subjects for judicial scrutiny and remedy. But the Supreme Court in 1972, without going into the merits of these cases, kept the courts out of the process for that election year. The Daley case (*Cousins v. Wigoda*) came to the Supreme Court for final determination in 1975, after the Illinois state courts had ruled that the Daley (Wigoda) delegates had been illegally denied their seats at the 1972 convention. In rejecting this ruling, the Court gave wide discretion to the national party in determining the character of the delegate selection process:

> The states themselves have no constitutionally mandated role in the great task of the selection of Presidential and Vice-Presidential candidates. If the qualifications and eligibility of delegates to National Political Party Conventions were left to state law ". . . each of the fifty states could establish the qualification of its delegates to the various party conventions without regard to party policy, an obviously intolerable result." *Wigoda v. Cousins,* . . . Such a regime could seriously undercut or indeed destroy the

[35] Reported in *Congressional Quarterly Weekly Report,* August 16, 1975, p. 1812.

effectiveness of the National Party Convention. . . . The Convention serves the pervasive national interest in the selection of candidates for national office, and this national interest is greater than any of an individual state.[36]

This decision does not mean that a national party can now force states to adopt certain laws, but it does make clear that national parties can refuse to accept delegates selected in a manner contrary to their own rules. The decision served to embolden those charged with implementing the Democratic Party's 1976 rules and gave them added leverage in dealing with the states. States could either acquiesce in the rulings of the national party or face the prospect of having their delegates refused a place at the convention.

The reform movement has thus successfully asserted the sovereignty of the national party over its state organizations and in some measure over state law. Democrats have chosen to exercise this prerogative in a vigorous way; Republicans have continued to allow a great deal of leeway to the states. As far as the Court is concerned, it now appears to be the case that the national parties have been designated as the supreme "legislator" for the presidential selection process. Although the reformers in the Democratic Party have used this power thus far to weaken the influence of existing state organizations and have made no effective provision for their replacement either by state organizations of a different sort or by a national organization, it remains that this power can now be used by the national party for a different purpose.

Turning now to the relationship of the reforms to the national party conventions, it must be acknowledged that it is still too soon to specify exactly what effects the reforms will have. The most one can offer are some reasoned guesses, based on an attempt to extrapolate from some of the tendencies inherent in the present system. The most obvious point with which to begin any discussion of the modern convention is with the observation that every presidential decision since

[36] *Cousins v. Wigoda*, S. Ct. 541 (1975), at 549.

1952 has been decided on the first ballot, the longest such string of first-ballot victories since the convention system began. But the implication which is often drawn from this fact, namely that the convention has lost its role as a deliberative body and serves now merely to ratify a previous choice, has probably been overstated. In at least two conventions during this period—the Republican conventions of 1968 and 1976—there was a genuine possibility of movement away from the eventual nominee. Nor should it be assumed that making a choice prior to the convention necessarily alters in a qualitative way the character of the decision-making process: it may be that the bargaining which formerly took place at the convention site is now, with modern communications, taking place in advance.

Yet this much, it appears, can safely be asserted: the use of the outside strategy, which grew in frequency over this period, has been coupled loosely with the view that the nomination should normally be decided in the primaries and go to the demonstrated popular favorite. Only in the event of a standoff in the primaries is it considered "legitimate" for the convention to exercise discretion. The reform movement, by making the outside strategy the necessary strategy and by tightening the connection between the selection of delegates and the expression of candidate preference, has contributed to the ascendancy of the primaries as the decisive stage. There is of course much that is vague in this view, not the least of which is the question of when a candidate has won enough primaries to become the popular favorite. Nonetheless, the general idea that the nomination is properly decided in the primaries has been gaining ground in the public mind, and to this extent the convention as a practical matter has lost a good deal of discretion. And not surprisingly, controversy over the fairness of the nomination process has tended to move back from the convention procedures to the procedures regulating delegate selection, since it is at this stage of the process that the real decision is now perceived to be made.

It would be paradoxical if the reform movement, which in a general way contributed to limiting the discretion of the convention, in fact made it more likely that the nomination decision would have to be made at the convention. Yet it was precisely this result that many observers predicted at the outset of 1976.[37] It was argued that the widespread use of proportional representation would fractionalize delegate support among the candidates, making it unlikely that any one candidate could win a majority; and since the bulk of the delegates would be committed to the various candidates, the stage would be set for a "brokered" convention. (In a use of language that defied all logic, though not expediency, the candidates who came to rely on a brokered convention as their only chance for winning the nomination referred to it as an "open" convention.)

Two broad strategies emerged in response to the new rules among the Democratic candidates for the 1976 nomination. On the one hand, candidates such as Jimmy Carter, George Wallace, and Morris Udall followed initially a "knock-out" plan. They believed that, notwithstanding proportional representation, the real decision would be made by those who won the primaries, especially the early ones. (Of course these strategies were adopted as much out of necessity as choice; Carter and Udall, both being long-shots, had to seek victories in order to establish any kind of credibility for their campaigns.) More important than winning delegates, early primary victories would establish one's claim to the nomination and, in a situation in which everyone still thought in terms of winners and losers, eliminate opposing candidates and establish momentum for the later primaries. On the other hand, Senator Jackson, a leading contender, adopted a strategy predicated on the assumption that the decision would probably be made at the convention. His objective in the

[37] These predictions were widely reported in the press, and according to Hamilton Jordan, Carter's campaign manager, most of the active contestants were basing their campaign on this assumption (*New York Times*, June 10, 1976).

primaries, accordingly, was to win some important races, establishing a partial claim to being the popular choice, and position himself to pick up second choice support. Others of lesser prominence, such as Senator Byrd, toyed with the idea of winning just enough delegate strength to "get one's hat in the ring," hoping for the best from a deadlocked convention. Hubert Humphrey, too, pursued a strategy based on a deadlock, though without entering any of the primaries.

Carter's victory has probably guaranteed that the aggressive "knock-out" strategy will remain the recommended type of outside campaign in the near future, even with the extensive use of proportional representation in the delegate selection process. Indeed, contrary to the predictions of most political analysts prior to 1976, there was a sense in which proportional representation actually helped to promote a first-ballot victory. This was because proportional representation was an integral part of the general reforms that emphasized the idea of a national candidate representation rather than representation of party organizations. Still, within the context of a system intended to emphasize national candidates, proportional representation does in fact tend to fragment the delegate totals among a larger number of candidates.[38] With the probable changeover of nearly all primary states to proportional representation by 1980, at least within the Democratic Party, this fragmenting effect could conceivably become much stronger and lead to a series of brokered conventions. Since the brokered convention remains at least a possibility, it is worthwhile to explore its possible character under a reform system.

One can distinguish three basic models of future decision-making under the conditions of a brokered convention. First, the decision might be reached through a bargaining process

---

[38] For a discussion of the complex effects of the use of proportional representation in the nominating process, see Paul David and James Ceaser, *Proportional Representation in the Presidential Nominating Process* (Charlottesville, Va.: University Press of Virginia, 1978).

among the candidates themselves, who by virtue of their own organizational efforts and the requirement in the Democratic Party for candidate approval of all delegates, should have strongly committed personal delegations. The result would then be a "top-heavy" convention in which a nominee is chosen by agreement among the major candidates. (In the past, a substantial portion of a candidate's initial support was made up of independent powers having interests of their own, and it was by the movement of these groups that deadlocks were broken.) A candidate-controlled convention would present an ironic outcome to the reform movement, which was originally justified on the grounds that it would make the decision-making process more open and democratic. The contradiction between promise and performance could lead to a challenge to the legitimacy of the convention system, especially if the candidate with the largest contingent of delegates was denied the nomination. One could then easily imagine the disappointed partisans of the defeated favorite making the charge of a "corrupt bargain" and attacking the convention system in the same vein as the friends of candidates defeated by "King Caucus" in the early nineteenth century.[39]

As a second possibility, the convention decision would be reached by bargaining from the "bottom" with national interest groups and constituencies, e.g. labor unions, blacks, women's groups, controlling groups of delegates. This model becomes more likely to the extent that groups perceive that no candidate will obtain a majority of delegates prior to the convention. This possibility runs counter to the general plebiscitary trend of the selection process, but it cannot be altogether discounted. Proportional representation offers groups the possibility to win delegates outright, since they need only secure a small share to obtain delegate support. They could

[39] For a description of delegate movement in past conventions, see Nelson Polsby and Aaron Wildavsky, "Uncertainty and Decision-Making at National Conventions" in Polsby, Denfler and Smith, eds., *Political and Social Life* (Boston: Houghton Mifflin, 1963).

obtain this share either under an uncommitted status or by running a "holding candidate" to represent their interests. Ellen McCormack's campaign indicated the possibilities for this strategy in the case of a national issue-oriented group, and some black leaders toyed with the idea prior to the 1976 convention of running a candidate of their own. It is significant, moreover, that while reformers pushed initially for proportional representation, the labor movement's National Coalition Clearinghouse was a prime mover for extending the principle of proportional representation at the 1976 convention, over the objections of the candidate Jimmy Carter. The obvious danger in any such bargaining process involving national groups is that the nominee would become too greatly beholden to one or more of them. Formerly, interest groups were represented in the nominating process through the party organizations; this gave these groups access, but also maintained a buffer between the candidates and the groups. If constituency blocs should ever become the principal arbiters of the nomination, it would contradict both the preference of the reformers and the grounds on which they declared the old system obsolete. The New Politics was founded on the assumption (or hope) that pluralistic influences were declining in favor of the activities of independent, issue-oriented individuals.

The final possibility would be an open convention in which neither of the kinds of blocs mentioned above would form or maintain cohesiveness. The decision of the convention would then be left to the individual delegates acting independently or to *ad hoc* groups and leaders forming at the convention. Although such a convention would be democratic in form, one must wonder about the quality of its deliberations. Democracy in so large an assembly could turn out to be chaotic and dangerous if the delegates are unable to bargain effectively or communicate with each other; alternatively, it could prove a sham if a few *ad hoc* spokesmen emerged to control the direction of the proceedings.

Thus a general problem future conventions may face will

be to establish the legitimacy of their choices. Reform was popularized in 1968 on the basis of giving the nomination choice to "the people," or at any rate to those who participated. The implication of this position was that the legitimate claim to the nomination derived not from the deliberation of the convention, but from the expression of the people's wishes prior to it. The convention was only to register what the people wanted even as the electoral college registers the people's choice in the general election. The new nominating system promises to live up to this ideal in the case of any candidate who wins a majority of those participating in the process. Otherwise, the convention is supposed to become a free deliberative body. But whether it can gain acceptance for its "deliberate" choice in the face of competing claims by some candidates to represent the people's choice is questionable.

AN EVALUATION OF THE REFORM MOVEMENT: A PRELIMINARY ANALYSIS

The reform movement should be evaluated first according to how well it accomplished the objectives of its own architects. The goal emphasized most in the reform commission reports was the restoration of legitimacy to the selection process. Legitimacy as we defined it earlier includes two aspects: first, in a formal sense, the existence of procedures widely regarded as fair and consistent with republican principles, and second, in an informal sense, the capacity of the system to produce a winner who appears to emerge from the entire process with a "natural" plurality of sufficient size to obviate the need for contrived mechanisms to creat a majority. These two standards refer to the selection process in its entirety, although both relate to the nominating process as well. The consideration of formal legitimacy applies directly. The issue here is whether the nomination process, taken in conjunction with the final election phase, is fair and consistent with republican standards. The consideration of informal legitimacy, on the other hand, is a concern that applies strictly speaking only to the result of the final election. But it is connected with the nominating process, for it has been the dominance of the two-party system since the 1830s which has solved the problem of informal legitimacy. There is a sense, then, in which this standard can be applied to the nominating process, in that the viability of the two-party system rests on the ability of the parties to obtain consensual choices and keep their various factions together. Nonetheless, it goes too far to tie the notion of legitimacy entirely to the capacity of the parties to win support from all segments of the party, which is the concept of legitimacy adopted by Denis Sullivan *et al.* in *The Politics of Representation*.[40] This concept is too restrictive in that the legitimacy of the final election outcome is not always threatened by the failure of one or another of the parties to win a consensus. While an institutional arrangement that discouraged the obtaining of a consensus would clearly threaten legitimacy, there are times when, even with consensus-promoting institutions, the various elements within the party cannot agree. A faction may then withdraw and sit out the election, join the opposition, or begin a third party. Such actions are an integral part, albeit an unusual one, of an open electoral process and have served to promote the long-term responsiveness of the two major parties. Legitimacy should not be defined to exclude them.

The reformers direct concern was with restoring a sense of formal legitimacy to the nominating process. How successful were they? The question is not an easy one to answer because of the difficulty of separating the effect of the "times" from that of the rules. Between 1968 and 1972 the political atmosphere was filled with talk of a crisis of legitimacy. By 1976 all was calm. An impartial analysis would probably demonstrate, however, that the change in the rules of selection was not entirely responsible for this shift in attitude. The times, too, had changed. The divisions within the party in

[40] Denis Sullivan, *et al., The Politics of Representation*, p. 127.

1968 and 1972 were much greater than in 1976. Had a New Politics candidate been denied the nomination in 1968 or 1972 under an open system, a great deal of bitterness would still have ensued. The existence of a particular set of rules, no matter how fair or democratic, does not mean that political division will disappear. The attack on the legitimacy of the selection system in 1968, as in the case of most such attacks in the past, was in some degree "partisan" in character, i.e. directed at attaining a certain political objective. Thus the challenge to the system would doubtless have subsided with a decline in the intensity of the political divisions within the party. At the same time, however, it must be conceded that reformers were able to make an issue of the legitimacy of the system; and unless one holds that the selection system will always be vulnerable to such attacks when passions run high, it must be acknowledged that a problem existed—either in the character of the existing process or in the way in which it was defended.

Whether all the changes made by the reformers were necessary to ensure legitimacy is certainly open to question. Indeed, if one takes the Democratic Party's selection system of 1972 as the reformers' "model," their efforts must be pronounced a failure. Even omitting consideration of the controversy over the quota issue, it is clear that the general system the reformers established, which in 1972 still included a large number of open caucuses, was subject to challenge. Groups such as the Coalition for a Democratic Majority charged that the formally open system was not democratic in its results because of different levels of political participation among various groups: in a highly charged political environment the issue-oriented activists were more likely to participate in caucuses than the "average" citizen.[41] The reformers' system may thus have been spared a crisis in legitimacy of their own making by the unanticipated shift of

[41] See Keech and Matthews, *The Party's Choice*, pp. 206-10. The campaign strategy of McGovern in the caucus states was based explicitly on this calculation of differential rates of participation.

many states to primaries. With the exception of the possible problems of legitimacy connected with a deadlocked convention discussed above, it is clear that the plebiscitary system is very difficult to challenge on the grounds of its formal legitimacy, as it is based on popular sovereignty, the strongest principle inherent in any democratic regime. Yet, though this title to formal legitimacy is clearly a strength of the system, it does not follow that the plebiscitary system is the only system capable today of winning public acceptance. More may have been conceded to popular rule than necessary, and a judgment about whether that was wise can be made only after assessing the effects of the plebiscitary system on the other objectives of the selection system, including its capacity to promote legitimacy in the informal sense.

The other goals of the reform movement differed according to the group of reformers in question. The ideological reformers, who sought to take control of the party and transform it into an instrument for expressing a clear and principled stand on the issues, succeeded in 1972, at least insofar as the nomination was concerned. But their success rested on a weak foundation—on the confusion over the meaning of openness, which many construed to imply a system that was thoroughly democratic but which in fact was designed to favor the issue-oriented activists. Only the politically naive—and the seasoned reformers on the party commissions were anything but that—would contend that a system open in the sense of providing all with the opportunity to participate will necessarily provide a result consistent with the wishes of the rank and file. It is a well-established finding in modern research into political behavior that as the event or activity becomes less visible or salient, the level of participation declines. Those left to participate in the less salient activities tend either to be the well organized, e.g. the party regulars, or the highly motivated, well-educated citizens "schooled" in the art of participation. The ideological reformers banked upon the latter, who were predominantly proponents of the New Politics, to overwhelm the former, and their expectations were certainly not disappointed in the highly charged political atmosphere of 1972.

Where these reformers were perhaps short sighted, however, was in their expectation that others would let them succeed in controlling the party in the name of democracy by a system that was not democratic in its operation. The opponents of reform appropriated the reformers' own democratic rhetoric in the push for primaries, and by 1976 the ideological reformers learned what they perhaps had always feared—that the people were not necessarily on their side. (This lesson had been brought home to them in the general election of 1972, but Watergate intervened to raise temporarily their expectations.) The initial worry of many in 1975 was that the people might follow George Wallace in a demagogic appeal to covert racial prejudices. Efforts were undertaken by some to repeal primary laws in Tennessee and North Carolina, but these were rebuffed by Wallace supporters. Governor Wallace himself even traveled to Tennessee to defend the primary in the name of popular rule, sparing no opportunity to attack the reformers for their alleged hypocrisy. After the Wallace campaign collapsed and the mildness of the political climate in 1976 became clear, the new concern of many ideological reformers was with the ability of Carter to seduce the people with appeals to "image" and to certain nebulous "valence" issues. This was hardly the issue-oriented politics that these reformers had sought, and this led some to have second thoughts, as typified by the following comments by Rick Stearns, a McGovern aide who played a major role in drafting the McGovern-Fraser Commission reform rules:

> If you regard a party as simply a custodian for a process with little role or discretion on the outcome, then you might conclude the system is working reasonably well. . . . But if you regard the party as something more, as an organization supposed to play some responsible role in gov-

301

ernment, then you might conclude the system doesn't work too well. It's hard to say the Democratic Party—the organized groups that make up the party and are its continuing strength—produced Jimmy Carter.[42]

The objective of the other major group, the establishment reformers, was to achieve an immediate reconciliation between the New Politics dissidents and the party regulars and to build over the long-run a structure that would maintain a coalitional type party. Given the policy differences that existed between the New Politics advocates and the regulars in 1972, the task of building a consensus was admittedly very difficult, if not impossible. That the establishment reformers failed to do so in 1972 should not therefore be taken as conclusive proof of the inadequacy of their views. But having said this, one must add that their theory of how to build a coalitional party was flawed in its conception. Reduced to its simplest terms, their idea was to push for the representation of all elements within the party in the delegate selection process on an equal footing on the assumption that representation produces reconciliation. Yet, while one might grant that representation is a necessary means to promoting reconciliation, it does not follow that any method of representation will promote harmony. In fact, it appears that the particular scheme the establishment reformers chose creates discord over and above the "natural" level caused by the actual political divisions.[43] It does so by turning over the selection of delegates to competition among the candidates each of whom is likely to value victory more than party harmony and who is just as likely to mobilize a constituency by accentuating party divisions as by building a consensus, a problem that was evident in the selection process in 1972. And the problem, if anything, was made worse from an in-

[42] *The Wall Street Journal*, July 9, 1976.

[43] This is the opinion of Nelson Polsby, *Congress and The Presidency*, 3rd ed. (Englewood Cliffs, N.J.: Prentice Hall, 1976), p. 180; and it is suggested by Keech and Matthews, *The Party's Choice*, p. 242.

stitutional perspective in 1976, though it was mitigated by the political influences of the absence of any divisive issues and the memory of the 1972 debacle. It might be said that it was by accident or luck and not by design that a consensus was achieved in 1976. The task of building a consensus under the present system is left to the candidates and the people, hardly the picture of an institutional structure designed to promote a coalition.

CONCLUSION

THE meaning of republican government has undergone a fundamental change since 1787. In the Founders' conception, republican government was a species of popular government designed to balance the requirement of rule by the people with certain restraints on outright democracy. Under this system elected officials would be given a substantial degree of discretion in carrying out policy, though they would ultimately be accountable to the people. The Founders contrasted this system with a democracy, by which they meant a form of popular government in which elected officials would claim to make policy in accord with the dictates of public opinion. Each of these regimes, the Founders argued, had its own ruling "spirit" or public philosophy: republicanism implied the idea of restraint on popular authority, while democracy was predicated on the concept of the active sovereignty of the popular will. Republicanism has as its goal for the political process the promotion of deliberation and statesmanship, democracy a quick and accurate response to expressed public demands.

Today this distinction seems to have been lost, and republican government has become merely a synonym for democracy. This change is more than semantic. It represents a loss or a rejection of the idea of republican restraint. Democratic standards are now held up as absolute, and checks on popular authority are everywhere called into question. This triumph of the democratic principle, it must be acknowledged, has often been one more of form than substance. At the same time that the democratic idea has been gaining as a principle in the public mind, the courts and the bureaucracy have obtained more power, often at the expense of traditional democratic institutions. But whatever new limitations have emerged in the practice of democracy, none has been justified by reference to the idea of republican restraint.

304

Indeed, just the opposite: the claims to power are cloaked under a rhetoric of democratic principles.[1]

The movement toward formal democracy has perhaps been most pronounced in the area of presidential selection. The call for "direct democracy" in the choice of the president has been met virtually in full in the nominating process, and the push for an amendment for the direct election of the president has recently gained new momentum. The selection process is spoken of, in the parlance of the day, as a "test" for our system—the occasion to see if America truly "deserves" to be considered a democratic regime. The idea of institutional restraints in the sphere of electoral politics seems altogether foreign to the understanding of most opinion makers today. Although the Founders' teaching about institutional checks and balances has enjoyed a new-found respect after Watergate, little has been said about their prescriptions for controlling electoral appeals. In fact, their understanding of restraint in electoral politics never really became an established part of the nation's public philosophy. Van Buren's case for restraint, though embodied for a long time in the working of traditional parties and understood and appreciated by many politicians and political scientists, also never penetrated fully into the public consciousness. The rhetoric that accompanied the creation of parties was democratic, which was justified in light of the democratic effect of party competition, but which failed to instill a general public understanding of the moderating influence of the party system.

In the absence of a public philosophy embodying the idea of restraint in the electoral sphere, it is hardly surprising that when traditional parties came under attack during this century in the two great waves of reform, their defenders were unable to mount any substantial opposition on the

[1] For a treatment of the rhetoric and reality of democratic government in the United States, see Ward Elliott's penetrating study, *The Rise of Guardian Democracy* (Cambridge: Harvard University Press, 1974).

305

plane of principle. "Right" had always seemed to rest exclusively with reformers, be it in the form of Robert La-Follette's exhortation to "go back to the people" or of the Democratic Party's recent call for "the opportunity for every Democrat to participate in the delegate selection process."[2]

Proponents of restraint have also been placed on the defensive by the bold claims reformers have made about the benefits that supposedly flow from a more democratic system. Whatever was wrong with the prevailing electoral system has been attributed to its undemocratic aspects—precisely the kind of argument that in a popular regime is likely to fall on sympathetic ears. Progressive reformers contended that democratization would destroy bosses and machines, cleanse the political process of all its evils, and raise civic concern from a mean preoccupation with material interest to an enlightened concern for the common good. Modern reformers claim that their changes will save the two-party system, end manifestations of "antipolitics," and build citizen virtue through participation in the political process. To this list the National Commission on the Causes and Prevention of Violence recently added the item of a possible reduction in assassination attempts—this despite the fact that two such attempts occurred during campaigns in which an outside strategy was followed.[3]

Where more democracy has not produced all the benefits promised—where, in fact, it has created certain problems—reformers have still managed to retain the offensive by shifting their ground from hardheaded pragmatism to pious principle. Democracy, it is said, requires an acceptance of certain risks; those who call for any kind of restraint are fainthearted and have no faith in the people. According to James

[2] Robert LaFollette, *Autobiography* (Madison: Robert LaFollette Co., 1913), p. 197; *Democrats All: Report of the Commission on Delegate Selection and Party Structure* (1973), p. 1.

[3] *Assassination and Political Violence: A Report to the National Commission on the Causes and Prevention of Violence* by James F. Kirkam, Sheldon G. Levy, and William J. Crotty (Washington, D.C.: Government Printing Office, 1969), p. 109.

306

Sundquist, a defense of anything but an open selection system is "impossible to justify in terms of the democratic ethic."[4]

Impossible to justify? Certainly this is the case if one accepts the particular understanding of the democratic ethic propagated by the Progressives and their heirs. Not all Americans, however, have been willing to yield to this easy definition of republicanism or delight in the transformation of republican government into an experiment in dangerous living. Some, taking their cue from pre-Progressive theorists, have been willing to define the problem of popular government not in terms of how it can be made more democratic, but in terms of how the general requirements of popular rule can be met in such a way as to produce good government.

In this study we have identified five normative functions of a sound selection system. The selection process, it has been said, should minimize the harmful results of the pursuit of power by ambitious contenders, help establish the proper kind of presidential leadership and proper scope of executive power, help secure a competent executive, ensure a legitimate accession, and provide for the proper degree of choice and change. Merely identifying these functions does not by itself answer the question of what is the best institutional arrangement for choosing the president. Each function must be interpreted, not only in respect to certain basic standards, but in respect to the particular needs of the times; and, where conflicts exist among the different functions, the proper "trade-offs" must be determined. But an awareness of these functions would at least provide guidance to legislators by focusing their attention on the full range of issues that are involved in the selection problem.

The theories of the Progressives and the modern reformers, both of which are based on a democratic interpretation of republicanism, have been criticized for ignoring the function of controlling candidate ambition and for interpreting

---

[4] James L. Sundquist, *Dynamics of the Party System* (Washington, D.C.: Brookings Institution, 1973), p. 307.

307

the function of influencing the presidency in a way that makes presidential authority rest on the foundation of a public opinion leadership. Both of these theories, in a word, have failed to see the selection process as a way of restraining or moderating the pursuit and exercise of political power. In the quest for electoral democracy, the notion of republican restraint was buried. In the case of the Progressives, at least as far as Woodrow Wilson was concerned, this choice was consciously made in order to enhance the power of the presidency; in the case of the modern reformers, however, it seems to have been adopted as a matter of course, without consideration for the effects of the selection process in these areas. The function the reformers emphasized was that of securing legitimacy; and on this issue their original position was that the only interpretation of republicanism that could meet the modern standard of legitimacy was full popular control over presidential nominations—a position that seems to have reflected their own preference rather than a genuine constraint imposed by public opinion.

In order to reestablish a restraining role for the selection system, it is evident that the problem must first be attacked at its roots, which is to say with calling into question the current ideology espousing the "democratic ethic." Given what might seem to some an inevitable drift in society toward support for direct democracy, an effort of this sort might appear futile. But the current selection system is still far from having won a firm endorsement from the American people; and should its consequences, many of which are still not fully known or appreciated, bring about widespread dissatisfaction, the way could be opened for a new approach. Advocates of electoral restraint must then be prepared to demonstrate that many of the problems in the current system are the result not of its closed aspects but of its very openness, and that a movement to curtail some of the formalistic aspects of democracy would not be inconsistent with traditional understandings of republican government. These arguments would serve as a prelude to a plan for strengthening political parties and restoring them to a central place in the selection process.

THE PROBLEM OF PRESIDENTIAL AMBITION

A great danger in the contemporary selection process is its failure to reckon with the force of political ambition. Beginning with the Progressives and culminating in the recent revision of the Democratic Party rules, the nomination process has encouraged candidates to pursue their ambitions by carving out personal constituencies through direct popular appeals. The candidate-oriented system was supported on the grounds that personal appeals would be elevated in their tone and would tend to promote a new consensus (Wilson's conception), or that they would address in a serious and responsible way the "hard issues" that confronted the nation (the reformers' conception). But the results of the plebiscitary system have not exactly corresponded with these optimistic expectations. Successful appeals, as the reformers are first now to concede, have been made on grounds other than high principle, be it by demagoguery or personal image appeals, and factional divisions within the parties have been exacerbated during some of the recent nomination struggles.

These results accord more with the view of nonpartisan popular elections described by early American theorists than they do with the ideals of the Progressives. According to the earlier viewpoint, unregulated candidate solicitation would tend to produce demeaning or immoderate appeals as contenders gravitated to the kind of campaign most likely to promote personal success. Even where candidates using such appeals did not win the nomination or the election, they could cause harm by introducing deeper divisions and imparting a more strident tone to political discourse. The Founders were also concerned that the understanding of political leadership that would emerge from such campaigns would be inconsistent with promoting the dignity associated with statesmanship. While their views here are clearly too

309

elevated in their pure form to be applicable to democratic politics today, many have nevertheless begun to wonder whether current arrangements, in which as many as nine or ten openly declared candidates begin their campaigns well in advance of the election, are finally not too demeaning for both the candidates and the electorate. Have we not, some have asked, confused means with ends and permitted our concern over the fairness of the pursuit of office to undermine the character of the office itself?[5]

The neglect of the qualitative aspects of leadership in recent reform thought may reflect in some degree the lack of concern for this issue in modern political science, where the primary effort in the recent past has been devoted to quantifying the relative strengths of issues, party, and candidate appeal in determining voter behavior. But it would be incorrect to say that all modern political scientists have ignored the qualitative dimension of leadership appeals. For the late V. O. Key, this issue was the center of concern in his last book, *The Responsible Electorate*. At the outset of this work Key asked, "what kind of appeals enable a candidate to win the favor of the great god, the People?" Key's ironic tone was indicative of a skepticism on his part about the mere formulae of democracy, a skepticism that was strongly in evidence in some of his earlier studies of the direct primary in state politics. Key raised the problem of the qualitative character of the electoral process by reference to a metaphor of an echo chamber: "The voice of the people is but an echo. The output of an echo chamber bears an invariable relation to the input."[6] The principal "input," Key makes clear, is the leadership appeals of the candidates.

Key was troubled by two types of democratic leadership appeals: image-building and extreme popular leadership or demagoguery. Image solicitation refers to appeals focusing

[5] See for example, McGeorge Bundy, *The Strength of Government* (Cambridge: Harvard University Press, 1968), p. 70.

[6] V. O. Key, *The Responsible Electorate* (New York: Random House, 1966), pp. 1-2.

on personal *character* attributes irrelevant to the proper exercise of political power. Demagoguery represents a form of *issue* appeal that evokes powerful and often lawless passions. These two appeals may be made by, or on behalf of, the same person, as when youth is combined with an appeal to extreme freedom or toughness with a call for unnecessary repression. For analytical purposes, however, it will help to treat the two separately.

Image

The problem of image candidacies, so closely associated today with the existence of sophisticated public opinion research and Madison Avenue advertising techniques, was not unknown in the past. The Founders expressed concern over factions that might form around persons "interesting to human passions," and many in the nineteenth century worried about the image aspects of campaigns involving military "heroes." It seems clear, however, that the potential for image campaigns has increased dramatically in modern times with the advent of mass media, opinion polling, and extensive research in the field of human behavior.

By concentrating on the role and use of these new factors, a school of thought in political science has grown up whose central thesis is that image techniques constitute the most important element of the modern campaign. Candidates, so the charge goes, allow themselves to be "packaged" and "sold" by crafty campaign consultants and unscrupulous ad men. Images are created that tap deep psychological needs, such as the longing for an authority figure, or evanescent moods, such as a desire for a "nonpolitician." The entire campaign, according to Murray Edelman, consists in "a superficial bemusement with personalities [that] substitutes for tough-minded analysis of problems and social structures."[7] If this contention were true, elections could not per-

[7] Murray Edelman, "The Politics of Persuasion" in James Barber, ed., *Choosing the President* (Englewood Cliffs, N.J.: Prentice Hall), p. 171.

form many of the crucial functions ascribed to them by democratic theorists. There could be no valid judgment on the issues nor any legitimate assessment of the competence of the candidates. It is necessary, therefore, to explore the extent to which image appeals actually determine electoral behavior.

Key was certainly concerned that superficial considerations such as "fatherliness" or "sincerity" might come to dominate electoral choice, especially if these were what political campaigns stressed: "Fed a steady diet of buncombe, the people may come to expect [it] . . . and those leaders most skilled in the propogation of buncombe may gain lasting advantage in the recurring struggles for popular favor." Key was troubled in particular by the possibility that existing social scientific theories of voting behavior, watered down and distorted in the transition from academia to the political world, might encourage this tendency. Candidates, laboring under the impression that image appeals were scientifically established as the most important determinant of voting behavior, would emphasize image appeals in their campaigns, confirming the "findings" of researchers and setting off a further round of reciprocal influence between the researchers and the candidates. (Many social scientists were not at the time used to thinking of themselves or their work as possessing the status of independent variables and did not take kindly to Key's criticisms.) But while Key warned of the dangers of image politics, his own empirical research—guided perhaps by his concern for maintaining the integrity of the electoral process—suggested that image was not the decisive factor. Key sought to save the political from the psychological by showing that the electorate was moved primarily by a concern for "the central and relevant questions of public policy, of governmental performance, and of executive personality."[8]

Not all political scientists, however, were willing to accept Key's findings. Fred Greenstein, writing in 1965, assigned the greatest weight in presidential voting behavior to the

[8] Key, *The Responsible Electorate*, pp. 7-8.

"purely personal aspects of presidential image."[9] More recently, in 1974, Murray Edelman argued that the critical swing portion of the electorate, consisting of those voters most susceptible to political persuasion, is made up of people who "lack stable and gratifying roles in their life," who possess "low self-esteem and inadequacy," and who act in politics in order to seek out the psychological roots that are absent in their private lives. For such people issues hold no genuine significance: "People for whom politics is not important want symbols and not information." The candidates, able in a weak party era to run their campaigns as they think best, have few qualms about gratifying these desires. The real villains, however, are not the candidates, but the campaign consultants, the mercenaries of modern electoral warfare. By allowing these legions to be turned loose, the result is that the "seduction of the public is most deliberate in precisely that part of the political process that symbolizes popular participation."[10]

With Edelman placing emphasis on how easily voters can be manipulated, one might think that he would entertain certain doubts about a fully open electoral process, if not about democracy itself. Yet he surprisingly proposes to increase the number of candidates on the grounds that some of the additional contenders, having no real chance of succeeding, would educate rather than manipulate. His faith in democracy remains unshaken. The blame for its failure in America lies with an elite that attempts to fool the people. Democracy can be saved, but only apparently at the expense of the current political system. Edelman's final solution to what is essentially the problem of restraining candidate ambition turns out to be, by his own account, a "drastic" one. He avoids any

---

[9] Fred I. Greenstein, "Popular Images of the President," *The American Journal of Psychiatry*, 122:5 (November, 1965): 523-29. The characterization in the reference is Greenstein's own. It appears in his article "What the President Means to Americans" in Barber, ed., *Choosing the President*, p. 141.

[10] Edelman, "The Politics of Persuasion," in Barber, ed., *Choosing the President*, pp. 156, 160.

analysis of the presidential selection process and flies directly to a system-wide solution:

> [The problem] lies in the norm of rewarding those who manipulate public attitudes while real social, economic, and international problems remain unsolved. . . . If business, the CIA, and behavioral psychologists subscribed to a norm that sanctions manipulation or dirty tricks, so will the institutions of government, for they reflect prevailing norms. Only a drastic restructuring of the functions, the objectives, and the rewards of our major economic and political institutions can cure the blight.[11]

It is not easy to settle the dispute between Key and Edelman since a good part of their disagreement stems from a different qualitative assessment of the character of certain leadership appeals. Edelman sets his standards in such a way that all the appeals of which he seems to disapprove, whether they relate to character or issues, are classified as instances of manipulation. If one disregards standards that are so difficult to define and operationalize and looks instead to the usual categories that have been employed in recent empirical studies, a consensus emerges now among researchers on voting about the relative weights of the candidate-related component and of issues in explaining voting behavior. (The candidate component is not the same as an "image" response because not all evaluations of candidate character are trivial or irrelevant; but since the candidate component includes the image factor, it can be used as an analytic tool in this context.) Recent findings have shown that the candidate component as an independent determinant of voter behavior played a significant role in the elections of 1952, 1956, 1960, and 1976. Its importance relative to issues was much less for the elections of 1964, 1968 and 1972. A good deal of negative reaction was registered in 1964 and 1972 against the persons of Goldwater and McGovern, but much of it was based on a "legitimate" concern about incompetence, and

[11] *Ibid.*, p. 172.

314

there is also some reason to suppose that the character re-actions in these two instances may have been strongly in-fluenced by the candidates' positions on the issues.[12] The data collected for nomination campaigns has not been nearly as extensive as that for the final campaigns, but the evidence for the last two Democratic races again suggests the possibility of great variation: in 1972 issue voting was of central im-portance, while in 1976 the candidate factor played a much greater role.[13]

The generally accepted interpretation of these findings among students of electoral behavior can be stated as fol-lows: the relative weight of issues and the candidate com-ponent (as well as that of party voting for the final election) will vary greatly from election to election, depending on the circumstances and the campaign strategies adopted by the candidates. Where strong issue differences among candidates become a part of the campaign, the issue component in voter response will be large; where issue differences are small, i.e. where the candidates occupy the same general issue space, the candidate factor is apt to dominate voter choice. The electoral process is indeed something of an echo chamber in which the behavior of the voters cannot be understood apart from the kind of noise the candidates make.[14]

The rediscovery of the importance of issues has invalidated those theories of voting behavior that were predicated en-tirely on the supposed psychological needs of the voters, as Greenstein has now conceded.[15] Of course, this does not mean that image-related responses are never decisive or that no increase is likely to take place in the use of personalistic

[12] Nie, Verba and Petrocik, *The Changing American Voter* (Cam-bridge: Harvard University Press, 1976), p. 340.

[13] Pomper, *The Election of 1976* (New York: David McKay, 1977), pp. 75-78.

[14] Gerald Pomper, *The Voter's Choice* (New York: Dodd Mead, 1975), pp. 165-85; Nie, Verba and Petrocik, *The Changing American Voter*, pp. 315-16 and 319-44.

[15] Greenstein, "What the President Means to Americans," in Barber, ed., *Choosing the President*, pp. 141, 143.

image campaigns. Nor does it mean that image techniques cannot be effectively combined with issue appeals, as in the case of the political "outsider" who attacks the "Establishment center." Used in this way, image appeals might not show up independently in general quantitative estimates of voting-determinants, though their effect could still be substantial. Overall, however, the finding that the issue component can be—and in many recent elections has been—decisive has vindicated Key's general attempt to save the political from the psychological in understanding voter behavior.

Yet this vindication would not by itself have satisfied Key as to the health of the selection process. It was not merely the fact of issue-oriented voting that was important to him, but the quality of the issues to which the voter responded. As compared with image responses, the existence of issue motivation held out for Key the prospect either of greater intelligence *or* greater depravity on the part of the voters. This point was one sometimes overlooked by recent researchers, who in their initial flush of victory in saving the American voter from the claim of issueless psychological motivation, too readily concluded that votes based on issue responses were proof of a healthy selection system.[16] If it is now accepted that voters are not completely dominated by deep psychological needs, then one must also "credit" them with the capacity for faulty and pernicious judgment. Key's normative conception of responsibility in the electorate included the idea of freedom from the influences of demagoguery as well as image-building. It might have been small consolation for him that his vindication came initially in response to evidence from the candidacies of Goldwater, Wallace, and McGovern. Proof of the electorate's "responsibility" as meas-

[16] See Pomper, *The Voter's Choice*, pp. 15-17. Initially Pomper celebrates the responsive voter, but by the end of the book, when he begins to consider the implications of this development, he adopts a much more cautious attitude.

316

ured by quantitative standards alone may only have been the first sign of a problem of its irresponsibility as determined by a qualitative assessment.

The matter of judging the selection system thus cannot be settled by a simple determination of whether institutions favor "issues" or "character." In the first place, each of these categories must be subdivided into its qualitative components. Thus issue appeals may be either demagogic or non-demagogic; and character appeals may focus either on misleading or irrelevant "image" characteristics or on attributes that are germane to a determination of executive competence. Secondly, given this more complex classification, there is no longer any reason to assume that any particular institutional arrangement of the selection system must encourage one of the principal categories at the expense of the other, i.e. issues at the expense of character or character at the expense of issues. Rather, a system may encourage different components of both categories. The evidence from the last two campaigns suggests the modern selection system places an increased reliance on demagogic issue appeals and on image-building. Both kinds of appeals thrive where parties are weak and where candidates are left to their own devices to build personal followings: both are potential replacements of moderate party-based issue stances and appeals to traditional partisan allegiances. The growth of these nonparty appeals owes a good deal to modern communications, which allow candidates to relate directly to the people, and to the existence of more educated voters who show a greater disposition to vote on the basis of issues rather than partisanship. But these factors by themselves cannot account fully for the new style of political campaigns. Behind the changes in leadership appeals stands a selection system that has weakened party loyalty and emphasized individual candidates and current issues. The problems of contemporary selection are thus largely political in origin and remain within the scope of influence of modern political decision makers.

Demagogic Appeals

Extreme popular leadership or demagoguery is the second dangerous form of democratic leadership appeal. It was of even more concern than image appeal to the statesmen who legislated on the selection problem before this century. The attention they gave to the potential of dangerous issue appeals reflected their view that citizens were moved more by political than "psychological" concerns and that the greatest threat to the political system therefore derived from political passions. Whatever their other differences on the question of selection, both the Founders and Martin Van Buren shared the fear that the people might be led in undesirable directions by ambitious politicians seeking to further their own interests at the expense of the common good. Both accordingly attempted to devise electoral institutions that would control and channel the appeals of potential aspirants.

This perspective on the selection problem differs completely from the modern view inaugurated in its basic form by the Progressives. According to the Progressives the two major problems of electoral politics were corruption and the existence of old and irrelevant divisions in our political campaigns. Both of these problems could be traced directly to the dominance of "old-style" political parties. Once parties were reformed, corruption would be eliminated and the electorate would be able to respond to contemporary issues. It was apparently assumed that the people would use their new freedom wisely and the leaders would exercise self-restraint in their appeals. Demagoguery was thus not considered a major problem. Perhaps the single greatest indication of the pervasiveness of Progressive views in modern times is that the issue of demagogic leadership appeals was never even raised in any of the literature of reform. The dismissal of all of the "darker" elements of democratic politics combined with a total confidence in the people has allowed reformers to enjoy the luxury of considering "fairness" and maximum participation as the chief issues of the selection problem. But reformers' own "private" views have not accorded with their

318

official optimism. Their dismay at seeing their own candidate rejected by the people in 1972 was followed by their frequently expressed concern in 1975 that George Wallace might appear as the people's favorite.[17] Instead of changing their idea of popular government to accord with their true conception of popular rule, some have responded with anger at their "betrayal," as if the people had willfully let them down. Perhaps the ultimate conclusion to this line of thought will be that the American people do not "deserve" democracy.

The term demagogue is frequently used as a weapon of partisan conflict to cast aspersion on a despised opponent. It is, admittedly, a vague term; but the fact that the bitterest partisans have been reluctant to use it to describe persons such as Taft, Hughes, Eisenhower, or Stevenson suggests that the term has at least a certain intuitive content. Even when used partisanly, it is applied only to a leader who divides on the basis of a strong issue appeal or who poses as a "friend" of the people, abandoning the normal degrees of reserve and distance. Its meaning can perhaps be refined further by tracing the term's origin and development.

The term demagogue was first used in Ancient Greece. Its literal root meaning is "leader of the people," and one finds that it was employed in Athens to refer to the head of the popular party. According to the aristocrats' conception of politics at that time, society was comprised of two basic "parties"—the "better sort" or the gentleman, and the commoners or merely "the people." The people were thought to be governed by passion and were therefore considered unfit to rule. Gentlemen alone should hold office, upholding gentlemanly values. The demagogue threatened these ideas by championing the people's claim to rule and by attacking the values and privileges of the gentlemen. The demagogue would often call for full personal power as a "temporary" measure to protect the people and to achieve their immediate demands. From this arose the view, accepted by many of the

[17] See David Broder's editorial in *The Boston Globe*, April 9, 1975.

Founders, that the likeliest source of tyranny in a popular government was from the demagogue and not the oligarch. Demagoguery was further understood to assume different forms, depending on the status of the leader. If the popular leader was a gentleman or a commoner who had achieved prominence by some singular deed, usually military, the appeal for the people's support might be a combination of demagoguery and image, known now by the name "Caesarism." If, on the other hand, the leader was a commoner simply, having no personal distinction or standing, his appeal would necessarily be reversed to vehement issue arousal, giving rise to demagoguery in its coarser sense.

In classical political philosophy, however, the concept of demagoguery was refined to refer to something more precise than leadership of the people.[18] It described a certain qualitative kind of leadership, one which, while perhaps most likely to be employed by the leader of the popular party, could also be used with other groups and even with society as a whole. It is this qualitative sense of the term that is of interest here, if only because nearly all contemporary leaders, conservative no less than liberal, actively claim to represent "the people."

Classical political philosophy understood demagoguery first in a "soft" sense, as leadership which engaged in flattery. Flattery, in this instance, referred to a leader who encouraged the constituency to which he was appealing to believe that it already possessed all attributes of political knowledge and excellence. Thus all wisdom, a leader might say, resides with the "better sorts" or with the people, or all virtue with the businessman or the working man. In the case of popular demagoguery, the ruler flatters the people by claiming that they "know" what is best, and makes a point of claiming his special "closeness," by manner or gesture. As James Fenimore Cooper remarked in *The American Democrat*, "The man who is constantly telling the people that they are un-

[18] Aristotle, *Politics* 1305a-13056, in Richard McKeon, ed., *The Basic Works of Aristotle* (New York: Random House, 1968).

erring in judgment is a demagogue."[19] With the ascendancy of democratic politics, this kind of flattery becomes inevitable in some degree. But the early objections to it are still worth considering, at least insofar as they may influence people's views about the degree to which such practices should be countenanced.

The central objection to flattery is that it undermines statesmanship. It conflicts directly with the notion that political leadership possesses (or can possess) a special knowledge about statecraft. This tension between flattery and statesmanship was recognized by the American theorists most concerned with establishing a statesmanlike discretion for leaders—the Founders and, in his own way, Woodrow Wilson. The Founders condemned flattery outright and sought to isolate the executive from the immediate influence of public opinion, though not ultimate popular judgment. The president would rely on the powers of his office, and the mode of selection would protect aspirants from the necessity or temptation of flattery by discouraging them from making popular appeals. Wilson, by contrast, believed statesmanship could be established by abandoning the formal aspects of power and opening up the selection process. The latitude apparently lost to the president by the breakdown of formal authority could be regained by the art of persuasion; and the danger of flattery would be obviated by the self-restraint of the leader. The ideal of leadership that emerged from this theory combined rectitude, popularity, and discretion (but not prudence) into the image of the inspirational moral leader. Rhetorical inspiration replaces official power and a respect for the office as the chief source of executive discretion.

Classical political philosophy also understood demagoguery in a second and more dangerous sense. Demagoguery was a particular method by which a leader would build and maintain his constituency. The demagogue rises and generates power by creating divisions and setting one group or

[19] James Fenimore Cooper, *The American Democrat*, ed. H. L. Mencken (New York: Alfred A. Knopf, 1931).

321

symbol against another; he rises by means of pitting his constituency against a force that allegedly threatens it. The demagogue's claim to power is based on the rectitude of the group's wishes and the threat to which that group is supposedly being subjected. Constituency support, not formal powers, form the justification for his authority. Demagogic appeals are "partisan" in the sense that they divide, but—applying the analysis to modern-day politics—they undermine the idea of partisan competition by their threats to "crush" any opposition. Lipset and Raab, who studied this form of demagoguery in American politics, indicate that these leaders project a "monistic" view, a rejection of all other opinions but their own, which is the very antithesis of Van Buren's ethic of partisan tolerance.[20]

Given the association of demagoguery with extremism, the effort is sometimes made to identify any new and disruptive appeal as demagogic. This association is obviously too broad, for disruptive appeals that call for fundamental changes may sometimes be justified. The true demagogic appeal is thus not only extreme but "bad" or pernicious in its intent or effect. It is impossible to specify the exact standards that would permit one to identify such appeals, but we can mention three types of appeals that American theorists have identified as potentially demagogic.

First, there is the class appeal that pits the poor or have-nots against the wealthy. Madison thought this kind of division the most likely and dangerous in modern politics, and the Progressives agreed. Many of the original Progressives, in fact, rejected Franklin Roosevelt in 1936 because of his deliberate efforts at class polarization—his welcoming of the "hatred" (Roosevelt's own word) of the selfish rich.[21] Appeals that divide people on the basis of property need not be

[20] Seymour Martin Lipset and Earl Raab, *The Politics of Unreason* (New York: Harper and Row, 1970), pp. 12-13.

[21] Arthur Schlesinger, Jr., ed., *History of American Presidential Elections*, 4 vols. (New York: Chelsea House, 1973), 3:2839.

limited to a strict war between classes. Indeed, for politics at the national level today an exclusive appeal to the poor could not hope to win the support of a majority and could easily lose votes by frightening away members of the larger middle class. Some, like George McGovern in 1972 and especially Fred Harris in 1976, experimented with a new "populism" that attacked the large corporations in the name of the working and middle classes. This sort of appeal is designed to entice not only those who stand to benefit materially from a redistribution of wealth, but also those who identify on the plane of ideology with the cause of income redistribution. Many welfare-state liberals accordingly find such appeals difficult to disavow, even when they realize their demagogic intent.

Second, there is division over cultural issues. Here the demagogue defends the orthodox against foreign or modernizing elements that allegedly are destroying society's traditional way of life. The law, being an integral element of tradition, is naturally claimed as part of that way of life and is defended against those who would destroy it. Demagoguery of this sort has been associated with distrust of those elements considered non-American, as in Know-Nothingism or Anti-Masonry, and with a suspicion of intellectuals who now often invite these attacks by making a point of their own cosmopolitan orthodoxies. The defense of a traditional way of life raises some of the most powerful human passions— fear and horror over the destruction of what has been known and violent anger directed against the alleged subverters of society. According to Lipset and Raab, such "preservatist" passions have exercised a very strong appeal in America, but have been kept out of the mainstream of our politics, even when they represented a potential majority, by the moderate character of the major parties.[22] As in the case of

[22] For an account of the strength of these currents in America, see Lipset and Raab, *The Politics of Unreason, passim.* For Lipset's view of the role played by American parties in controlling these

the class appeal, a legitimate group, the conservatives, may find itself hard pressed to disavow this form of extremism. Demagogic defenses of traditional values support in a distorted way many of the views of traditional conservatives, and as a consequence conservatives are sometimes slow to condemn them.

A third form of demagoguery is characterized by appeals based on excessive encouragement of morality and hope. The division generated is between the righteous (understood progressively) and the backward, or between those who have compassion and those who are insensitive. Appeals of this type stretch politics into the realm of morality, offering images of new worlds or holding out the hope of self-realization through political action. Because such appeals evoke nobler passions, it is likely that those making them will explicitly deny any demagogic intent. Demagoguery, they might say, is an appeal to fear and anger, while moral leadership is an appeal to hope and to what is "best" in us. There is doubtless some truth in this, but inspirational leadership carried to excess possesses an extreme character of its own, including at times a scorn for political restraints.

Demagoguery is always dangerous, but in rare instances it may be justified. It represents an extreme tool of the statesman, one which, if it ever became the norm rather than the unspoken of exception, would undermine statesmanship itself. Responsible leaders contemplating the use of a demagogic appeal must consider not only the immediate passions it sets loose but also the precedent it establishes for the general style of politics. Nothwithstanding these dangers, there may be instances when demagoguery is necessary, as when one must build support for an essential goal or when one must counteract the appeals of truly dangerous leaders. Thus some defenders of Franklin Roosevelt justify some of his extreme

---

movements, see Seymour Martin Lipset, "The Paradox of American Politics," *The Public Interest* 41 (Fall 1975): 154-59 and 163-65.

rhetoric on the grounds that it stole the thunder of genuine demagoguery.[23]

Demagoguery has many formal similarities with the extraordinary but "legitimate" form of popular leadership that goes into building new movements or parties, or into reformulating the character of old parties. James Sundquist has said of all past periods of realignment that "political discourse took place in language charged with a passion that in the intervening periods of stability would have been unconvincing and unacceptable."[24] Polarization is a necessary component of building constituencies anew, something which is evident from the appeals of the originators of the Republican Party and from those of the Founders themselves at the time of the Revolution. Leadership in such instances cannot be distinguished from demagoguery by a clear standard. Only by analyzing the intentions, the rhetoric, and the actions of the relevant actors in each particular case can a judgment be made.

Both demagoguery and the legitimate but exceptional popular leadership that "renews" the political process take place beyond the normal restraints of the electoral process. Both dissolve existing voter alignments and existing states of affairs. There is no institutional arrangement that is capable of distinguishing between them. The institutional choice is either to place a damper on all such extraordinary forms of leadership or to open the system to them. The danger that the Founders, Jefferson, and Van Buren perceived in the dangerous kinds of appeals led them to devise institutional arrangements that were deliberately designed to limit leadership. Under these plans for restraint, exceptional leadership would not be excluded, but it would have to establish itself in the face of strong institutional deterrants. These theorists cal-

[23] Morton J. Frisch, "Franklin Delano Roosevelt" in Frisch *et al.*, eds., *American Political Thought* (New York: Charles Scribner's Sons, 1971), p. 226.

[24] Sundquist, *Dynamics*, p. 278.

culated that this was the best institutional approach, since the dangers inherent in allowing and thereby encouraging extreme appeals outweighed the benefits of making it easier for exceptional popular leadership to have its way. Perhaps they may even have thought that the presumption against extraordinary leadership appeals was the best way to test the need for a legitimate leadership of renewal: when it was truly required, it would be able to clear the existing impediments and have its way.

The institutional solution that Van Buren devised and that served the nation until the recent reforms was predicated on the dominance of the electorate by two stable parties and on nominations controlled chiefly by established party leaders. Yet this system was to remain open to a challenge by new parties and thereby to either the replacement or regeneration of one of the major parties. In formal terms, the system could be described as an open electoral process dominated by two closed, i.e. organizationally controlled, parties. The usual dominance by the major closed parties was the institutional check on demagoguery; the openness of the electoral system was one avenue for promoting necessary change. Of course new parties operated at a considerable disadvantage, but this was not thought a weakness but rather a strength of the system. Precisely because politics outside the major parties was open to the possibility of extremism—as illustrated, for example, by the policies of the Know-Nothings, the Populists, and the American Party—the natural disadvantages faced by new parties could be considered a benefit which gave the nation the time for "more cool and sedate reflection."[25] Yet for all this the minor parties were still a legitimate part of the system, presenting demands for change when the major parties might resist. Their ultimate effect in influencing the behavior of the major parties is such that, to quote Key, they "must be regarded, somewhat paradoxically, as integral elements of the so-called two-party system."[26]

[25] *The Federalist*, #70, p. 432.
[26] V. O. Key, *Politics, Parties and Pressure Groups*, 5th ed., p. 307.

It is thus not correct to say, as many critics of the traditional and mixed systems have charged, that the restraints these systems placed on leadership were intended chiefly to protect the *status quo* from the possibility of significant change.[27] Rather, the basic intent was to discourage dangerous forms of leadership which bred in the same institutional environment that encouraged change. Moreover, these systems were based on the premise that fundamental change, insofar as it derives from the selection process, is not needed in each and every election, but rather only periodically. There was no need, accordingly, to encourage regular change by institutional stimulation. Under the modern understanding of selection, in contrast, the restraints on leadership appeals have been removed in order to allow for constant change on the assumption that change is necessary for the well-being of the system. In Wilson's thought—and modern thought generally—it is held that this emphasis on change incurs no significant risks, that open parties will serve to institutionalize the most elevated form of popular leadership on a regular basis and at the same time avoid the problem of demagoguery. This expectation, it now seems fair to say, is chimerical on both counts.

THE CONTEMPORARY QUEST FOR THE BEST MAN

Votes based on a character assessment of the candidates should not all be dismissed as irrational responses to image politics. They may reflect a valid concern for what Key called "executive personality" and for what has been identified throughout this study as the function of promoting a competent executive. If there was a tendency among political scientists before Watergate to collapse all concern about character into the category of trivial image considerations, this has now changed. Post-Watergate scholarship, shocked into

[27] See, for example, the comments of James Sundquist, *Dynamics*, p. 306; and James MacGregor Burns, *The Deadlock of Democracy* (Englewood Cliffs, N.J.: Prentice Hall, 1963), p. 266.

normative analysis, now takes very seriously the question of good character. A "nonpartisan" perspective on selection has returned. Indeed, the author of the most widely read current book on the presidency, James Barber, implicitly rejects the assumption of the Progressives and modern reformers that the chief function of elections is to make policy choices. Barber, sounding more like the Founders than the Founders, argues that the issue dimension should be a secondary consideration and character the primary one. The message of his book is to "look to character first":

> Before a President is elected, debate centers on his stands on particular issues, his regional and group connections, his place in the left-right array of ideologies. After a President has left office and there has been time to see his rulership in perspective, the connection between his character and his Presidential actions emerges as paramount.[28]

Barber's work stands out as the boldest contemporary attempt to deal with the question of presidential character. Although it has been treated by most as a text on the presidency, it is in reality directed chiefly at the problem of presidential selection: "This book is meant to help citizens cut through the confusion and get at some clear criteria for choosing Presidents."[29] In the broadest sense, Barber's intent is to make the essential aspects of character "visible" to the average citizen and thereby to resolve the age-old problem of securing a "good" man by popular choice. Barber's extraordinary attempt to become the nation's tutor for the selection of the president rests on three premises. First, he claims to have discovered a theory that can predict reliably the elements of character which can explain much about a candidate's subsequent behavior in office. Until now, he implies, citizens had no rigorous method to assess candidates and were thus forced to rely either on their perceptions of a

---

[28] James Barber, *The Presidential Character* (Englewood Cliffs, N.J.: Prentice Hall, 1972), p. 445.

[29] *Ibid.*, p. 3.

candidate's record or on traditional biographic sketches. But with his new theory, citizens have available a tool that can be used to classify candidates into meaningful character types. Second, Barber believes that his theoretical model is simple enough to become a practical guide for opinion makers and average citizens. Because Barber wants to have a direct public impact (and not merely address his fellow scholars), the criterion of simplicity is at once sensible and essential. A complicated typology, no matter what its accuracy, would stand little chance of influencing citizens or opinion makers. Finally, Barber asserts that his typology is not only descriptive but normative as well. Of his four types, there is clearly a worst and a best one, with the other two ranking in an unspecified way in between.

Barber's plan to make character assessment the touchstone of the selection process derives from a deep pessimism regarding the current state of affairs in presidential selection. Like Edelman, Barber believes that the typical presidential campaign is a "sham," filled with "kitsch and fakery." Character is concealed beneath images cleverly devised by campaign consultants, and issues are reduced to slogans and "abstract moralisms" designed to tap subconscious mass needs.[30] From the depths of this pessimism, Barber rises to the grand hope that the voters can be educated to focus on character properly understood, thus allowing them to get beneath image and demagoguery. While no one would wish to quarrel with so noble a goal, the hard questions still remain: is Barber's remedy practical? does it in fact instruct us about good character and how to identify it? and is it based on an adequate understanding of the selection problem as a whole?

The most striking point about *Presidential Character*, insofar as it is a book about presidential selection, is its complete neglect of the institutions of the selection process. No arrangements are suggested that would tend to encourage the

---

[30] *Ibid.*, p. 452; "Introduction" to James Barber, ed., *Choosing the President*, p. 6.

selection of Barber's preferred character type as over and against the ones he dislikes. Instead of offering institutional advice, Barber evidently believes that the problem of securing a competent executive can be solved by establishing through public education a set of norms that journalists and citizens could use to understand and judge political character. This is an intriguing approach, but one that is unlikely to have very much success. Few teachings in politics are self-executing; they require the support of institutional arrangements to bring them to fruition. In all past efforts to "legislate" the promotion of certain character attributes in the selection process, a combination of norms and institutions was employed.

Of course, it may well have been that Barber avoided offering any institutional advice for fear of where it might lead. Since his categories are finally predicted by psychological characteristics, the institutional remedy that immediately comes to mind is some kind of board of psychiatrists and psychologists which would screen the candidates according to certain prescribed psychological attributes. Indeed, it was to just this conclusion that Erwin Hargrove came when he followed through the logic of attempting to make a connection between securing a best character type (defined principally by psychological characteristics) and devising institutional arrangements to promote it. Apparently shocked by his own suggestion for a board of "elite gatekeepers," Hargrove quickly retreated to the innocuous safety of advocating, like Barber, a general norm.[31]

As a further criticism of this theory's neglect of institutions, it may be suggested that a style of leadership is not entirely fixed by character but is in some measure learned through the institutional framework in which aspirants operate. One decisive difference between Barber and the Founders is that while both emphasize the importance of securing a good character, the Founders also sought to establish insti-

[31] Hargrove, "What Manner of Man?" in Barber, ed., *Choosing the President*, p. 33.

tutional arrangements that would channel and control politicians, so that a less than ideal person would be "taught" to avoid a dangerous leadership style.

A second and more important problem in Barber's theory is that its standard for judging character is inadequate. Barber's four fundamental categories are correlated with (and predicted by) certain associated personality characteristics. The most important of these is the degree of self-esteem a person possesses, for it is this quality that best explains the extent to which a leader is flexible or adaptable. It is not too much to say that adaptability is the highest standard by which Barber judges political character.[32] In focusing on adaptability, Barber seems to have been groping toward the virtue of the statesman as defined according to classical standards, namely prudence. The difficulty in Barber's analysis, however, is that adaptability is not the same thing as prudence and therefore cannot be predicted by the degree of self-esteem (even if one assumes that self-esteem correlates with adaptability). Prudence, like adaptability, requires a temperament that allows an individual to judge affairs without the interference at every point of considerations of ego. But above and beyond this, prudence is an intellectual virtue that depends decisively on the nature of person's principles—his understanding of human nature, politics, and the character of his own society. These last elements Barber includes under the rubric of "world view," but they play no independent role in his standard for judging political character. The key, again, seems to be the level of self-esteem and the degree of adaptability. By this standard, the melancholic Lincoln (prior to assuming the presidency) would almost certainly have come out a poor second to the ebullient and adaptive Douglas.[33] By making the essential criteria for judging character

---

[32] The terms adaptability and flexibility come up continually in the descriptions and praise of the active-positive. See Barber's initial description of the category in *Presidential Character*, p. 12.

[33] I am indebted on this and other points relating to Barber's work to a study being made by Jeffrey Tulis, research associate at the White Burkett Miller Center of Public Affairs.

depend on psychological attributes, Barber denies the importance and autonomy of principles, meaning here not necessarily the stand on issues in a given campaign but rather the fundamental content of a world view. Moreover, his standard also overlooks the importance (and autonomy) of other moral attributes, a criticism made against Barber in the aftermath of Watergate by Erwin Hargrove. (Hargrove himself underwent something of a transformation in his position after Watergate, adding to his previous list of attributes of a healthy executive personality the traditional qualities of "integrity" and "old-fashioned morality."[34]) There is no doubt that by excluding principles and moral attributes from his character typology Barber has gained the advantage of simplicity; but the merit of this advantage is dubious, as it comes at the expense of ignoring the most important factors for judging political character. The popular standard of judgment, formed in part by traditional moral and political theory, may be more reliable in the most crucial respects than theory derived from popularized psychology.

Finally, while Barber's emphasis on the importance of character is a useful corrective to the modern reform view that elections should always be decided on "hard" issues, he undoubtedly goes too far in ignoring the programmatic dimension of elections. "Executive personality" is one valid consideration in the selection process, but not the only one. While it is foolish to hold the electorate to the standard of "issues" where no important issues are at stake, there are nevertheless occasions when elections do perform a crucial role in initiating or consolidating major shifts in domestic and foreign policy. At such times, considerations of character, within tolerable limits, may properly be subordinated to policy.

Barber's pessimism about the people's present ability to judge character is implicitly called into question by Stephen Hess, another modern student of selection who regards char-

[34] Hargrove, "What Manner of Man?" in Barber, ed., *Choosing the President*, p. 32.

acter as the central issue of the selection process. Hess, unlike Barber, focuses directly on institutional questions and seems more than satisfied with the ability of the people to make sound judgments under the current open nominating system. For Hess the current system is geared, as he feels it should be, to producing "political presidents." The Nixon case disturbs Hess, but he dismisses it as an aberration because Nixon was not at heart a politician and therefore does not represent the type of candidate that the system tends to promote. (That Nixon was deft at feigning to be what he was not, however, is a difficulty Hess fails to deal with.) The open nomination process, in Hess's view, offers the best means for testing the mettle and character of presidential aspirants. "What Americans have constructed, mostly by accident, is a *partial simulation* of the presidency," and through this simulation Americans are provided with "much necessary data with which to measure politicians, as well as time to make an assessment." Hess would like the president to possess a range of political, personal, and executive qualifications. But of the three, if the processes must test one, priority should be given to the personal, "for they are the most immutable, the least likely to be changed by experience in office." The list of qualities Hess proposes is a strange mixture of traditional moral attributes with a heavy overlay of the Wilsonian virtues of the "leader." It includes "a transcending honesty," "intelligence," "stamina," the capacity to "inspire public trust" and the ability to "dream grandly." These are precisely the qualities, according to Hess, that the open process tests and encourages.[35] Hess, it is clear, operates entirely within a Wilsonian framework, coming very close to equating the qualities of the campaigner with those of the office holder and to narrowing or collapsing the distinction between the pursuit and the exercise of power.

If Barber underestimates the capacity of the people to respond to valid considerations of executive character, Hess

[35] Stephen Hess, *The Presidential Campaign* (Washington, D.C.: Brookings Institution, 1974), p. 42; p. 22; pp. 4-22.

surely seems to go to the opposite extreme. Hess proceeds as if all that the people care about is character, as if the partisan or issue component of the preconvention struggle presents no obstacle to the public's sifting dispassionately through the "data" that the open process provides. The people resemble the original electors in their wisdom and disinterestedness. Hess in the end qualifies his argument by conceding that the open process supplies the people with the "knowledge we need to make the best decisions possible. . . . There can be no guarantee that voters will act wisely."[36] Indeed, there cannot be. But then, the real question is whether they do act wisely—or rather whether the present system actually tends to promote good character. For all his concern with character, Hess does little to convince us that the present system actually succeeds in producing good persons as distinct merely from generating the "data" by which they might be judged. If character is so well tested in the nomination process, how is it—even excluding the case of Richard Nixon— that in 1972 so many people considered character incompetence by a major nominee as a major issue, and that in 1972 major leaders refused to support their party's candidate because they considered him untrustworthy? Of course, no system is foolproof and instances of possible failure do not conclusively prove a point. But if Hess wanted to investigate thoroughly the character "output" of different selection systems, he should have considered the performances of other systems of selection, themselves no less "political." Had he done so, it is at least questionable whether he could have proven the current reformed system superior to a more closed system.

To Hess's view of a test before a public audience, one might oppose a test before a more restricted group consisting of people who make politics a calling and who possess direct knowledge of the aspirants' characters and qualifications. Perhaps our greatest success in consistently elevating men of upstanding character came under the closed systems of the

[36] *Ibid.*, p. 113.

original electoral system and the Congressional caucus. The connection between these systems and the promotion of certain aspects of sound character may not have been simply coincidental. Hugh Heclo investigated the differences between the American and the British selection systems and concluded that it was precisely the closed aspects of the British system that have contributed to its elevation of persons of high integrity.[37]

Of the five functions of selection identified in this study, promoting a "good person" is the most difficult for which to specify satisfactory standards and to institutionalize any standards that might be agreed upon. "Virtue" or good character is a slippery concept which is impossible to "see" objectively. As Adam Smith observed in a discussion of the general problem of leadership recruitment, qualities of character are "invisible . . . always disputable and generally disputed."[38] Nor is it easy to imagine any institutional mechanism that could be so finely tuned as to promote any particular character type. Perhaps because they were aware of these difficulties, past theorists of selection avoided defining any single "psychological profile" and proceeded instead to encourage their desired character attributes by specifying a certain kind of political leadership that could in some measure be institutionalized. These leadership roles would tend to "correlate" with certain character attributes. Thus for the Founders the selection system was designed to promote a person with maturity, experience, and proven capacity for administration, while for Wilson the system should be designed to favor someone who possessed inspirational qualities.

What is most striking about the modern concern for character in the selection process as illustrated in the writings of both Barber and Hess is the degree to which the selection

---

[37] Hugh Heclo, "Presidential and Prime Ministerial Selection" in Donald R. Matthews, ed., *Perspectives on Presidential Selection* (Washington, D.C.: Brookings Institution, 1973), pp. 36-38.

[38] Adam Smith, *The Wealth of Nations* (New York: Modern Library, 1937), p. 671.

problem as a whole is defined in terms of looking for a *direct* means for finding a "good person." These attempts run immediately into the difficulties that seem to be inherent in any such endeavor. Barber's categories are explicit but seem incapable of informing the debate on institutional arrangements. His clarity, one might say, is achieved at the cost of political relevance. Hess claims some relationship between existing arrangements and his essentially Wilsonian ideal of good character, but offers no real evidence that these arrangements actually meet his standards. While the difficulty inherent in defining and implementing good character is no reason to give up on the attempt, it surely makes one wonder about the wisdom of making it the central focus of an institutional study of the selection process. So long as a plausible case can be made that a given system promotes good character—and the case on behalf of the mixed system is as strong as that on behalf of the plebiscitary system—it would seem reasonable to judge systems by reference to other criteria. In particular, if there are grounds for supposing that the attempt to obtain some notion of good character comes at the expense of other desirable objectives, there is all the more reason for taking other considerations into account.

The idea of balancing considerations of character against other more tangible objectives has been implicit in the development of the selection process at least since the time of Van Buren. Once the Founders' nonpartisan system with its emphasis on individual virtue broke down and the pursuit of the presidency became the focal point of factional struggles, Van Buren argued that parties were necessary in order to restrain ambition and weld the diverse factions into potential majorities. In order to maintain parties, the quest for the best man had to be weighed against the value of finding a candidate who could serve as an acceptable representative of the elements of a diverse coalition. The "statesman" had in some measure to give way to the "politician." While the politician could meet the minimal requirements of political competence, integrity, and sound mental health, he might

336

lack the polish and illustriousness of the man of virtue that the Founders had envisioned. To relate this same consideration to the modern understanding of the best man, the politician might lack the singular inspirational qualities now frequently associated with greatness—what Hess identifies as the capacity to "dream grandly" and what Erwin Hargrove calls "positive moral leadership." These qualities, which have their origin in Wilson's ideal of the popular statesman who appeals beyond mere partisanship, point to the dissolution of parties. If parties, as Hess claims, are "essential to the governance of free societies," then it follows that some weight must be given to the kind of leadership that maintains them. Parties cannot be treated on the one hand as mere nominating agencies that bestow their label on the winner of a plebiscite and on the other be expected to exist as strong and vigorous institutions. Party maintenance may extract a certain price in terms of "greatness," although one must add that the current notion of greatness may be so empty and the current attempt to secure it so unsatisfactory that parties might offer the better prospect for obtaining able and reliable leadership.

Neither Barber nor Hess, moreover, considers what effects a selection system based on finding the "best person" might have on restraining the authority of the executive. From the Founding, the restraint of executive authority was understood to rest on both formal and informal checks. Even the best men, according to the Founders, required powerful restraint once in power because political virtue would generally exist in conjunction with high ambition. The formal check on the president in the Founders' system would come from the institutional division of power, the informal from the popular prejudice that existed linking the executive power with monarchism. Although the Founders did not envision the selection process as a part of the informal system of checks on the executive, neither did they view it as an enabling device. Selection for the Founders was to be "neutral" with respect to presidential power, making the office neither more nor less powerful than intended by the Constitution. Once, however, the presidency came to be regarded as a popular and not a monarchic institution, and once election was considered an empowering and not a neutral process, the chief informal restraints the Founders envisioned were lost. The nineteenth-century substitute was the political party, consisting of identifiable persons—bosses and power brokers—who were known to have a "say" in presidential nomination and who by virtue of this power could exercise an informal check on executive authority. The party, so understood, continued to exercise this function through much of this century. By the time of Richard Nixon's campaign in 1972, however, traditional party leaders could be completely ignored. Nixon was able to run a campaign with his own organization, which disregarded the wishes of party leaders and in a number of instances actually assisted Democrats.[39] In the Democratic Party, meanwhile, reformers deliberately wrote party organization leaders out of the selection process on the grounds that they were unrepresentative.

The quest for the best man as embodied in the thought of Woodrow Wilson is tied directly to a selection system designed to remove all restraints from executive power and to provide the executive with the full informal claim of being the leader of the people. Wilson's goal, realized in this instance, was to sweep away the restraints of the traditional party and power brokers and allow the executive to rule by virtue of a personal mandate. It is true, of course, that in the aftermath of Watergate an effort has been made to reinstitute some restraint on executive authority. Many formal restrictions have been proposed and some have been implemented. But informal restraints, despite much talk about their importance, have not been restored, with the single exception of the growth of a temporary barrier of public suspicion against executive power in response to the Watergate crisis. The idea of using the selection system as a pos-

[39] The Ripon Society and Clifford W. Brown, Jr., *Jaws of Victory* (Boston: Little Brown, 1973), p. 71.

338

sible instrument of restraint has thus far made little head-way, and such reforms as have recently been made in the selection process, even since Watergate, have only hastened the changeover to candidate based parties. Indeed, the one reform of the selection process made explicitly in response to Watergate, the Campaign Finance Law of 1974, does nothing to curb presidential authority; if anything, it adds further support to the rise of candidate supremacy by fun-neling public funds directly into the candidates' personal organizations. Without limiting the president's claim to full personal popular authority, which results in large measure from the way in which he is selected, we should not be too surprised by the eventual recurrence of imperial tendencies in our highest office.

The Case for Stronger Political Parties: Restraining Executive Authority and Controlling the Pace of Change

Beyond its immediate effect on the fortunes of Richard Nixon, the Watergate crisis led many Americans to reex-amine their views about the role of the presidency. The po-litical crisis was the result of the actions of a conservative President, but the intellectual crisis has been most acute for liberals, for it was the liberals who led the way throughout this century in championing the virtues of a strong execu-tive. The lesson Richard Nixon succeeded in teaching his life-long enemies was that of the need for restraint on po-litical power, even when—as was the case with Nixon—that power enjoyed the overwhelming support of the na-tion's voters. But although this much was evident, the ex-perience of the Nixon presidency did little to offer any in-struction about what form the needed restraint should assume.

Following Watergate, many political scientists and com-mentators began to call for fundamental changes in the Con-stitutional position of the executive. Proposals were set forth

339

to limit the president to a single six-year term, to allow the dismissal of the president after a negative vote of confidence by three-fifths of the members of each branch of the Congress, and to replace the single executive by an executive by a committee.[40] At the same time, many within the Congress spoke of the need for a return to full-fledged Congressional government in which the Congress would take the lead in formulating national public policy. The heirs of Woodrow Wilson were demonstrating, if nothing else, their willingness to entertain "growth" in the Constitutional system, even if it came at the expense of their own long-cherished goal of presidential government.

Led by more sober advice, however, liberal thought quickly abandoned these radical proposals. While some adjustments in the formal powers of the presidency were called for (and needed), critics of Nixon as strong in their views as Arthur Schlesinger, Jr. maintained that a strong executive was still a necessity. Energetic power and unity of purpose in its command remain requisites of good government in modern society. The attempt to check the abuse of power by eliminating it altogether may be an appealing solution in the aftermath of a crisis such as Watergate, but its long-range effects are certain to produce more harm than good.[41] Realizing this, many began to see that the only sensible way in which to restrain the executive was to restore certain "informal" checks on presidential power, checks which would leave the basic legal authority of the office intact but render it less likely that that authority could be exercised in an arbitrary fashion.

One institution that immediately came to mind for performing this function was the political party. Had not parties in the past imposed constraints on the president's au-

[40] These proposals are discussed in Arthur Schlesinger, Jr., *The Imperial Presidency* (New York: Popular Library, 1973), pp. 359-440.

[41] Schlesinger, *The Imperial Presidency*, pp. 359-440, and Bundy, *The Strength of Government*, p. 30.

thority and actions, and were not these same constraints now conspicuously absent? As Arthur Schlesinger noted, "when parties were strong—Presidents were objects of respect but not veneration. . . . As the parties wasted away, the Presidency stood out in solitary majesty as the central focus of political emotion. . . ."[42] The idea of strengthening parties also proved attractive upon consideration of the immediate origin of the Watergate crisis. The "caper" at the Watergate and the assorted other dirty tricks of the Nixon campaign which were subsequently exposed were the work of a personal organization committed to a single man; they might never have occurred, many argued, if the presidential campaign had been run by "professionals" and party regulars.[43] Parties, then, could serve the functions of checking executive power and assuring a degree of moderation and fair play in the pursuit of the office.

In spite of the apparent soundness of this analysis, liberals have been reluctant to swallow the medicine that many of their own doctors have prescribed. Any move to strengthen political parties would run counter to the principle on which the recent reformers based their public appeal—the right of the people to choose presidential nominees. However much liberals or reformers may attempt to avoid or deny the fact, it remains that the open selection system is what creates the necessity for contenders to build full organizations of their own; and it is the open system that destroys the intermediary power brokers within the party who can offer an effective check to the president's power. From the vantage point of the president, the open party consists of an amorphous mass whose only means of resistance is a periodic message sent through political polls. The public may eventually humble an incumbent by denying him renomination, but it cannot, like the political power broker, negotiate with him, sit in his cabinet, or tell him that its support will be contingent on certain actions. Until the last moment, a president may think

---

[42] Schlesinger, *The Imperial Presidency*, p. 210.
[43] Hess, *The Presidential Campaign*, pp. 95-98.

that he can win back his following by the use of dramatic personal actions or persuasion, a fact which probably encourages the verbal excesses that have become so characteristic of modern presidential rhetoric.

If one looks, moreover, at the justifications advanced in the liberal and reform proposals to strengthen parties during this century, it is clear that restraint on political power was never their objective. The "old" liberal plan for party government, championed by such people as E. E. Schattschneider and James MacGregor Burns, was based precisely on the elimination of the formal checks on presidential power built into the Madisonian system; and while some emphasis is given, in Burns's words, to the "powerful balances and safeguards that are built into a system of majority rule and responsible parties," one can hardly feel comfortable with a system that would rely almost entirely on informal restraints.[44] In fact, since Watergate, one hears little of the party government position in the pure form in which it was originally advanced. Burns has apparently abandoned his former animus against Constitutional checks and balances and is now singing the welcome song of using responsible parties to restrain executive authority.[45] Similarly, if one looks at the reform literature supporting the stronger parties, no mention can be found, at least before Watergate, of the idea of restraint. According to the authors of a recent paean to reform, John Saloma and Frederick Sontag, its primary objective is to increase citizen participation in politics as a means of building citizen virtue.[46] As this defense is accompanied by a warm endorsement of the open selection process of today, it leads to the very vacuum in electoral politics that is one source of the "personal presidency." Finally, the one sense in which the Democratic

[44] James MacGregor Burns, *The Deadlock of Democracy*, p. 6.

[45] James MacGregor Burns, "Introduction" to Saloma and Sontag's *Parties*. In this short introduction Burns does not make his usual attack on the Madisonian system. In his discussion of parties, the emphasis is placed on using parties to restrain the presidency.

[46] Saloma and Sontag, *Parties*, p. 374.

Party has been strengthened along the lines advocated by reformers—namely greater control of the national party over the state and local affiliates—poses even a graver potential threat to restraint on the executive. A Democratic president, who can usually win control over the national party apparatus, would now control the decision-making authority for the entire party, without facing the resistance from state and local organizations.

In order to strengthen parties, and to strengthen them for the correct reasons, one must begin from a different premise than that found in recent reform thought. The basis of the now position must be the republican idea that there are certain values, such as restraint on the pursuit and exercise of power, that are more important than adhering to the formulae of full democracy. If the existence of parties with intermediary power brokers—modern bosses if you like—can provide an informal check on the presidency and discourage candidates from going to the roots in quadrennial crusades, then the cost in terms of a deviation from some abstract notion of the "democratic ethic" is well worth bearing. The recommended direction of reform, in short, must be to "close" our political parties while opening the electoral process.

One can anticipate three objections to any plan that would give the party back to the organization. They are: that it is fundamentally undemocratic, that it would promote weak and incompetent presidents, and that under modern circumstances it would not produce the desired results but lead instead to control of the electoral process by extreme ideological parties. The first objection is difficult to take seriously in view of the fact that regimes universally recognized to be democratic have "closed" nomination systems. Our own regime, as Walter Dean Burnham has argued, was by many standards most democratic when parties were controlled by the organizations.[47] It is not clear,

---

[47] Walter Dean Burnham, "The Changing Shape of the American Political Universe," *American Political Science Review* 59 (March 1965): 24.

moreover, that the open system is as democratic in substance as it appears to be in form. Many modern political scientists have demonstrated the technical impossibility of arriving at a purely democratic choice where more than two alternatives are involved.[48] For a choice to be fully democratic, some method must be found to take into consideration the rank preferences of the voters for all the candidates. On this count, there is no reason to suppose that delegates selected in primaries or by an open process can better represent the party's will than delegates selected by a closed process. More important is the objection of Jefferson and Van Buren that a nonpartisan selection process is not an especially democratic procedure because it accords an advantage to those having the time, money, knowledge, and, for whatever reason, the ability to organize quickly. (Public financing up to the fixed limit of spending obviously removes the advantage of money, though it also puts a higher premium on the other factors; its effect may therefore be to replace one kind of nondemocratic influence with others.) According to Jefferson and Van Buren, elections would best serve the cause of "true" majority rule if the people were presented with a managed choice by organizations which over time had demonstrated their fidelity to a certain constituency.

It goes without saying that the groups and interests which dominate in such organizations will have greater influence than those that are outside. But the pertinent questions are whether they abuse this power by making choices objectionable to the party's constituency and whether they do so more often than would occur under an alternative system. Certainly the election of 1912 illustrates that an organization can deviate from the wishes of its constituents. But 1912 stands out as a major exception in a system that has represented the interests of the various components of the party constituency in tolerable relationship to their strength within the party.

[48] See Donald R. Matthews, "Presidential Nominations" in Barber, ed., *Choosing the President*, p. 37.

Of course party organizations will not necessarily represent every new current of opinion in exact relationship to its general electoral strength. In this sense, party organizations respond "undemocratically." But far from constituting a reason for destroying them, this is one of the most important reasons why they should be maintained. The "leverage" that parties possess enables them to withstand, at least temporarily, undesirable currents of opinion and extreme movements. If it is known *a priori* that the centers of power in a party are closed to certain opinions, leaders interested in higher office will be more apt to leave them alone.

The power to exclude or ignore certain movements, like any other power, is one that can be abused. Legitimate movements whose "time has come" may be denied their say in the major parties. But there is a check against the total exclusion of any movement from the political process. This check derives from the fact that parties are not official Constitutional institutions. The Constitution does not assure the continuing existence of any particular party or guarantee that it will remain competitive. The only Constitutionally regulated procedure in the presidential selection process is the final election. From the Constitution's neutral perspective, the nation is served just as well by Party A as by Party B. Translated into practical terms, the check on a major party's abuse of its gatekeeper role with respect to new political demands is the threat that it will be defeated by its opposition or replaced by a new party. The history of party development in this country, including the vital role that has been played by third parties, provides ample testimony to the reality of this threat. If the objection to closed parties is the age-old question of who guards the guardians, the answer is still the people. The Constitutional system as it presently exists calls by its very neglect of parties for an open electoral system. Every political regime faces the need for periodic renewal—for an infusion of new ideas, programs, and approaches—and if the established parties are sometimes tardy in meeting such demands, which is the price of their other virtues, the open electoral system provides the needed stimulus to make them respond in the end.

One well-known defender of the current nominating system, James Sundquist, has downplayed the role of third parties. For Sundquist, as for the McGovern-Fraser Commission, activity outside the two existing parties is considered automatically to be a dangerous challenge to the political system:

> Throughout our history and the history of other countries, those who have been denied a full right of participation in the party system have taken their case to the streets . . . if zealots and extremists are to work within the party system, they must be granted the right to take control of a *major* party if and when there are enough of them.[49]

It is little wonder that a defender of open parties identifies third-party activity as antisystemic. If the major parties are thought of as the sole allowable nominating agencies, then "fairness" must be observed. Certainly the state, or an entity that is regarded as a public institution, cannot openly establish certain groups in the electoral process and exclude others.

Another way of considering the matter, however, would be to say that a major party does have the right to exclude "zealots and extremists" at its own peril; and that such persons, "if and when there are enough of them" may take their case to the people in the form of a third party. As Sundquist's analysis indirectly testifies, the third party—and especially the equal right of a third party to form—is the friend of "closed" parties: the third party preserves a legitimate justification for the existence of closed parties in that while any particular party may be closed, the electoral system as a whole remains open. In practice, of course, a third party stands at a *de facto* disadvantage because of the very logic of a winner-take-all system, which makes a ballot cast for a minor party candidate seem wasted. But this disad-

[49] Sundquist, *Dynamics*, p. 307.

vantage is a natural consequence of the electoral system and does not appear as a deliberate or invidious attempt on the part of the state to discriminate against a particular group wishing to form a party. Furthermore, the disadvantage to third parties imposed by a winner-take-all system is not insuperable. Although only one third party in our history has replaced a major party, third parties have often succeeded in pressuring the major parties to change their positions, as recently, in fact, as 1968. The concept of the open electoral system is thus not—or need not be—a legal myth. There is every justification for a public teaching which holds that any group that is dissatisfied with the major parties has an equal opportunity to take its case to the people *within the system*. This teaching is undermined to the extent that the two major parties are viewed as permanent "public" institutions and begin on this basis to grant themselves certain legal privileges, as in the recent campaign finance legislation. It is accordingly in the long-term interest of the defenders of strong parties to resist any attempt at official establishment of the major parties and to keep the electoral process formally open.[50]

[50] The threat to an open electoral process came initially after the turn of this century when various states used their control over access to the ballot to impose severe obstacles on new parties. These laws impeded the efforts of LaFollette in 1924 and Henry Wallace in 1948. In 1968 George Wallace and the American Party challenged a restrictive law in Ohio and won a favorable ruling in *Williams v. Rhodes*, 393 U.S. 23.

This victory for an open electoral process was almost immediately offset, however, by the campaign finance legislation of 1974. The threat to the third parties posed by this legislation may be greater than the ballot restrictions, if only because the ballot restrictions were acts of the individual states and did not apply in every case. The campaign finance legislation, on the other hand, is national in its scope; the restrictions it places on individual contributions would seem to make it very difficult for a third party to collect the funds sufficient for conducting a national campaign. In the event, however, that a third party does succeed in obtaining more than five percent of the vote, the law guarantees the party a share of campaign funding in the succeeding election, thus providing an incentive to keep the

The second possible objection to strong parties is that they would limit the discretion of the president, binding him to narrow platform provisions or forcing him to make concessions to the power brokers who may influence his chances of being renominated. These were among the reasons that led Woodrow Wilson to attack the nineteenth-century parties. But while such concerns about excessive party domination had some basis in the late nineteenth century, when parties were at their strongest and the presidency at its weakest, they have much less foundation today. The decisive change since Wilson's time has been the growth in the power and visibility of the presidency, a growth due not only to the bold assertions of political scientists and certain for a powerful executive, but also to the greater need for executive action given the expanded role of the United States in world affairs and the increased involvement of the federal government in domestic policy-making. With these changes in the requirements of governing, the presidency inevitably becomes the dominant institution in the modern political system. Its power and visibility guarantee an incumbent a substantial degree of independence from his party in the conduct of his duties and assure him that he will not be de-

---

party alive. Since third parties are often "one-shot affairs," e.g. the Progressive Party in 1912 and, for all practical purposes, the American Party in 1968, the legislation may have the tendency to perpetuate deviation beyond its normal course. In both of its effects, then, the law has tampered significantly with the "natural" tendencies of the open party system—and in both instances its influence appears to be undesirable.

The general problem with such regulation, as with almost all cases of government regulation, is that the regulation in the end is likely to favor the interests of the most powerful groups that are regulated —in this case, the major parties. Even William Crotty, a strong advocate of finance legislation, has expressed grave concerns about this possibility: ". . . should the commission take to promoting the interests of one party to the detriment of another or should it favor major parties (a more likely occurrence) to the exclusion of minor parties, the whole experiment might well be doomed" (*Political Reform*, p. 187).

nied renomination if he has performed well. Moreover, any final election in which an incumbent is involved will almost certainly turn on the people's retrospective judgment of his record. The presidency in its official constitutional position remains a nonpartisan office, and any modern president having a modest amount of pride and determination should have no difficulty resisting extreme partisan encroachments.

There is therefore no need in modern circumstances to devise electoral arrangements to assure the president an adequate means for establishing a personal constituency to counteract the influence of his party. The problem today is rather to establish some means by which to place his personal constituency within certain boundaries and ensure that it does not become the chief source of his claim to authority. Nor does it seem necessary, as Wilson believed, for a new president to possess a *personal* mandate in order to maintain the powers of the office. The official powers of the president are substantial, and the president, even without being selected primarily on a personal basis, can still appeal directly to the American people for support for his programs. The widely held view that Gerald Ford could not function effectively as president because he did not receive a personal electoral mandate is exaggerated as well as misleading: Ford, in fact, was able to protect the essential prerogatives of the office under very difficult circumstances; and to the extent he encountered unusual resistance, it can be attributed to the large size of the opposition party in Congress and to the reaction against executive authority that followed after Watergate. The attempt to arm the president with a full personal claim to represent the people thus goes beyond what is needed to guarantee the president a reasonable degree of discretion and increases the risk that he may assert unnecessary presidential prerogatives. In saying this, no attempt is being made to deny the president a right to assert a limited mandate on the basis of his electoral victory. The additional energy that derives from this source is a valuable and by now accepted supplement to formal presi-

349

dential power. The problem today is to prevent this supplement, especially in its highly personal form, from becoming too much the basis of presidential authority. Placing the party "prior" to the candidate would be an important step in restraining this tendency.

The object of this restraint, it must be emphasized, is not to weaken or hobble the president. Indeed, it has been pointed out that the executive's claim to full and plenary power based on his personal role as representative of public opinion has in certain respects had the paradoxical effect of diminishing effective executive authority. The populist claim erodes the discretion of the office, not to mention its majesty, while the personalistic basis of the claim has served to weaken the political parties and thus to deprive the president of his partisan basis of support among the people and within the Congress. Lacking this solid support, the president is forced to turn more and more to mass persuasion and is perhaps more likely to assert bold claims to having a personal, "special relationship" with the people. His weakness thus becomes one reason for his overarching assertions.

The third and final objection comes from those who sympathize with the idea of restraint but who believe that strengthening parties under modern circumstances would achieve the opposite result. Parties, in this view, would inevitably be taken over by ideologically motivated amateurs which in turn would lead to more strident conflict. With the destruction already of many of the traditional party organizations and with the decline of patronage, the incentives to join and participate in parties are primarily purposive. The prototype of the modern party organization is found in the aggressive amateur organizations of the candidates, and indeed in many cases these amateurs have already taken over segments of the official organization. Considering, then, the nature of these organizations, the best solution ironically might be the *most* open one—the national primary. National primaries—or perhaps the simpler nonpartisan two-stage election once suggested by Andrew Jackson—would be more moderate than a system in which ideological organizations dominate. The national primary would focus the greatest attention on the candidates and stimulate the average citizen, whose attitudes are less ideological than those of the amateur organizational participant, to turn out and vote. The people, in short, would be used to circumvent the parties for the explicit purpose of moderating the selection process.

This objection to stronger parties is not without merit, and depending on the way parties evolve, it could prove decisive. But it is an undesirable solution, one that can be justified only on the grounds of being the lesser of two very serious evils. Moreover, instituting a national primary would be a nearly irreversible decision because it would require a Constitutional amendment. Such an amendment would almost certainly be justified on democratic grounds, thus detracting still further from the chance of reestablishing the idea of restraint in the electoral process.

The strongest response to this objection, however, is that there is not yet enough evidence for accepting the "worst case" assumption about the character of future party organizations. Amateurs have admittedly gained ground since the 1950s, but groups, shifting as always with changes in society, maintain a vigor of their own and continue to seek representation in the political process. Indeed, after the period of "movement politics" from the mid- to the late-sixties, the nation has experienced a partial resurgence of "pluralist" politics. Nor can one as yet be certain that amateurs, once they become regular participants in the party organizations, will continue to behave as uncompromising ideologues. There is probably some truth to the idea that yesterday's amateur is tomorrow's professional. Once secure in his place within the party organization, the amateur might begin to assume responsibility for the well-being of the party as a whole. The energy he formerly employed in attacking the entrenched organization within the party might now be given to defending the party against its opponents. At a

351

minimum, if an organization controls the nomination, even if it is an amateur organization, the selection system possesses something of the character of an institution; it retains some capacity for institutional memory by virtue of the fact that a group of persons exists who can learn from past mistakes and be in a position to apply these lessons the next time around. The reform goal of harnessing amateur motivations to the political process is thus not in itself objectionable. It is only when this goal is justified on the grounds of promoting the "democratic ethic" that the damage is done, for a plebiscitary system in the nomination process will in the end destroy a political party in any meaningful sense.

The idea of recreating "establishments" within the parties that would have real power in influencing nominations may by now seem impractical. Apart from the difficulty of persuading a party of the desirability of such a change, how could such a plan be carried out in practice? Would it require a Constitutional amendment that would fully nationalize the nomination process and bring it under full legal control? Fortunately, the practical obstacles are not as great as one might suppose. The reforms in the Democratic Party proceeded under the assumption that the national party, rather than state law or state party regulations, had final control over the manner in which delegates are selected, and this idea has very nearly been endorsed by the Supreme Court. A full acceptance of this view would mean that a party *could* write its own delegate selection rules with a view to closing the delegate selection process. There is thus no reason in theory why a national party could not now begin openly to encourage states to abandon primaries and even, if necessary, place an upper limit on the number of delegates chosen by this means, perhaps by alloting them on a rotating basis to those states preferring this method. Nor is there any reason why a national party could not allow or even encourage the selection of some portion of a state's delegation on an *ex officio* basis or by "untimely" processes in advance of the election year. A party might even establish its own rules for campaign financing during the nomination stage, banning if it wished the use of public funding. And finally, since the legitimacy and fairness of closed parties is enhanced when the electoral system as a whole is open to all parties, a closed party in its own long-range interest might want to oppose any form of discrimination against third parties, something that would require at the very least some major changes in existing campaign finance legislation. If parties are viewed as fully public agencies and become an official part of the legal system, they cannot expect to be in a position to resist pressures to adhere strictly to the procedures of democracy. Taken together these reforms would help place restraints on candidate appeals and build an institution that could offer an informal check on presidential power.

It is apparent that these changes would have to be supported by a campaign to convince people of the virtues of strong political parties. Perhaps one of the parties might find in such a campaign part of a general philosophy of republicanism that it could oppose to some of the defects and excesses in our current conception of democracy. The division thus inspired, which might require an act of exceptional leadership, could lay the foundation for a safe but vigorous partisanship in the years ahead.

BIBLIOGRAPHY

Books

Adams, John. *The Works of John Adams*. Edited by Charles Francis Adams. 10 vols. Boston: Little Brown, 1850-56.

Adams, John Quincy. *The Memoirs of John Quincy Adams*. Edited by Charles Francis Adams. 12 vols. Philadelphia: J. B. Lippincott, 1874-77.

————. *Parties in the United States*. New York: Greenberg, 1941.

Agranoff, Robert. *The New Style in Election Campaigns*. Boston: Holbrook Press, 1976.

Ambler, Charles. *Thomas Ritchie*. Richmond: Bell Books Stationary, 1913.

Aristotle. *The Basic Works of Aristotle*. Edited and Introduction by Richard McKeon. New York: Random House, 1968.

Bailyn, Bernard. *The Ideological Origins of the American Revolution*. Cambridge: Harvard University Press, 1967.

Banfield, Edward C. and Wilson, James Q. *City Politics*. New York: Vintage Books, 1963.

Banfield, Edward C. *Political Influence*. New York: Free Press of Glencoe, 1961.

Barber, James David, ed. *Choosing the President*. Englewood Cliffs, N.J.: Prentice Hall, 1974.

————. *The Presidential Character*. Englewood Cliffs, N.J.: Prentice Hall, 1972.

Basset, John Spencer. *Correspondence of Andrew Jackson*. 2 vols. Washington, D.C.: Carnegie Institution, 1927.

Best, Judith. *The Case Against the Direct Election of the President*. Ithaca: Cornell University Press, 1975.

Bickel, Alexander. *The New Age of Political Reform*. New York: Harper Books, 1968.

354

Bonney, Catharina. *A Legacy of Historical Gleanings*. Albany: J. Munsell, 1875.

Brown, William. *The People's Choice, The Presidential Image in the Campaign Biography*. Baton Rouge: Louisiana State University Press, 1960.

Bryce, James. *The American Commonwealth*. 2 vols. London: Macmillan, 1889.

Bundy, McGeorge. *The Strength of Government*. Cambridge: Harvard University Press, 1968.

Burnham, Walter Dean. *Critical Elections and the Mainsprings of American Politics*. New York: W. W. Norton, 1970.

Burns, James MacGregor. *The Deadlock of Democracy*. Englewood Cliffs, N.J.: Prentice Hall, 1963.

Calhoun, John C. *A Disquisition on Government*. Indianapolis: Bobbs-Merrill, 1953.

Campbell, Angus; Converse, Philip E.; Miller, Warren E.; and Stokes, Donald E. *The American Voter*. New York: John Wiley and Sons, 1964.

Carter, Nathaniel H., and Stone, William L. *Reports of the Proceedings and Debates of the Convention of 1821: Assembled for the Purpose of Amending the Constitution of the State of New York*. Albany: E. and E. Hosford, 1821.

Chambers, William Nisbet and Burnham, Walter Dean, eds. *The American Party Systems*. 2nd ed. New York: Oxford University Press, 1975.

Chase, James. *Emergence of the Presidential Nominating Convention*. Urbana: University of Illinois Press, 1973.

Cooper, James Fenimore. *The American Democrat*. Edited by H. L. Mencken. New York: Alfred A. Knopf, 1931.

Croly, Herbert. *Progressive Democracy*. New York: Macmillan, 1914.

Crotty, William J. *Political Reform and the American Experiment*. New York: Thomas Y. Crowell, 1977.

David, Paul and Ceaser, James W. *Proportional Representa-*

tion in the Presidential Nominating Process (Charlottesville, Va.: University Press of Virginia, 1978).

David, Paul T.; Goldman, Ralph M.; and Bain, Richard. *The Politics of National Party Conventions.* Washington, D.C.: Brookings Institution, 1960.

Davis, James W. *Presidential Primaries: Road to the White House.* New York: Thomas Y. Crowell, 1967.

De Tocqueville, Alexis. *Democracy in America.* Edited by J. P. Mayer. Translated by George Lawrence. New York: Doubleday, 1969.

Diamond, Martin; Fisk, Winston Mills; and Garfinkel, Herbert. *The Democratic Republic.* Chicago: Rand McNally, 1966.

Dodd, Lawrence and Oppenheimer, Bruce, eds. *Congress Reconsidered.* New York: Praeger, 1977.

Dudden, Arthur P., ed. *Woodrow Wilson and the World of Today.* Philadelphia: University of Pennsylvania Press, 1957.

Duverger, Maurice. *Political Parties.* Translated by Barbara and Robert North. New York: John Wiley and Sons, 1963.

Eidelberg, Paul. *The Philosophy of the American Constitution.* New York: Free Press, 1968.

Elliott, Jonathan, ed. *The Debates in the Several State Conventions on the Adoption of the Federal Constitution,* 2nd ed. 5 vols. Philadelphia: By the Editor, 1861.

Elliott, Ward. *The Rise of Guardian Democracy.* Cambridge: Harvard University Press, 1974.

Farrand, Max, ed. *The Records of the Federal Convention of 1787,* rev. ed. (New Haven: Yale University Press, 1937).

Flexner, James Thomas. *George Washington.* 2 vols. Boston: Little Brown, 1965-72.

Foner, Eric. *Free Soil, Free Labor, Free Men.* New York: Oxford University Press, 1970.

Frisch, Morton J. and Stevens, Richard G., eds. *American Political Thought.* New York: Charles Scribner's Sons, 1971.

Gammon, S. R., Jr. *The Presidential Campaign of 1832*. Baltimore: The Johns Hopkins Press, 1922.

George, Alexander and Julliette. *Woodrow Wilson and Colonel House*. New York: Dover Publications, 1956.

Goldwin, Robert A., ed. *Political Parties, U.S.A.* Chicago: Rand McNally, 1961.

Graham, Otis. *An Encore for Reform: The Old Progressives and the New Deal*. New York: Oxford University Press, 1967.

Hall, Van Beck. *Politics Without Parties, Massachusetts, 1780-1791*. Pittsburgh: University of Pittsburgh Press, 1972.

Hamilton, Alexander; Madison, James; and Jay, John. *The Federalist. Papers*. Edited and Introduction by Clinton Rossiter. New York: New American Library, 1961.

Hamilton, Alexander. *The Works of Alexander Hamilton*. Edited by H. C. Lodge. 12 vols. New York: G. P. Putnam's Sons, 1904.

Hargrove, Erwin C. *The Power of the Modern Presidency*. New York: Alfred A. Knopf, 1974.

Herring, Pendleton. *The Politics of Democracy*. New York: W. W. Norton, 1965.

Hess, Stephen. *Organizing the Presidency*. Washington, D.C.: Brookings Institution, 1976.

———. *The Presidential Campaign*. Washington, D.C.: Brookings Institution, 1975.

Hofstadter, Richard. *The Idea of a Party System*. Berkeley: University of California Press, 1969.

Israel, Fred L., ed. *The State of the Union Messages of the Presidents*. 3 vols. New York: Chelsea House, 1966.

Jefferson, Thomas. *The Works of Thomas Jefferson*. Edited by Paul Leicester Ford. Federal Edition. 12 vols. New York: G. P. Putnam's Sons, 1905.

———. *The Writings of Thomas Jefferson*. Edited by Andrew A. Lipscomb and A. Ellery Bergh. Washington, D.C.: Thomas Jefferson Memorial Association, 1905.

Jensen, Richard. *The Winning of the Midwest*. Chicago: University of Chicago Press, 1971.

Johannsen, Robert, ed. *The Lincoln-Douglas Debates.* New York: Oxford University Press, 1965.

Keech, William R. and Matthews, Donald R. *The Party's Choice.* Washington, D.C.: Brookings Institution, 1976.

Key, V. O., Jr. *Politics, Parties and Pressure Groups.* 5th ed., New York: Thomas Y. Crowell, 1964.

————. *The Responsible Electorate.* New York: Random House, 1966.

————. *Southern Politics.* New York: Alfred A. Knopf, 1949.

Ladd, Everett, Jr. *American Political Parties.* New York: W. W. Norton, 1970.

————. *Transformations of the American Party System.* New York: W. W. Norton, 1975.

LaFollette, Robert M. *Autobiography.* Madison: Robert M. LaFollette Company, 1913.

Lipset, Seymour Martin and Raab, Earl. *The Politics of Unreason.* New York: Harper and Row, 1970.

Lowi, Theodore. *The End of Liberalism.* New York: W. W. Norton, 1969.

Madison, James. *Letters and Other Writings of James Madison.* Edited by William C. Rives and Philip R. Fendall. 4 vols. Philadelphia: J. B. Lippincott, 1865.

————. *Notes of Debates in the Federal Convention of 1787.* Edited by Adrienne Koch. New York: W. W. Norton, 1969.

————. *The Writings of James Madison.* Edited by Gaillard Hunt, 9 vols. New York: G. P. Putnam's Sons, 1903.

Maine, Henry, Sir. *Popular Government.* London: John Murray, 1885.

Malone, Dumas. *Jefferson and the Ordeal of Liberty.* Boston: Little Brown, 1962.

————. *Thomas Jefferson as Political Leader.* Berkeley: University of California Press, 1963.

Mansfield, Harvey C., Jr. *Statesmanship and Party Government.* Chicago: University of Chicago Press, 1965.

Marcus, Robert. *Grand Old Party.* New York: Oxford University Press, 1971.

Matthews, Donald R., ed. *Perspectives on Presidential Selection*. Washington, D.C.: Brookings Institution, 1973.

May, Ernest. *The Making of the Monroe Doctrine*. Cambridge: Harvard University Press, 1975.

May, Ernest R. and Fraser, Janet, eds. *Campaign '72, The Managers Speak*. Cambridge: Harvard University Press, 1973.

Mayhew, David. *Congress: The Electoral Connection*. New Haven: Yale University Press, 1974.

Mazmanian, Daniel L. *Third Parties in Presidential Elections*. Washington, D.C.: Brookings Institution, 1974.

Meyers, Marvin. *The Jacksonian Persuasion*. Stanford: Stanford University Press, 1960.

Miller, Warren E. and Levitan, Teresa. *Leadership and Change*. Cambridge: Winthrop, 1976.

Monroe, James. *The Writings of James Monroe*. Edited by S. M. Hamilton. 7 vols. New York: G. P. Putnam's Sons, 1898-1903.

Neustadt, Richard. *Presidential Power*. New York: John Wiley's Sons, 1976.

Nichols, Roy F. *The Invention of the American Political Parties*. New York: Free Press, 1967.

Nie, Norman H.; Verba, Sidney; Petrocik, John R. *The Changing American Voter*. Cambridge: Harvard University Press, 1976.

Overacker, Louise. *The Presidential Primary*. New York: Macmillan, 1926.

Pierce, Neil. *The People's President*. New York: Simon and Schuster, 1968.

Pitkin, Hanna. *The Concept of Representation*. Berkeley: University of California Press, 1967.

Polsby, Nelson W. *Congress and the Presidency*. 3rd ed. Englewood Cliffs, N.J.: Prentice Hall, 1976.

Polsby, Nelson W. and Wildavsky, Aaron B. *Presidential Elections*. 3rd ed. New York: Charles Scribner's Sons, 1971.

Polsby, Nelson W.; Dentler, Robert A.; and Smith, Paul A.,

359

eds. *Political and Social Life.* Boston: Houghton Mifflin, 1963.

Pomper, Gerald. *The Election of 1976.* New York: David McKay, 1977.

―――. *Nominating the President.* New York: W. W. Norton, 1966.

―――. *The Voter's Choice.* New York: Dodd Mead, 1975.

Porter, Kirk H. and Johnson, Donald Bruce, eds. *National Party Platforms 1840-1964.* Urbana: University of Illinois Press, 1966.

Ranney, Austin. *Curing the Mischiefs of Faction: Party Reform in America.* Berkeley: University of California Press, 1975.

―――. *The Doctrine of Responsible Party Government.* Urbana: University of Illinois Press, 1962.

Remini, Robert. *Martin Van Buren and the Democratic Party.* New York: Columbia University Press, 1959.

Richardson, James D., ed. *A Compilation of the Messages and Papers of the Presidents.* 10 vols. Washington, D.C.: Bureau of National Literature, 1897-1913.

Ripon Society and Brown, Clifford W., Jr. *Jaws of Victory.* Boston: Little Brown, 1973.

Roosevelt, Theodore. *Campaigns and Controversies.* New York: Charles Scribner's Sons, 1926.

―――. *The New Nationalism.* Englewood Cliffs, N.J.: Prentice Hall, 1961.

Roseboom, Eugene H. *A History of Presidential Elections.* New York: Macmillan, 1970.

Saloma, John S. and Sontag, Frederick H. *Parties: The Real Opportunity for Effective Citizen Politics.* New York: Random House, 1973.

Schattschneider, E. E. *Party Government.* New York: Holt, Rinehart and Winston, 1942.

Schlesinger, Arthur M., Jr., ed. *History of U.S. Political Parties.* 4 vols. New York: Chelsea House, 1973.

―――. *The Imperial Presidency.* New York: Popular Library, 1973.

Schlesinger, Arthur M., Jr. and Israel, Fred, eds. *History of American Presidential Elections 1789-1968.* 4 vols. New York: Chelsea House, 1971.

Sindler, Allan P. *Political Parties in the United States.* New York: St. Martin's Press, 1966.

Smith, Adam. *The Wealth of Nations.* New York: Modern Library, 1937.

Stanwood, Edward. *A History of the Presidency from 1788 to 1897.* Boston: Houghton Mifflin, 1898.

Stroud, Kandy. *How Jimmy Won.* New York: William Morrow, 1977.

Sullivan, Denis G.; Pressman, Jeffrey L.; Page, Benjamin L.; and Lyons, John J. *The Politics of Representation.* New York: St. Martin's Press, 1974.

Sundquist, James L. *Dynamics of the Party System.* Washington, D.C.: Brookings Institution, 1973.

Thach, Charles, Jr. *The Creation of the Presidency, 1775-1789.* Baltimore: The Johns Hopkins Press, 1969.

Thompson, Charles. *The Rise and Fall of the Nominating Caucus.* New Haven: 1902.

Tugwell, Rexford G. and Cronin, Thomas E. *The Presidency Reappraised.* New York: Praeger, 1974.

Van Buren, Martin. *The Autobiography of Martin Van Buren.* Edited by John C. Fitzpatrick. Annual Report of the American Historical Association, Washington, D.C.: 1918.

————. *Inquiry into the Origin and Course of Political Parties in the United States.* New York: Hurd and Houghton, 1867.

Verba, Sidney, and Nie, Norman H. *Participation in America.* New York: Harper and Row, 1972.

Washington, George. *Writings of George Washington.* Edited by John C. Fitzpatrick. 39 vols. Washington, D.C.: Government Printing Office, 1931-41.

Weber, Max. *The Theory of Social and Economic Organization.* Edited by Talcott Parsons. New York: Oxford University Press, 1947.

361

White, Theodore. *The Making of a President 1960*. New York: Atheneum, 1961.

———. *The Making of the President 1972*. New York: Bantam Books, 1973.

Wiebe, Robert H. *The Search for Order*. New York: Hill and Wang, 1967.

Wildavsky, Aaron. *The Revolt Against the Masses*. New York: Free Press, 1971.

Wilmerding, Lucius. *The Electoral College*. New Brunswick, N.J.: Rutgers University Press, 1958.

Wilson, James Q. *The Amateur Democrat*. Chicago: University of Chicago Press, 1962.

———. *Political Organizations*. New York: Basic Books, 1973.

Wilson, Woodrow. *College and State, Educational Literary and Political Papers (1875-1913)*. Edited by Ray Stannard Baker and William E. Dodd. 2 vols. New York: Harper Brothers, 1925.

———. *Congressional Government*. Boston: Houghton Mifflin, 1885.

———. *Constitutional Government in the United States*. New York: Columbia University Press, 1908.

———. *Leaders of Men*. Edited by T.H.V. Motter, Princeton: Princeton University Press, 1952.

———. *The New Freedom*. Introduction and Notes by William E. Leuchtenburg. Englewood Cliffs, N.J.: Prentice Hall, 1964.

———. *The Papers of Woodrow Wilson*. Edited by Arthur S. Link. 18 vols. Princeton: Princeton University Press, 1966–

Wood, Gordon. *The Creation of the American Republic 1776-1787*. New York: W. W. Norton, 1969.

Young, James Sterling. *The Washington Community 1800-1828*. New York: Harcourt, Brace, and World, 1966.

Assassination and Political Violence: A Report to the National Commission on the Causes and Prevention of

Violence. By James F. Kirkam, Sheldon G. Levy and William J. Crotty. Washington, D.C.: Government Printing Office, 1969.

Democrats All: A Report of the Commission on Delegate Selection and Party Structure. Barbara A. Mikulski, Chairwoman. Washington, D.C.: Democratic National Committee, 1974.

Mandate for Reform: A Report of the Commission of Party Structure and Delegate Selection to the Democratic National Committee. George S. McGovern, Chairman. Washington, D.C.: Democratic National Committee, 1970.

Openness, Participation and Party Building: Reforms for a Stronger Democratic Party, Report of the Commission on Presidential Nomination and Party Structure. Morley A. Winograd, Chairman. Washington, D.C.: Democratic National Committee, 1978.

Report of the Commission on the Democratic Selection of Presidential Nominees reprinted in The Congressional Record, vol. 114, part 24, 90th Congress, 2nd Session, 1968.

ARTICLES AND PAPERS

American Political Science Association. "Toward a More Responsible Two-Party System," the Report of the Committee on Political Parties. *American Political Science Review* Supplement vol. 44 (September 1950).

Burnham, Walter Dean. "The Changing Shape of the American Political Universe." *American Political Science Review* 59 (March 1965): 1-28.

Greenstein, Fred I. "Popular Images of the President." *American Journal of Psychiatry* 122:5 (November 1965): 523-29.

Jackson, John S. "Some Correlates of Minority Representation in the National Conventions 1964-1972," *American Politics Quarterly* 3 (April 1975): 171-88.

Kayden, Xandra. "The Political Campaign as an Organization." *Public Policy* 31 (Spring 1973): 263-90.

Key, V. O., Jr. "A Theory of Critical Elections." *Journal of Politics* 17 (February 1955): 3-18.

Lipset, Seymour Martin. "The Paradox of American Politics." *The Public Interest* 41 (Fall 1975): 142-65.

Mansfield, Harvey C., Jr. "The Modern Doctrine of Executive Power." Paper delivered at the Midwest Regional Meeting of the American Society for Eighteenth Century Studies, October 26, 1973.

Morgan, William G. "The Origin and Development of the Congressional Nominating Caucus." *Proceedings of the American Philosophical Society* 113 (April 1969): 184-96.

Nichols, Roy F. "Adaptation versus Invention as Elements in Historical Analysis." *American Philosophical Society Proceedings* 108, no. 5, 1964: 408.

Orren, Gary and Schneider, William. "Democrats versus Democrats: Party Factions in the 1972 Presidential Primaries." Manuscript.

Ostrogorski, Moise. "The Rise and Fall of the Nominating Caucus, Legislative and Congressional." *American Historical Review* 2 (December 1899): 281.

Ritchie, Thomas. "Congressional Caucus No. 3." *Richmond Enquirer* January 2, 1824.

Snowiss, Leon. "Congressional Recruitment and Representation." *American Political Science Review* 60 (Fall 1966): 627-39.

Soule, John and Clark, James. "Amateurs and Professionals: A Study of Delegates to the 1968 Democratic National Convention," *APSR* 64 (September 1970): 888-99.

Wallace, Michael. "Changing Concepts of Party in the United States: New York 1815-1828." *American Historical Review* 74 (December 1968): 453-91.

Wildavsky, Aaron. "The Past and Future President." *The Public Interest* 41 (Fall 1975): 56-76.

INDEX

Adams, John, 61n, 97
Adams, John Quincy, 119, 120n,
 150, 166; on antipartisanship,
 125
Agranoff, Robert, 7n
Aiken, George D., 12n, 258
amateurs, 4, 242, 265-76, 350;
 and reform, 269-71
ambition, 10-13, 29, 309-27
Ambler, Charles, 138n
Antimasonry, 323
Aristotle, 320n

Bagehot, Walter, 179
Bailey, Steven K., 23n
Bailyn, Bernard, 47n
Bain, Richard, 28n
Banfield, Edward, 17n, 22, 22n,
 68n, 180n, 198n, 257, 257n
Barber, James David, 5n, 6n,
 10n, 12, 12n, 18n, 93n, 245,
 245n, 257n, 327-34, 328n,
 329n, 330, 330n, 331n, 332n,
 337
Bayh, Birch, 22n
Bell, John, 139
Best, Judith, 44n
Bickel, Alexander, 272n
Bonney, Catharine, 126n, 133n
Bowdoin, James, 68n
Broder, David, 319n
Brown, Clifford W., 13n, 338n
Brown, Jerry, 251
Brown, Thad A., 246n, 248n
Brown, William, 165n
Bryce, James, 162, 162n, 167,
 168n
Buckley v. Valeo, 239
Bundy, McGeorge, 310n, 340n
Burnham, Walter Dean, 23n,

 115n, 170n, 206, 206n, 218,
 254, 254n, 343
Burns, James MacGregor, 23n,
 60n, 209n, 264, 327n, 342,
 342n
Burr, Aaron, 61n, 232
Byrd, Harry, 294

Calhoun, John C., 157, 157n
campaign finance legislation, 13,
 225, 238-40, 338-39, 344, 347-
 48
Campbell, Angus, 213n
candidate supremacy model, 214,
 217-27, 236-54, 255-56. *See*
 plebiscitary model
Carrington, Edward, 48n, 61n
Carter, Jimmy, 8, 241, 243, 248-
 54, 301; 1976 campaign strategy, 293-94
Carter, Nathaniel, 69n
caucus system, 11, 103-04, 113-
 21, 286; effect of, 118-19; relation to one party system,
 120; shift from caucus to
 convention, 148-49
Ceaser, James, 294n
character, as a consideration in
 selection, 33, 327-39
Chase, James, 115n, 118, 118n
Choice School on the role of
 political parties, 22-24
Clark, James, 267n
Clor, Harry M., 172n
Congressional selection of President, 19, 21, 43-44, 78-83, 113,
 144
consensual school on the roles of
 political parties, 22-24
Converse, Philip, 213n

365

Library of Congress Cataloging in Publication Data

Ceaser, James W.
  Presidential selection.

  Based on the author's thesis, Harvard, 1977.
  Bibliography: p.
  Includes index.
  1. Presidents—United States—Election—History.
2. Presidents—United States—Nomination—History.
3. Political science—United States—History.   I. Title.
JK524.C4   329'.00973   78-70282
ISBN 0-691-07602-2